Independence Hall

Sam^{el} Huntington

SAMUEL HUNTINGTON,
PRESIDENT OF CONGRESS

LONGER THAN EXPECTED

A NARRATIVE ESSAY ON THE
LETTERS OF SAMUEL HUNTINGTON 1779–1781

BY

GEORGE KELSEY DREHER

Library of Congress Cataloging-in-Publication Data

Dreher, George Kelsey, 1919–
  Samuel Huntington, President of Congress longer than expected: a narrative essay on the letters of Samuel Huntington, 1779–1781 / by George Kelsey Dreher.
      p. cm.
  Includes bibliographical references (p. 188) and index.
  ISBN 0-9601000-5-9 (hardcover). — ISBN 0-9601000-6-7 (paperback)
  1. Huntington, Samuel, 1731–1796. 2. Huntington, Samuel, 1731–1796—Correspondence. 3. New England—Church history—18th century. 4. Legislators—United States—Biography. 5. United States. Declaration of Independence—Signers—Biography. 6. United States. Continental Congress—Biography. 7. United States —History—Revolution, 1775–1783—Religious aspects. I. Title.
E302.6.H914D74 1995
973.3'12'092—dc20
[B]   95-45949
                                                                      CIP

Published by Iron Horse Free Press, P.O. Box 10746, Midland, TX 79702
Imprint for Longshanks Book, Mystic, CT

Typesetting by AV Communications, Mesa, AZ

Printed in the United States of America

DEDICATED TO

my motherly friend, the late Hortense B.C. Gibson,
who told me I should write this book,
and I felt appalled by any such notion.

S HUNTINGDON,

President of the Congress.

Drawn from the Life by Du Simetiere in Philadelphia.

Publish'd May 10ᵗʰ 1783 by Wᵐ Richardson 174 Strand.

Table of Contents

John Adams

Richard Henry Lee

FOREWARD

This book started in the 1960's when I heard of a signer of the Declaration of Independence whose home back then was rather near mine now. I could not find out much about him in print, so I began collecting copies of his manuscript letters.

During the 1976 Bicentennial, I prepared a talk and delivered it to a few groups, entitled, "Samuel Huntington for First President." It took off from a friendly debate between Maryland and Connecticut over an insoluble question—whether John Hanson or Samuel Huntington had the office first. Any solution depends on how you set up the semantic criteria.

Then, with encouragement from a few people including my wife, who could not have foreseen the whole consequence but has tolerated it gallantly, I applied for and received a fellowship at Yale Divinity School in 1980, to research further into "The Presidency of Samuel Huntington, 1779–1781, in the Light of New England Religion." My church granted me a part-time sabbatical for it. So that year I worked part-time at the Divinity School library, the downtown libraries of Yale University, and in a paper-laden corner at home, and when the year of the fellowship ended, continued working by visits to the Connecticut College library, Mystic Seaport library, and local public libraries. I am particularly indebted to Assistant Dean Harry B. Adams of Yale, and librarian Brian Rogers of Connecticut College, but also to a score of others, parishoners and friends, whose support braced me.

As the bibliography attests, I owe debts to many scholars, especially to John T. McNeill (the officiant at my wedding) for his important studies of Calvinism, and to Herbert D. Foster, who in his essay "International Calvinism through Locke and the Revolution of 1688"[1] traces a line through "nine Calvinist revolutions" including the 1640 and 1688 in England, implying (pp. 147, 163) that the American Revolution was another. The five points of "political Calvinism" which he

---

[1] American Historical Review, April, 1927.

describes (pp. 163–178)[2] were basic tenets of Huntington and many of his colleagues.

Otherwise I have not proposed or argued big conclusions from what follows in this book. You will discover a viewpoint. I think the data show that "civil religion" during the American Revolution, while passionately patriotic, subordinated its nationalism, as in the Declaration of Independence, to biblical or sometimes deistical inclusivism. Also, that an isolationist, imperial tendency was subordinated to engagement in the alliance with France, with a shrewd eye on the interplay of European politics; militarism, subordinated to republican civilian authority in the interest of the whole population; a tempting monarchial style, subordinated to a new consensual style. Mainly I am content to narrate some events which show a tenacious patience during passage of our nation from colonial adolescence to early adulthood. It wasn't easy.

—G.K. Dreher

A List of events in Samuel Huntington's Life
1731, June 3, born in Scotland (then Windham), Connecticut
1754, admitted to the bar
1760, moved to Norwich to practice law
1761, married Martha Devotion, daughter of the Rev. Ebenezer Devotion
1764, elected to the Connecticut Assembly
1765, King's Attorney for the Colony of Connecticut
1775, chosen a delegate to the Continental Congress
1776, July 4, signed the Declaration of Independence
1779–1781, President of the Continental Congress*
*1781, after passing the Articles of Confederation called "The United States in Congress Assembled"
1784, elected Deputy Governor of Connecticut
1786, elected Governor and re-elected for ten years
1796, January 5, died and laid to rest in Norwichtown

---

[2] "Through Locke there filtered to the American Revolution five points of political Calvinism held by hundreds of Calvinists," he states, "but clarified through his Civil Government: fundamental law, natural rights, contract and consent of people, popular sovereignty, resistance to tyranny through responsible representatives." In the subsequent pages of his essay, Foster treats each of the five points separately.
Among consonant treatments of later date, see Christopher Hill, Intellectual Origins of the English Revolution, Oxford U. Press, 1965. Pp. 284–287.

LONGER THAN EXPECTED

"As I find myself under a necessity to remaining in Congress much longer than I expected, for it was my wish and full expectation to have returned home in October last, I am under the necessity of requesting that one hundred pounds in hard money may be sent me..."

— **Samuel Huntington to John Lawrence**
(treasurer of Connecticut).
December 1, 1780

SLOW OVEN

What is to be done when the loaf has not risen?

You are in a front room, the carpeted and brightly furnished room, waiting with the friends you asked in to share with you a fresh bread-smell coming from the oven, a taste of buttered hot slices new out of the oven. But it has not happened. You can last a short time on the anticipation of smell and taste, excited and impatient. Then you face each other, bravely lasting longer by words of gossip, comical words, smiles. Someone exits, murmuring an apology. Bravery is ebbing. Of course, we cannot wait all day.

The heat of the oven has been too low. The loaf is still raw each time you prick it urgently. It will come out late. Who can take lateness? What is to be done? The letdown is a wisp of calamity or an ache of vague reminders about thwarted wishes and broken loves.

What is to be done after children have played tree tag until some of them are tired of playing? Do you want to play 'red rover' now? No, not I. 'Pirate ship' is a better game. Let's go home.

What is to be done when, one frost after another, the town workers don't fill the holes in our local roads?

What is to be done when the war has not ended? Our strong spurt of early desire was not enough. Lexington, Saratoga, and still they stay, firing their muskets at us. They left Boston, and took New York. They marched into Philadelphia and stayed a while. They'll take Charleston.

Our paper money is silly. Our winters in camp are chill. Too many of us die. Shall we end it by a mere collapse? Let's go home. Shan't we ever try the frontier, or at least plant more seeds of corn in the fields our parents and grandparents worked before us? Shan't we watch for a day when somebody runs a steamboat up our rivers?

How much time can we reserve for one long-foiled purpose? Maybe we were wrong to crave the liberty and pursue the happiness outrageously. We have tolerated delay. Our babies have learned to walk without much applause from us while we made hot oratory around the liberty tree and expected our enemy to run away. Sly neighbors who did not pledge an equal sacrifice were meanwhile earning money to put new roofs on their houses. Some of them laugh at us. And are we certain that more time will make a difference if we consent to tug the immense weight of the war in the direction we started years ago?

"The period that confined me to my present painful situation is almost expired, and as I have been long absent from my private affairs, and my health somewhat impaired with the burthen and fatigue of business, I hope to obtain leave of absence in about one month..."
—Huntington to Governor Jonathan Trumbull,
September 4, 1780

"Indeed the weight and burden of business is continually increasing and like to increase while the war continues."
—Huntington to James Cogswell,
July 22, 1780

"The burden and fatigue of the business, to which you are no stranger, makes me doubtful whether I can endure it much longer."
—Huntington to John Jay,
the immediate past President,
October 6, 1780

Note: all boxed verse is from the author.

"George Washington freed our country."
"Hear, hear!" "No. Ben Franklin did it."
"No, no. Adams did." "LaFayette!"
"Bah. Robert Morris turned the trick."
Perhaps the people helped do it?
"Helped whom? Morris or Washington?"
The people helped Horatio Gates.
The people helped Nathaniel Greene,
They privateered, sang Billings' songs,
They quoted Jefferson and Paine.
"Aha! State governors did it.
Jefferson... Trumbull, Clinton, Reed..."
The states created a Congress.
"But does talk make a victory?"
One Congress met — one, not thirteen,
A basket for our messages,
A blending-pot for our consent.
"Well, Congress tried to help him win.
You must remember Valley Forge;
George Washington, alone in snow."
"Hear, hear!" "Remember Gates!" "No. Greene!"
"Remember Jay... or Rochambeau..."

His Excellency S. HUNTINGDON Prefident of Congrefs.

Pub.^d May 15.th 1783, by R. Wilkinfon N.º 58 Cornhill London.

Huntington in the Chair

"The history of man clearly shows that it is dangerous to intrust the supreme power in the hands of one man. The same source of knowledge proves that it is not only inconvenient but dangerous to liberty, for the people of a large community to attempt to exercise in person the supreme authority. Hence arises the necessity that the people should act by their representatives; but this method, so necessary for civil liberty, is an improvement of modern times."

—Huntington to Connecticut convention
debating the Constitution.
January 9, 1788

"I find one consolation very necessary in public life: that is, to believe or at least act as if I did fully believe there are many wise men who can judge better than myself on important subjects, and I have the happiness generally to unite in promoting their determinations, as far as duty requires in any sphere I am called to act in."

—Huntington to Jonathan Trumbull, Jr.
January 3, 1780

When on March 1, 1781, the thirteen states completed their breakaway from Great Britain by formal confederation, a serene and temperate man from Connecticut thereby became, in an odd sense of the title, the first President of the United States. Samuel Huntington had far fewer duties and powers than soon would be vested in President Washington. Still, his leadership contributed to the country's integrity at its very start.

Although Huntington's name is scarcely known, his face is possibly more familiar. In the often-reprinted painting 'The Signing of the Declaration of Independence' by Huntington's younger compatriot from Connecticut, John Trumbull, the President's table is prominent. John Hancock sits to our right of it presiding. Secretary Charles Thomson

1

stands by it. The painter significantly places Huntington nearest Thomson and Hancock. We have seen him there often, one of the unidentified familiar faces in the image-glut we experience these days.

Most members of the Continental Congress sat in Windsor chairs, but the President sat on a platform, two steps above floor level, in a graceful, tall-backed walnut armchair. Built on a restrained version of Chippendale lines, the arms curved gently and the outer slats of a somewhat decorous layout of three uprights curved away from each other. The crestpiece on the headrail became famous a few years later from a remark by Benjamin Franklin about the round design painted on it: "I have been wondering if that were a rising or a setting sun. Now that we have succeeded in drafting the Constitution here, I believe it is a rising sun."

Seated in this chair behind a desk, the President faced a semicircle of thirteen walnut tables, each covered with green cloth. There were grouped the delegates of the states. At a desk to the President's right sat Secretary Charles Thomson.

The first occupant of the chair had been Virginia's proficient elder statesman, Peyton Randolph. Then, not counting the few days of Middleton, followed three sparkling personalities, one from each of the country's three regions. John Hancock, a Harvard-educated merchant from Boston, popular, ostentatious. Henry Laurens, Charleston trader and planter, a genial, peppery Whig. John Jay of New York, trained for law at King's College (Columbia), well-married, sharp-minded, conservative. Now a contrast. Samuel Huntington, calm, self-educated lawyer from Connecticut. He did not seek the Presidency but he was ready for it. Like a runner who goes out on the road regularly and by hard exercise keeps his legs in shape without thinking of special laurels, he was ready to preside.

He had not felt content to stay on the farm, earlier in life at Windham, nor in the cooper's trade which his father had offered him as an alternative to farming. Instead he drove himself through the disciplines of study, learning to sort facts from untested assertion, to grasp precedent and procedure, to read human nature and plan feasible settlements or persist toward fair judgments. He found a mode of spiritual discipline, too, as we shall see.

Looking back from our time, it seems remarkable that in his time Huntington's move into the chair was almost not remarked. It was like a stone's merely falling into the vacancy when you remove one pretty pebble from your jar of pretty pebbles. You make a space and another stone falls in. John Jay was chosen our first minister to Spain, leaving the President's chair empty.

On September 28, 1779, he was elected. The next day John Jay wrote to Governor George Clinton: "Mr. Huntington of Connecticut is now President of Congress, and I am persuaded will fill that office with propriety." It does not sound as if he felt excited.

After the vivid personal colors which Hancock, Laurens, and Jay gave to the presiding role, members of Congress probably felt relief now that they could rise and address a milder, steadier occupant of the chair.

Besides that, why did they choose him? Granted, after Laurens and Jay it was New England's turn again on the regional rotation, after Hancock Connecticut's turn among states of the region. But there is more of an answer.

For one thing, he was alert to other people. His fellow-Congressmembers sensed it. For instance, back in February, 1776, he had tactfully opened correspondence with the eldest of the young Trumbulls, Joseph Trumbull, Commissary-general of the Continental army: "Col. Dyer not being continued in Congress was unexpected and disagreeable to me; but as I am at present stationed here, shall be happy in the favour of your correspondence during my residence at this place." Dyer, Trumbull's father-in-law, had been communicating from Philadelphia to the Commissary-general's post. Huntington did not shut out the feelings which crackled underneath when Dyer was displaced. Dyer and Trumbull would both be touchy about it. (Trumbull tended to be touchy about most situational changes. He was touchy just then about the displacement, too, of his clever young friend Silas Deane, Connecticut delegate with Dyer in 1775). Joseph Trumbull accepted Huntington as a correspondent. "Give me leave to congratulate you," Huntington was writing him in July, "on the success of American arms at S. Carolina."

Not only Trumbull but the delegates on scene at Philadelphia were finding Huntington aware and amiable, as a gray-newsy paragraph from the February letter may suggest: "This morning at about eight o'clock the worthy Mr. Lynch of South Carolina was taken with an apoplectic fit. Remains very ill tho' his reason is restored and speaks so as to answer questions. May God restore his health and usefulness. Through divine goodness I am restored to health so as to give constant attendance to business."

So in addition to friendliness, Huntington's reliable attention to the tasks of Congress was a second reason for the members' confidence in him. "The Congress are crowded with business," he wrote his kinsman

Jabez Huntington in 1776. "I have enjoyed as much health as could be expected with the fatigue of business during the sultry season in the stagnate air of this city," he wrote three homestate colleagues.

By 1779, when they needed to move a new person into the President's chair, Congressmembers had long since felt the amiable scrutiny of Huntington's eye toward them each, and prized his diligence.

———————

Most important of the reasons why Congress chose Huntington when the chair became vacant was their need for a harmonious house.

Immediately surrounding their sessions had been turbulence of the political factions in the city of Philadelphia and the state of Pennsylvania. Meanwhile personal splits within Congressional delegations tinged the general atmosphere: among others, John Hancock and the Adamses, Henry Laurens and William Henry Drayton.

Members had divided heatedly between partisans of Schuyler and Gates; between critics and supporters in late 1777 into 1778 of Washington's generalship; between critics and supporters of the ambitious, brilliant, volatile Benedict Arnold, who had not yet defected.

After the alliance, some members trusted the French minister Gerard, others resented him.

Some challenged, others defended the expenditures of the quartermaster department and commissary department.

But most bitter of all was the spill into Congress of the quarrel between Silas Deane and Arthur Lee, American emissaries to France. The year 1779 opened in shock over the recent, incensed resignation of Lee-supporter Henry Laurens from the office of President. Then it moved to a snarling climax in the spring voting over the recall of Ralph Izard, William and Arthur Lee, and Benjamin Franklin, as well as postponement of a verdict on Deane. Huntington, with Roger Sherman and other Connecticut delegates, tended to support Lee against Deane, irrespective of the Connecticut tie. But Jay supported Deane and on his departure it was again the turn of a Lee supporter to be President.

Huntington had few enemies. Congress believed he could help them focus properly on the tasks to be done rather than widen the issues which had divided them.

Two months after he assumed the chair, he wrote to his friend Oliver Wolcott an assessment of the changed climate: "I have the pleasure to inform you that as great harmony and concord subsists in Congress as ever I knew or can be expected in such a body."

The perception, that is, was of a comparative, not of an absolute harmony. If tensions and tugs continued around him, the present climate was better than the past. As a longtime participant in Connecticut town meetings and Congregational church meetings; as an insider at the sessions of state Assembly and Council and at the Committee of Safety meeting at Governor Trumbull's "War Office," he was not expecting perfect poise and euphony.

His perception, furthermore, was not private. A substantial array of others saw things the same way. In January, 1780, Oliver Ellsworth wrote Governor Trumbull; "Greater unanimity has at no time perhaps prevailed in Congress than at present, or ever been more necessary."

At about the same time James Varnum was writing Governor Greene: "Party intrigues have some share in our councils, but they are far from influencing in matters of general utility. Whenever they are attempted, they appear rather under the garb of expiring struggles than in the expectation of success."

Thomas McKean, among others: "Harmony seemed to be restored in some measure, upon the appointment of Messrs. Jay and Carmichael. The death of Mr. Drayton and the considerable change about that time of the members, several of them not having been re-elected, left us pretty quiet ever since, tho' prejudices still too much prevail."

Congress apparently turned to Huntington because they predicted he could temper his own feelings and soberly point their deliberations toward the main issues. His principal assets for their purpose, besides friendliness and attentive workmanship, were his judicial background (which we shall note soon) and his attitude of persistent hope. Given the public plight, they needed a leader who was not easily discouraged. Congress had no money. Washington had pointed out the problems of keeping a Continental army together. The states were preoccupied with their own needs. A President would have to contend with all that.

Huntington's attitude is suggested by the frequency of the word "hope" in his vocabulary. "Am sensible you labour under many difficulties," he wrote to Jeremiah Wadsworth, the current Commissary-general, July, 1779, "...but hope for the best circumstances will admit of."

"I hope the wisdom of Congress and of the several states," he wrote to Wolcott in November, "will lead to such measures the ensuing winter that we may be prepared for peace or war as events may be. But I most sincerely wish the former."

During the weeks immediately preceding Huntington's election, his contribution to the work of Congress had spurted. Beyond normal attendance at daily sessions and at the pre-session committee meetings, he gave enough leadership to gain in the confidence of other delegates.

On September 6, for instance, a committee he chaired had reported on the situation of officers and citizens who were held prisoners on Long Island. The report remains on record in his handwriting. He told Congress his committee thought the British had no right by the law of nations to imprison citizens not taken in arms. Therefore, he proposed recommending to the states whose citizens were prisoners "to make such provision for their relief and comfortable subsistence as they shall judge necessary and expedient, and to keep an account of such expenditures." At the final settlement of accounts, British would be expected to pay.

The plight of Americans held as prisoners of war was tricky to address. Everybody knew the horror-stories about their living conditions, especially on prison ships in New York's East River: filth and disease, tedium and resentment. The first problem was that King George wanted them treated not as alien enemies but as defiant subjects. Under international codes they would have been better treated as enemies.

Not only did Huntington's committee report show a humane concern for the prisoners — a concern which he would be mentioning later in presidential letters. Also it held out inducement to the states to spend money, which the Congress was in no shape to do, for prisoners' upkeep. Congress, frustrated by a problem which had seemed insoluble, welcomed his constructive idea.

For another instance, Huntington was serving on the Marine Committee, a committee on which he had first served in 1776. Connecticut had engaged him in marine-related chores at times when he was not attending Congress.

On September 8, a French fleet of 33 ships under Admiral d'Estaing arrived off the mouth of the Savannah River. News of their arrival did not reach Philadelphia, however, until about the date of the presidential election. Everybody surmised that something big was going to happen. The Marine Committee was closer to the details than were others in Philadelphia.

On hearing of d'Estaing's movement, the Marine Committee ordered all frigates and other Continental armed vessels readied for sea, with three months' provision on board, "to join the French fleet or to such other places as may be directed by General Washington or the Count d'Estaing," cooperating with each other. But three frigates had, on September 22, been ordered to Charleston "for a very important service." Charleston *and* Savannah. Excitement rose.

Another instance involved Huntington more especially. On September he wrote to Governor Trumbull: "Committees appointed to prepare the proper resolutions for constituting Courts of Appeal for the final decision of all admiralty causes, and a proper Board of Admiralty, have not yet made their reports."

Huntington was himself chairman of one of the committees. It put him at the center of attention because Congress was in the midst of a wrangle with Pennsylvania over the power to determine appeals. Unknown to themselves, two natives of Connecticut were thus making Huntington prominent just at the time when Congress had to elect a new President. They were Gideon Olmstead, a privateersman, and General Benedict Arnold.

Olmstead, a native of East Hartford, had claimed prize money in the Admiralty Court of the state of Pennsylvania. He and three companions, after being captured and impressed by the British, had overpowered the crew of the sloop *Active* while sailing from Jamaica to New York. They headed for the mainland. At one point their captives briefly pushed loose for a shootout, and Olmstead received a pistol wound before forcing them back into the hold. Then the suppressed crew jammed the ship's rudder until they grew so hungry and thirsty that they yielded by reactivating it. As they neared land a Pennsylvania armed ship took the *Active* to Philadelphia. To Olmstead's bitter surprise, their escort counter-claimed the prize money.

In Pennsylvania, as in many states, such cases were tried by jury. It was a safeguard against the tyranny of the old British admiralty courts where, allegedly, arbitrary judges had treated the colonists unjustly. But in cases where local people contested the claims of people from elsewhere, jury members tended to favor their neighbors. The Philadelphia jury awarded one-fourth of the prize to Olmstead and his companions. The rest went to Pennsylvanians. The red-blooded Olmstead did not submit. He had suffered too much for that prize to lose it by a dubious award.

Eventually he made a deal with Arnold, who was then the military commander of Philadelphia. For the pledge of half interest in the proceeds, Arnold loaned them money and agreed to support their cause. He approached the Congress and won them an appeal.

There was in Congress a standing "committee of appeals" for such a purpose. Huntington had participated in its design. Back in 1776, when appeals in cases of capture initially came to Congress and there was as yet no standing system for them, Huntington was appointed in succession to the first three special appeals committees. As a judge of the Superior Court of Connecticut, he was an obvious choice for them. Then in October, 1776, Congress appointed a committee to review appeals procedures and offer suggestions for improvement. Huntington served on that review, which recommended establishing the standing committee. In February, 1778, he arrived in Congress for a second term. The day after he arrived, he was appointed a member of the standing committee of appeals.

And now that he was on his third round of congressional duty he was deemed the one fit to be chairman of a committee, appointed August 26, 1779, in the midst of the wrangle over the sloop *Active*, to report out a "plan for establishing one or more Supreme Courts of Appeal in all maritime cases within these United States."

His committee probably went to work during the month before he was elected President — after which date he was spared committee chores. We catch a signal of this from his words to Governor Trumbull, "Courts," plural. The constituting act had said, "One or more Courts." The first committee report, read October 29, after the election, and written by William Paca, an original committee member with Huntington, proposed two Courts, one for eastern and northern districts, the other for middle and southern districts. This probably reflected the first thinking of the committee at the time when Huntington was chairing it. By December, the reported plan spoke of one Court only.

If the October 29 version does indicate Huntington's concept, its ample design, most of which survived in the later enactment, must have gained him prestige. Particularly, its vigorous assertion of Congress' prerogative over Pennsylvania's or any state's prerogative.

Whether members of Congress sided with General Benedict Arnold or Council President Joseph Reed in their long temperamental and political feud at Philadelphia, most members were ready for language directing state courts to obey the judgments of Congress' standing committee. They were upset over the argument of the late George Ross, judge of Pennsylvania's Admiralty Court, refusing to accept the decision of Congress' committee because, he thought, its authority did not extend to the point of overruling state law. Pennsylvania law stipulated a conclusive trial by jury, without appeal.

They were upset equally over the refusal of the marshal of the Pennsylvania court to heed an injunction of Congress' committee, ordering him to hold the prize money until they could direct him further as to its disposal. Instead, he gave the money to the state treasurer, who kept it; later his executrixes kept it till in 1809, Chief Justice Marshall, for the U.S. Supreme Court, awarded it to Olmstead.

Although Congress for tactical reasons did not ultimately adopt the vigorous words, and Paca perhaps used bolder words than Huntington would have used, most members liked the explicit statement that judges of the proposed federal Court would have "all the powers of a court of record in fining and imprisoning for contempt and disobedience; and judges of courts of admiralty and all officers of the said courts, pay obedience to the decrees and orders of the Courts of Appeal under pain of being guilty of contempt and subject to be imprisoned."

In another major tier of congressional business during 1779, Huntington had distinctly participated. When he arrived in May to resume his seat at the Connecticut table after a ten-month absence, he found a debate underway regarding the terms of eventual peace with Great Britain. The subject was an old interest of his.

He probably by then had bought and read the pamphlet *Considerations on the Mode and Terms of a Treaty of Peace with America,* printed the previous year in London and reprinted at Hartford in 1779. His copy, with his signature on the cover page, is preserved at Yale University. (See note at the end of this chapter).

Back in 1778, he had proposed a resolution that Congress are "not averse from entering into a treaty for peace and commerce" between the U.S. and Great Britain, "for the mutual interest and benefit of both, upon terms not inconsistent with the freedom, sovereignty, and independence of these States..." It was an indication, first, of his longing for peace. Also it was timed for a practical effect. At about that time he was writing to Governor Trumbull about news from Tirana, "that Spain have taken a decided part and joined their armaments with France, in consequence thereof, as is suspected in France, Great Britain are sending emissaries to America to offer us a truce and withdraw their forces if America will renounce all connection with France."

The coming of emissaries was a signal that the British government hoped to deal with America in time to forestall the treaty then developing between the U.S. and France. Their terms would be recognition of Congress, cessation of hostilities, repeal of all obnoxious laws concerning the colonies, and an American voice in Parliament. Those terms were no longer sufficient. But if the sovereignty and independence of the U.S. were mutually included in the terms, might peace be arranged before a French treaty greatly complicated Anglo-American relations? Such a possibility was the aim of Huntington's proposed resolution.

The proposal was too late. Simeon Deane arrived from France bearing the texts of two treaties which France had approved. Congress ratified both quickly, and on June 17, Huntington was voting for the unanimous congressional reply to the British emissaries led by Lord Carlisle which rejected the insufficient terms they had offered. And immediately Huntington began to view the French alliance with hope.

By now, in 1779, Congress took the alliance into account when making all decisions. The formulation of specific peace aims was an initiative of Conrad Alexandre Gerard, first French Minister to the U.S. Both France and Spain wanted to know how close their own aims were to those of the U.S. Congress. Formulation would affect the French commitment of manpower and money as well as a possible Spanish peace mediation.

Gerard furthermore had advised Congress to compromise that the U.S. would not make peace with Great Britain apart from the consent and guidance of France. He encouraged giving assurance that Spain might regain the Floridas and dominate commerce on the Mississippi River. He discouraged claims to western land by any state, opposing Virginia's claim by investing his own money in a land company with opposite claims. He sought to protect contractors who were profiting from the supply of French armed personnel. And he desired fishing benefits for France off the coast of Newfoundland and a fishing base in the Gulf of Havana.

Huntington acquainted himself with the peace terms debate underway. He learned that in February, a committee under the chairmanship of Gouvernor Morris, an able young New Yorker who was inclined to collaborate with Gerard, had reported a terms proposal which Congress had been discussing at intervals ever since. The primary requirement, to Huntington's satisfaction, was to be British recognition of the independence and sovereignty of the U.S. Other favorable ultimata were to be territorial boundaries from Canada to the Floridas, and west to the Mississippi River; evacuation of all British forces from the territory of the states; unmolested fishing rights off Newfoundland; free navigation of the Mississippi to the southern U.S. boundary and free commerce on the Mississippi south of the boundary; a territorial claim to Nova Scotia, if the allies agreed to it.

Marquis de Lafayette at Yorktown

Negotiable items were to be ceding Nova Scotia for other consider-ations; forgoing territorial reach beyond the treaty boundaries; yielding the Floridas to Spain. Perhaps Spain would give a subsidy for American troops to help conquer the Floridas. The U.S. would accept Spanish possession of the Floridas in return for free navigation of the Mississippi.

On March 19, Congress had agreed to Gouvernor Morris' proposals on boundaries and evacuation of all British forces. The two principal questions which remained were fishing rights, which New England states counted as important, and navigation of the Mississippi, desired by the southern states. Huntington soon entered the discussion. He decided that both the fishing rights and the navigation rights were valuable. Both fitted into his vision of the future of the nation.

Gouvernor Morris and others were trying to restrain the demand, articulated especially by Elbridge Gerry of Massachusetts, about fish-ing. They were willing to give it a high priority without making it an absolute requirement for a peace settlement. The practical need of the moment was for Congress to find a generally satisfactory formula. Huntington understood the nicety. On a June 12 vote, he broke with his New England colleagues including Roger Sherman, senior member of his own state's delegation, to join the middle and southern states in a minor softening resolution. Eventually Congress would decide to say that in no case would the rights be given up, a statement consid-ered to be something less than an ultimatum.

Just then, however, Congress was talking less about the peace treaty than about an accompanying treaty of commerce with Great Britain. In the treaty of commerce, should fishing rights become less than an ultimatum? Huntington believed not. On July 17, he moved a pragmatic amendment: "No treaty of commerce shall be entered into, or any trade or commerce whatsoever be carried on with Great Britain, without an explicit stipulation on her part not to molest or disturb the inhabitants of the United States of America in taking fish on the banks of Newfoundland, and other fisheries in the American sea anywhere, excepting within the distance of three leagues of the shores of the ter-ritories remaining to Great Britain at the close of the war, if a nearer distance cannot be obtained by negotiation." They debated his amend-ment for a time during the session, when he moved it, then adjourned. On July 22, they agreed to it by a voice vote and then enacted the main motion as now amended: the motion for fishing made and ardently promoted by Gerry. Eight states votes yes. Maryland, Virginia, and North Carolina voted no.

Then Congress returned to the formula for an eventual treaty of peace. Was the phrase "in no case to be given up" tough enough? Or should the stipulation which Huntington won for the treaty of commerce be adopted also for the treaty of peace?

On July 29, Huntington seconded a motion by Thomas McKean (who had seconded his amendment a week before). It was tough, but not quite so rigid as an ultimatum: "If after a treaty of peace with Great Britain, she shall molest the citizens or inhabitants of any of the United States in taking fish, on the banks and places described in the resolution passed the 22nd day of July, instant, such molestation (being in the opinion of Congress a direct violation and breach of the peace) shall be a common cause of the said states, and the force of the union be exerted to obtain redress for the parties injured." The eight states voted yes. The three, plus South Carolina, no.

By this time, the members of Congress were viewing Huntington as a man with lively concerns about foreign affairs. On August 4, he was named (as was McKean) to a committee chaired by Morris for drafting instructions to the commissioners whom Congress would appoint to negotiate a peace treaty. Those instructions were to summarize the agreed results of Congress' whole peace terms debate. On August 14, the committee reported a proposed set of instructions and their proposal was adopted. They had avoided the question of navigation on the Mississippi. Agreements during the course of the debate so far, steered mainly by Morris but also by Gerry, Huntington and McKean, were the substance of the instructions. But, in September, Congress returned to the navigation question. A possibility of alliance with Spain, more than the eventual treaty with Great Britain, was its occasion.

Congress wanted the Spanish alliance. Yet they were concerned also about the future development of the American west, including commerce on the Mississippi. Gerard told them that Spain would not like them to press states' land claims west of already recognized state lines; nor, to press for the river navigation.

Back in August, Meriwether Smith of Virginia had successfully inserted the words "the free navigation of the river Mississippi" into a congressional measure. Huntington had voted for the insertion, Morris against it. Smith was preparing to push hard for the principle.

September 6th, when they resumed considering it, John Dickinson, now a member from Delaware, tried a restatement which Spain might like better: "But if his Catholick Majesty shall positively insist" on concessions, "it is not the desire of Congress to continue the war" for the goals under consideration. If Spain obtains the Floridas from Great Britain, the U.S. will guarantee the Floridas to Spain. Also the U.S. will deliver masts for the Spanish navy. The Minister to Spain should endeavor to procure from Spain, for its part, annual payment of "a certain sum of money." After Dickinson's motion had been debated for a time, Huntington gained its postponement and offered the decisive substitute motion. Smith seconded. It was debated and amended in part. Its final form was adopted on September 17. Thus Huntington ended up the effective shaper of the last one of the 1779 peace terms plan.

His effectiveness was in shrewd dealing with the interests and attitudes of fellow members. For instance, on September 10 his motion included language which appealed to the south: Provided that his Catholic Majesty shall "establish on the said river, at or somewhere southward of the thirty-first degree north latitude, a free port or ports, under such regulations and restrictions as shall be agreed on between the Ministers plenopotentiary of his Catholick Majesty and the United States." The language was removed by amendment on the 17th. Smith deplored its removal and sought to reinstate a modified form of it, but on record vote his attempt failed. Even Huntington voted against it, probably as a tactic to preserve the main features of his motion.

For another instance, his motion had included a promise of war supplies: If his Catholic Majesty think proper to attack the Floridas, "these United States will aid and assist his Catholick Majesty in such enterprise with such provisions and naval stores as shall be required by his Catholick Majesty and can be furnished by these states." That promise was removed, too, by amendment.

Perhaps Huntington sensed better than his colleagues the lack of Spain's enthusiasm for alliance with the U.S. after France had pledged support for the main Spanish goals. The promise of war supplies might have functioned as an incentive to Spain. His phrase "and can be furnished by these states" was a hedge which Congress could appreciate; his own correspondence with his friend from Connecticut, the Commissary-general Jeremiah Wadsworth, shows his awareness that the continent's store of supplies was lean at the moment. Further, his limiting the promise to supplies and not manpower suggested his distaste for military involvement if there was a worthy alternative. He thought that a political rather than a military acquisition of the Floridas was possible for Spain ("by cession or by war, with or without the assistance of the allies," words also excised by amendment). Cession was possible by treaty if the war ended, or if the war continued even as a desperate lure offered by Great Britain to attract Spain away from France and the U.S. Thus a military attack by Spain, to gain the Floridas, was imaginable but not inevitable.

The final form of the resolution which he initiated said that if Spain allied with the U.S. and did obtain the Floridas, "these United States will guarantee the same to his Catholick Majesty, provided always that the United States shall enjoy the free navigation of the river Mississippi into and from the sea." In the peace terms discussion, Huntington had advocated the causes of both New England and the south. It enlarged his reputation for promoting the continental interest above state or sectional interests.

Benjamin Rush thought of Huntington as "a sensible, candid, and worthy man and wholly free from state prejudices."

—————>●<—————

NOTE

Considerations on the Mode and Terms of a Treaty of Peace with America. London: 1778. Hartford: reprint, 1779. A copy of this 23-page booklet with Huntington's signature on the title page is in the Pequot Collection at the Beinecke Rare Book and Manuscript Library, Yale University.

The writer thinks that the use of force against America has been found to be ineffectual. Parliament should soon treat with Congress, through the diplomats in Paris, or else Europe will interfere. Both America and Great Britain need peace. America possibly will concede such points as trade around Cape Hope and Cape Horn, trade with Africa, possession of the West Indies (America needs no more lava), engagements about fisheries, non-interference in British Hudson's Bay trade. But the prior condition for any agreement is American independence.

The writer warns of Spanish and Dutch involvements following more delay in an application for peace. As for the opinion that it is wiser to seek a treaty with France and to avoid recognizing the independence of America, France will choose to gain Canada and fishing rights off Newfoundland and "gold" from an independent United States rather than benefits from Great Britain, while America will react in disgust by stopping future commerce.

British peace commissioners have told Congress that France is "insidious." Princes of every country, however, act for their own interest.
He who trusts to any other behavior on their part "is a poor politician." Thus, "when Great Britain offers to America everything but
independence, she shows the extreme folly of insidiousness. She
gives everything, only to gain the right and power of retracting everything."

Spain, interested in Gibraltar and Jamaica, and Holland, interested in
commerce, would arise as Britain's adversaries if France were qui-
eted. So all powers are interested in American independence, and
America is now able to baffle every attempt against it.

—————◆—————

"God made all men naturally equal."

—John Locke

*"We hold these truths to be self-evident, that all men are
created equal, that they are endowed by their Creator with
certain unalienable rights."*

— Declaration of Independence

THE UMPIRE

And is this president partial
To his home state or to your state
Ahead of the union of states?
"He's not partial. He wants union."
Is he partial to Deane or Lee?
Washington, Conway, Mifflin, Gates?
"He has his leanings, but meanwhile
He views the outside of a roil.
He listens, abates ill tempers,
Guides everyone toward household peace."

"Whereas almighty God, in the righteous dispensation of his providence, hath permitted the continuation of a cruel and desolating war in our land...

"...that it may please almighty God to guard and defend us against our enemies, to give vigour and success to our military operations by sea and land; that it may please him to bless the civil rulers and people, strengthen and perpetuate our union, and in his own good time establish us in the peaceable enjoyment of our rights and liberties..."

—**Resolve of Congress,**
drafted by Daniel Roberdeau with
Samuel Huntington and
Nathaniel Scudder,
commending April 22, 1778,
as a day of national fasting,
humiliation, and prayer

Drawn from the life by Du Simitier in Philadelphia.   Engraved by B. L. Prevost at Paris.

Huntington's Family and Connecticut Religion

"It is disagreeable to be so long removed from my famaly and friends. However I most cheerfully obey the calls and dictates of Providence without repining.

"... Please to present my duty to Madam, my kind respects to Br Justin Devotion; and let me request an interest in your prayers, that I may be enabled faithfully to perform the trust reposed in me, and in due time be returned to my famaly and native land in peace."

— Huntington to James Cogswell,
March 30, 1776

S amuel Huntington had been admitted to the bar in 1754. He moved to Norwich in 1760 and opened law practice in that larger, more complex community. His longtime pastor back in the town of Windham, the Reverend Ebenezer Devotion, solemnized marriage vows between daughter Martha Devotion and Samuel the next year. For ten years they attended the First Church in Norwich but did not become members until after Devotion's death in 1771. Then they joined by letter of transfer.

Their pastor at Norwich, Joseph Strong, later said of Huntington, "For many years a professor of religion, he appeared to delight both in the doctrines and ordinances of the gospel. A constant attendant upon public worship, he was occasionally the people's mouth to God, when destitute of preaching."

The same pastor reported Huntington's final testimony, "Amid re-peated and very feeling declarations of his own personal unworthiness, he avowed unwavering trust in God through his Son, in full belief that he would keep what he had committed to him."

In the Continental Congress, Huntington was considered a mem-ber interested in religion. Once before and once after his presidency, he was named to committees charged with composing the 1778 Fast Day resolve and the 1783 Thanksgiving Day resolve. He had voted in favor of adopting and commending to the states the 1776 Fast Day resolve shortly before writing his first letter from Philadelphia to his stepfather-in-law, the Reverend James Cogswell. Chief author of the resolve was William Livingston, now of New Jersey, "Desirous…to have people of all ranks and degrees duly impressed with a solemn sense of God's superintending providence and of their duty devoutly to rely, in all their lawful enterprizes, on his aid and direction, do earnestly rec-ommend that Friday, the seventeenth day of May next, be observed by the said colonies as a day of humiliation, fasting, and prayer; that we may with united hearts confess and bewail our manifold sins and transgressions and by a sincere repentance and amendment of life, appease his righteous displeasure and, through the merits and media-tion of Jesus Christ, obtain his pardon and forgiveness; humbly implor-ing his assistance to frustrate the cruel purposes of our unnatural enemies; and by inclining their hearts to justice and benevolence, pre-vent the further effusion of kindred blood."

Or if there must be war, "to crown the continental arms."

Devotion's death having left vacant the pulpit of the Scotland church (town of Windham) which he had served, his longtime friend and col-league in nearby Canterbury, James Cogswell, became pastor there and also husband of the widow.

———⟫●⟪———

François Barbe-Marbois, writing to the French foreign Ministry at the close of Huntington's service as President, July, 1781, offered comments about the situation in America and the stance of each state's delega-tion to Congress. He stated that Connecticut held to the league of eastern states, somewhat independently, and to the religious tie which unified all of the "Presbyterian" delegates from the northern part of America. The Presbyterian sect dominated, he wrote, if not by their constitution at least by the large number attached to it by their "ap-plication" and the "systematic spirit" which motivated them.

His comment enlightens our understanding of the scene he observed. The words "if not by their constitution" were probably not intended to minimize the importance of presbyterial church government for the development of civil government in America along republican lines. Rather, they were an acknowledgement of the various distinctions of organization and particular practice among the main church bodies with a Calvinist heritage.

From his location in Philadelphia, the Marquis de Barbe-Marbois, an alert diplomat who later would be negotiating the sale of Louisiana to the U.S., had enough evidence of a "Presbyterian" dominance. The secretary of Congress, Charles Thomson, was a Philadelphia Presbyterian. So was James Wilson, influential whether in or out of Congress. Most of the presidents of Congress shared a basic Calvinist view and owned membership in Calvinist bodies. Rancock and Huntington were New England Congregationalists. After the Saybrook Platform of 1708, Connecticut church people were willing to label themselves either "Congregational" or "Presbyterian" due to their consociational pattern. Laurens and Jay, while members of the Church of England, were marked by their Huguenot heritage; Jay married Sarah Livingston, a Presbyterian like others of her family. McKean and Boudinot were Presbyterian.

Meanwhile Harvard's stamp on the Adamses and the Trumbulls; Yale's on Oliver Wolcott, Lyman Hall, and the leaders of the New York "Presbyterian faction" William Livingston and John Morin Scott; and Princeton's on James Madison (although he belonged to the Church of England), Joseph Reed, Benjamin Rush and William Churchill Houston, all affected the nation's complexion.

Alexander McDougall, Abraham Clark, and numerous other middle states Presbyterian laymen doubtless impressed Marbois, as surely the Reformed tie of Robert R. Livingston, Jr. and numerous Dutch and German laymen did. The church ties of Yankee leaders from New England were plain. Connecticut, for instance, sent to Congress not only Huntington but Roger Sherman, treasurer of Yale, brother of two Congregational ministers, who himself relished talk and correspondence with the theologian Samuel Hopkins; Jesse Root, a Princeton graduate who had studied theology before turning to law; Oliver Ellsworth, likewise a Princeton man who studied theology, then law.

One of the chaplains of Congress, the Reverend George Duffield, was pastor of the third Presbyterian Church in Philadelphia. John Adams had described Duffield, with Boston bias: "A preacher whose principles and prayers and sermons more nearly resemble those of our New England clergy than any I have heard."

The Rev. Dr. John Witherspoon, who is seated alongside Huntington in the John Trumbull painting of signers, probably because they were strong friends and heart-mates, was influential not only as President of Princeton. The only clergyman to sign the Declaration of Independence, he exemplified application and systematic spirit in Congress. Marbois singled him out for mention by name when commenting in the July, 1781 dispatch on New Jersey delegates' orientation.

According to a study published in 1844 by Robert Baird and still commonly cited by historians, at the time of the American Revolution there were 700 Congregational churches, 140 presbyterian, 60 each Dutch Reformed and German Reformed, and 20 Associate Presbyterian. Most of the 1140 clergymen of those affiliations were active for the cause of independence.

The importance of Congregational, Presbyterian, and Reformed membership strength would have been difficult for Marbois to summarize briefly. He could have assumed it lay at least in the precedents of the English Civil War and the Parliamentary opposition to Royal rules the American Revolution, viewed from one angle, was an extension of the Cromwellian struggle and the Glorious Revolution, precedents in which religion had counted. Further, there were close similarities between the religious doctrine of "covenant" and the political idea of "compact." All authority, ecclesiastical and civil, was held to subserve the divine law or at least the law of nature. Accordingly the theory was widespread that resistance to actual tyranny is not anarchic but a valid expression of good order. Huntington's family and friends in church life were vehemently interested in the covenant and the compact.

Two letters which Samuel Huntington wrote to the Reverend James Cogswell are now in the Manuscript Collection of the Historical Society of Pennsylvania. They reveal some of his personal concerns while he was a member of Congress.

Cogswell, pastor at Scotland (town of Windham), was more than eleven years his senior. By the date of the first letter, Cogswell was 56 years old and owned status as head of the family. The father of sons and a daughter by his first marriage, three years ago he had taken Martha Lathrop Devotion as his second wife. Huntington's relationship as stepson-in-law to Cogswell was woven into other relationships.

He was virtually the foster parent of Cogswell's third son Mason, later a prominent Hartford physician, a minor figure among the "Hartford Wits," and a leader in the rounding at Hartford of the pioneer "Asylum for the Deaf and Dumb" due to his intense caring for his own nonhearing daughter. Mason lived in the Huntington home a few years before entering Yale.

In fact, although Samuel and Martha Devotion Huntington were childless, their home was usually filled with young. In addition to Mason, there were young Samuel and Frances ("Sammy" and "Fannie"), children of the Reverend Joseph Huntington and the deceased Hannah Devotion Huntington — two Huntington brothers having married Devotion sisters. Those children lived in the Samuel Huntington home since 1771. At times, other youngsters, too.

Regarding Cogswell's family status, Joseph became explicit when writing a letter of condolence in 1790, "The united family of which you are now the parent, by nature and affinity, was when I first entered the scenes of public life far more alluring to me than any connections on earth beside, and in the two families now united have been the dearest prospects and, for a time (alas! how short) by far the greatest pleasures that ever I have tasted in all sublunary things."

The tone of Samuel's 1776 letter from Philadelphia suggests a similar sentiment. "I take this opportunity to pay my respects to you." Also, "Please to present my duty to Madam, my kind respects to Br Justin Devotion..." And he wished to be returned "to my famaly."

"My business," he explains, "is very arduous as well as important. We commonly set from ten in the morning until between four and five in the afternoon, intent on business, without any refreshment. It was very tedious at first but by usage is become tolerable."

Cogswell would have felt sympathetic about the arduousness of such sessions added to committee meetings, extramural raps, correspondence, and all. "I have by divine blessing enjoyed a very good state of health," Huntington assured him, "ever since my recovery from the small pox."

(Six weeks earlier, writing to Joseph Trumbull, he had reported similarly: "Through divine goodness I am restored to health so as to give constant attendance to business.")

There were also mental costs: "I cannot forget my native country, and praise Conecticutt higher than ever I did before." He was homesick. "...However I most cheerfully obey the calls and dictates of Providence without repining."

In using God-talk, Samuel was not merely deferring to the style of a clergyman. If some of his contemporaries were deists, believing that God is the august planner of the cosmos, remote from human itches, fevers, and funks, Huntington was not so. Both health and cheer were particularly sent gifts. Daily work was a personal calling, dictated and sustained providentially for his own case.

"There are devout, pious people in this city," he wrote Cogswell, "a number of pious and excellent preachers…" (George Duffield would be named a chaplain to Congress a few months after this observation.)

"He who does not live a virtuous and religious life here must amuse himself. Every man has liberty to pursue the dictates of his own conscience." A few days before he wrote those words, he had to think about an issue they touched. Congress authorized the Reverend John Carroll, Roman Catholic, to accompany the mission of Benjamin Franklin and others to Canada. Instructions to the commissioners included: "You are further to declare that we hold sacred the rights of conscience." Accordingly, the people were to be promised freedom for the undisturbed exercise of their religion.

Now Huntington, disclosing some astonishment, described a St. Patrick's Day parade he had recently seen. Having been culturally secluded before now in his home state, he found the parade novel and remarkable. (See the quotation, pg. 26).

New England Congregationalists went to Congress thinking that most Anglicans were loyal to Great Britain, thus cool toward American independence. The stereotype dissolved when they became acquainted with George Washington, Richard Henry Lee and numerous other members of the Church of England who ardently favored the cause. William White, afterward the first Protestant Episcopal Bishop of Pennsylvania, would soon become a chaplain to Congress along with Duffield. Huntington later, when Governor of Connecticut, was going to make friends with Bishop Samuel Seabury and make a famous gesture of concord, scheduling the state's official Fast Day on Good Friday, a day which then was more important to Episcopalians than to Congregationalists, rather than during Easter week as had often been the schedule in the past.

Befriending Presbyterians, especially John Witherspoon, enriched Huntington's experience during his congressional years. It was a small step, compared to authorizing freedom for Canadian Catholics. The fact that Connecticut and the middle colonies had sent clergymen of both bodies to yearly meetings from 1766 to 1775 was a major symbol of possibility, both interchurch and intercolony. To people back home in the local churches it was also a new sign of the plural religious traditions which were headed toward encounter as the American people mingled increasingly.

If Congregationalists and Presbyterians were rivals in the time of Oliver Cromwell, the Saybrook Platform arranged a middle polity between the stricter Congregationalism of Massachusetts and the inherited Presbyterianism of the middle colonies. Connecticut thus felt both a continuity of kinship with Massachusetts and a reach in the other direction, too. Significantly, the Connecticut churches would soon be entering into cooperation with Presbyterians for stimulation and support of new churches on the western frontier, via a Plan of Union in 1801. If such cooperation eroded later in the 19th Century, by the middle of the 20th it had resumed via many ecumenical programs including both traditions.

Huntington's experiences with tolerance at Philadelphia were doubtless consistent with some impulses he already knew beforehand. As a teenager he had heard arguments favoring tolerance, voiced in his home town by Solomon Paine and others. But those arguments had come from opposition to his colony's established church and his family's church of preference. Ebenezer Devotion and the congregation at Scotland, Connecticut, felt stung by the uprising of the "Separates."

Before Huntington's birth, when the uniformity of the Saybrook Platform was legalized, Connecticut had already provided toleration for "sober dissenters" so that, while the dissenters were still taxed for the upkeep of the local Congregational church, they could obtain a permit to worship apart. A little later, first Anglicans, then Baptists and Quakers, were allowed to divert their tax payments to the coffers of their own churches. And in 1750, aggressive itinerant preaching having abated and the consequent divisions in established parishes having lessened, Connecticut had lifted certain 1742 regulations enacted against "abuses" and to correct "disorders in ecclesiastical affairs."

Huntington doubtless had heard talk, moreover, of Cogswell's going to New Haven in 1767 and attending a remarkable meeting inclusive of Congregationalists and Presbyterians, both wary of Anglican designs in America. Delegates from the "consociated churches" in Connecticut met with delegates from the Presbyterian Synod of New York and Philadelphia. It was the second such meeting. A year before, at Elizabethtown, N.J., although few from Connecticut attended, those present agreed "to unite our endeavors and counsels for spreading the gospel and defending the liberties of our churches." They began work on a plan of union. The special concern which tended to unite them was a campaign of some Anglican clergy in the colonies to obtain the appointment of a bishop in America. They worried about that. How broad would the powers of such a bishop turn out to be? Would his powers be the same as those of a bishop in England, including civil functions connected with marriages, wills, and the adjudication of scandals? If so, suggested the writer of a letter accompanying the minutes of their meeting, tyranny might threaten. A tyrannical bishop could "harass our country and make our lives bitter by fines, imprisonments, and lawless severity." The letter alluded to "the numerous colonists who came hither for the sake of freedom from ecclesiastical oppression."

At New Haven, eighteen Connecticut clergymen had been present. Cogswell became acquainted with Presbyterian men from the middle colonies, George Duffield among them.

———◆———

ST. PATRICK'S DAY PARADE

"On Sunday morning, the 7th instant, my attention from my chamber window was suddenly called to behold a mighty cavalcade of plebians marching thro' the street with drums beating, and at every small distance they halted and gave three huzzas. I was apprehensive some outrage was about to be committed, but soon perceived my mistaken apprehention and that it was a religious exercise of the Sons of Saint Patrick, it being the anniversary of that saint. The morning exercise was ushered in with the ceremony above described. However, sir, should I leave you to judge of the religion of this city from the above story only, it would not be just."

—Huntington to Cogswell,
March 30, 1776

———◆———

James Cogswell preached the annual "election sermon" to the General Assembly of Connecticut, May, 1771. A reader of the sermon today finds him reticent to treat the tension between the colonies and Great Britain, compared to later election sermons by other preachers. "The attention of Americans," he does say, "has of late been uncommonly roused, and deeply engaged, about the public good. We have looked on our invaluable liberties and important privileges to be in danger."

However, "the public good" as such is a recurring theme in the sermon. He is explicit:

> Indeed the chief and ultimate design of religion, as it respects mankind, is to deliver us from the fatal effects of the Apostacy, and to fit us for a state of perfect holiness and happiness in the coming world. But this is not all.

> Godliness has the promise of the life that now is, as well as that which is to come. And it tends to the present happiness not only of individuals, but the love and practice of it has a most friendly aspect in public weal, and the neglect of it the most direct tendency to the misery and destruction of a state.

Such an assertion poses a number of further questions. But at least it distinguishes his position at the start from that of the religious privatists who saw religion as wholly a concern of individuals, not of communities, or wholly a preparation for eternity, not an involvement in the temporal relations of human history. Cogswell did not place himself with the Christian sects who, during the days of the Great Awakening, divided Connecticut by their highly individualistic tests of true faiths ecstatic outcries, bodily jerks, and "tongues." He argued rather from a viewpoint which seriously encompassed the prophetic teaching of the Old Testament.

In this sermon his reference text is Jeremiah 18:7–10, the parable of the potter — an affirmation of the wonder of divine power over history. God intends, according to this parable, to pluck up and pull down a people, or to build and plant them, in ratio to their doing good or doing evil.

Thus Cogswell puts a tag on God which is typical of much 18th Century theology: "the moral Governor of the world." God approves virtue and holiness, hates sin and wickedness. "So it is reasonable to believe he will show his approbation, favour and protection to the one, and frown upon and punish the other."

Here the situations of individuals and communities differ. The future state is the time of retribution for individuals. Civil communities, by contrast, have no existence outside this age. God shows "visible marks of approbation of public virtue" here and now. God frowns upon and punishes a sinful people here and now. Having sketched the viewpoint, Cogswell elaborates it at some length. He wants to make clear that he is not talking about polite virtues. He is talking, rather, about "a right temper of heart," "a supreme love of God," "a disposition to be subject to his will." He sees virtue of that sort as a possibility conceived in the traditional Christian faiths as a consequence of "redemption" needed after the "creation" and "fall" of humanity. He confines his discussion of those vast concepts to the central theme of his message in short, the "religion of Jesus Christ forms men to such a temper as powerfully inclines them to promote the interest of the public."

It may seem curious to 20th Century readers, accustomed to religious pluralism and its courtesies, that a colony's legislature would assemble and listen to so particular a plea. Since Cogswell's time we have disused the simple similitude between institutions of government and of religion. But in his time a continuity was still intact:

> We have the honour to be descended from ancestors who really deserved the name which was given them in derision. I mean that of 'Puritans.' They were indeed fast friends of liberty, but abhorred licentiousness. They were inviolably attached to purity and strictness in faith, in worship and conversation.

Conversation, in the Puritan view, encompassed citizenship.

Cogswell speaks of virtuous rulers, naming examples from the Old Testament (Moses and Nehemiah, Hezekiah and Josiah), also examples from Connecticut history. Toward the end of the sermon he briefly eulogizes the late Governor William Pitkin; and also, a recently deceased member of the upper house, one Zebulon West, of Tolland.

As he catalogs the virtues of rulers who were under the influence of religion — fidelity to duty, justice, guardianship of subjects' rights, paternal tenderness, unrestrained benevolence—we wonder if he hints a contrast with the conduct of British Tory rulers. Is he invoking the "opposition" philosophy of Whigs on both sides of the Atlantic? "What like religion will arm those in power," he asks, "against the temptations to pride and luxury, venality and oppression, which an elevated station particularly exposes to?"

Evidently he does intend a contrast with pure populism. The Puritan preference for an aristocracy of morally and spiritually fit persons over a sheer democracy appears in his rhetorics "When nothing but the testimony of an unreproaching conscience and the plaudit of the omniscient Judge can yield support, what but this will support them (the virtuous rulers) when repayed with ingratitude for their noble and self-denying exertions for the good of their country?"

A pertinent issue, still.

After speaking of rulers, he speaks of subjects:

> When men are wholly intent on private advantage, grudge every
> farthing which goes beside their own coffers, "and coil themselves
> up in the narrow and dirty shell of private interest," the public
> will be neglected. The State cannot prosper. Religion is calculated
> in the highest degree to cure this distemper. It enlarges the heart,
> greatens and sublimates the views of the mind. That benevolence
> which is the very life and soul of the religion of the gospel em-
> braces the whole system of beings thro' the universe in the arms
> of disinterested love. This then will be the noblest principle of
> public spirit, 'twill engage and dispose us to love our neighbors as
> ourselves.

From pleading for religion, he proceeds to the inverse, the dreadful
tendencies of irreligion, and an appeal for repentance and reformation.

Samuel Huntington grew up under the influence of a religion similar to Cogswell's. His father Nathaniel had settled alongside Merrick's
Brook in Scotland, the southeast section of Windham, before there was
a church nearby. Residents interested in forming a new society, officially
the "Third Ecclesiastical Society in Windham," met in his home, 1732.
They accepted from him the donation of a quarter-acre of land for the
site of a meetinghouse. From then on, the family were active in church
life. Eventually four of Samuel's brothers became Congregational ministers, and his sister Sibyl married a Congregational minister.

Samuel was received into membership of the Scotland Congregational Church in November, 1751.

Before the Reverend Ebenezer Devotion was Samuel's and Joseph's
father-in-law, he was their minister. Called to be the first minister of
the new church, three years after Samuel's birth, he stayed in this
charge until his death when Samuel was 40. When he started, the parish had about 70 families. During his pastorate that number doubled.

Ezra Stiles deemed him "a gentleman of solid understanding,
extensive reading, and eminent for every kind of merit. A great divine,
a pious man, an able politician."

His considerable private library was a principal means of Samuel's
early education.

There is a portrait of him by Winthrop Chandler, 1770, which shows
him a heavy man in a white wig, black suit with white bands, seated

in front of his library books. He holds a bound volume in one hand, the knuckles of the other hand propped on one knee so that the elbow bends away from the body. He neither smiles nor scowls, but seems poised indominately. His eyes are fearless, his jowels thick, chin forward.

A Yale graduate himself, his son Ebenezer and two sons-in-law, Joseph Huntington and another, also were Yale graduates. He became known outside his parish for speaking and writing. In May, 1753, for instance, he was invited to preach the annual election sermon before the General Assembly. In that sermon he somberly treated the paradox that civil rulers are at once honorable and mortal. About 1761 he led his congregation to adopt the "New Version" of metrical psalms for their singing at worship. That version, by Tate and Brady, seemed smoother and finer than the "Old Version" by Sternhold and Hopkins. (A few of its verses survive in modern hymnals, such as "As Pants the Hart for Cooling Streams" and "Through All the Changing Scenes of Life.") The decision to adopt it seemed a step in liturgical courage as well as in literary preference.

Devotion was thought to be the author of some anonymous pamphlets disputing Joseph Bellamy's argument against the practice of "half-way covenant" in the churches. Those pamphlets, published in 1769 and 1770, support Baptism of persons who assent to Christian doctrines, lead decent lives, and wish to be baptized even if they do not claim the experience of rebirth. In terms of the great theological and ecclesial debate of those times. Devotion was an "Old Light." Upon Yale President Clap's decision in 1754 to form a new college church connected with a new professorship of divinity, the Old Light faction in New Haven tried to salvage what they could of the First Church by proposing a compromise. One of their conditions was that Ebenezer Devotion be appointed the new professor. But Clap had other plans.

During the challenges of the "Separate" churches, in eastern Connecticut and elsewhere, Devotion upheld the regular Congregational churches. Thus, when the nearby Canterbury church was in turmoil because of one such challenge, he upheld Cogswell, who was six years younger but theologically similar; he upheld the pastor and the John Dyer faction of that church. Soon he felt upset because a Separate group emerged in Scotland, too. He resisted stoutly, summoning the dissenters to a disciplinary hearing in January, 1746, and before a hearing of the entire Association in February, 1747. But not even his own publication, "An Answer of the Pastor and Brethren of the Third Church in Windham to Twelve Articles, Exhibited by Several of Its Separating Members, as Reasons of their Separation," prevented a walkout. They charged that Devotion's preaching did not accord with their understanding of religion; that the church admitted unconverted persons to the Sacraments; that the church was anti-Christ. Devotion, standing on his own convictions and his legal prerogatives, sent his servant every Sunday to the "Brunswick Church" formed by Separates, with a paper prohibiting their worship service. Of course, they ignored the paper.

Samuel Huntington was a teenager when this turmoil swept his village. The Huntington family stayed with the regular, unseparated part of the church. On November 15, 1749, Samuel's eldest brother Nathaniel was ordained to the pastorate at Ellington, Connecticut. Probably Samuel and all the family attended. Preaching the ordination sermon, Devotion warned the candidate to expect "difficulties from men that are under the government of their lusts, prejudice, and ill affections, who won't bear sound doctrine, nor faithful treatment." Shifting from the negative to the positive, he testified: "You will serve the best of masters in the noblest business... The work is...of the last importance to men, that upon which their present peace and future bliss very much depends." He urged declarations of the Word of God which are weighty, plain, and well-stated—declarations in grave language, free from bombast or from grovelling; sublime but not out of the people's reach, with authority, not careless, hurried, nor merry.

⟫●⟪

In 1765, the town of Windham elected Ebenezer Devotion their representative in the lower house of the state legislature. This fact later caused more than one remark by Ezra Stiles, who was eager to praise the usual habits of Connecticut including proper bounds for clergy in relation to government. Rarely in all New England did clergy take seats of government. Ordinarily they were alert observers and unofficial advisors, but not power-wielders. Devotion's status in the assembly was, wrote Stiles, "a very singular instance."

The population of the colony in September of 1762, according to Governor Thomas Fitch's information to the British government's commissioners for trade and plantations, was 141,000 whites, 3,587 blacks, and about 930 Indians. Manufactures were "inconsiderable, the inhabitants being chiefly imployed in subduing, fencing, and improving the land." Revenue was by taxes on lands, polls, and personal estate.

Ordinarily it amounted to about 4,000 pounds sterling, of which about one-eighth was appropriated for schools. "But," reported the Governor as if he was concerned about the portent, Connecticut had met "extraordinary expense" beyond the usual appropriations for government "annually arisen during the course of the present war." The colonies were pleased by their success over the French, but distressed by its cost, and this one senses by Fitch's word "but." Devotion would sit in the lower house amongst men who opposed heavier taxes for the extraordinary expense. The lower house reflected the mind of farmers, while the upper house, with more lawyers and merchants, believed a tax increase was necessary.

Before the British Parliament passed the Stamp Act, Fitch tried to dissuade them by presenting polite legal arguments. He published his arguments to appease public anger at the Stamp proposition. But Parliament passed the Act, and in Connecticut during Devotion's term the house labeled it "unpresedented and unconstitutional." The whole of their resolve contained a preamble and eleven enumerated points.

A printed pamphlet appeared in 1766, subtitled: "In Answer to a Letter from a Gentleman in London to his Friend in America, 'The Claim of the Colonies to an Exemption from Internal Taxes imposed by Authority of Parliament, Examined.'" The title of the answering pamphlet: *The Examiner Examined: a Letter from a Gentleman in Connecticut to his Friend in London*. No author is named, either on the title page or within the pamphlet, but the work is commonly attributed to Devotion. One strong reason for this attribution is a copy in the Yale Library; penned on its title page in the handwriting of Samuel Huntington are the words, "By the Rev. Eben. Devotion, Pastor the church in Scotland only." At the foot of the page is penned, "Saml Huntington, Book."

The "examiner" whom Devotion examined was William Knox, agent in Great Britain for Georgia and East Florida. He had published (London, 1765) *The Claim...Examined*, identifying himself merely as "a landowner in America" who lies under "obligations to many gentlemen in your province." It reads less like a letter than like an essay. Devotion quotes a fair amount of Knox's argument and follows along his opponent's plan of organizing ideas. His examination reads more nearly like a letter, using phrases like, "it would be unkind in me not to believe you, but..." "Your reasoning, sir, slides by the colonies' claim." "But, sir, as you are determined to make thorough work with American liberties, you proceed..."

Readers in America must have focused on Knox's views: another lively reply to him was issued by Daniel Dulaney.

Knox did not really attempt to persuade those who claimed colonial tax exemption; he aimed to fortify those who denied the claim. He was especially effective in appealing to Americans who felt inclined to accommodate the tax, crediting the goodwill of George Grenville, Chancellor of the Exchequer.

Still less did Devotion attempt to persuade. His pamphlet was simple propaganda, designed to strengthen the spirit of American resistance. As in the pulpit he was used to confirming and celebrating the faith of those who had it already, so in this pamphlet he appealed to patriots who already disliked accommodation. He added nothing to the main arguments which had been developed in the resolves of several legislatures and in the declarations and petitions of the Stamp Acts Congress held in New York. Yet he gave those arguments special force by his own suppositions and style.

Knox asserts "that the Parliament of Great Britain has a full and compleat jurisdiction over the property and person of every inhabitant of a British colony." Devotion takes those words as a formula for "the slavery of millions of people who have ever until now thought themselves free-born."

Knox asserts that "the common law of England, the Great Charter, or the bill of rights, are so far from justifying any British subject in his claim of exemption that they with one voice declare the subject shall not be taxed by any other authority than that of Parliament." With relish, Devotion replies: "Sir, I don't know whether you attended to the sophism in this argument... i.e. the Parliament only have the right of taxing the subject, and therefore they must necessarily tax every subject. The reasoning would be the same if one should say, within a colony the supreme court have the exclusive right of hanging a man, therefore they have right to hang every man in the colony."

Devotion, further, contends that common law and Magna Carta are the basis for exemption. Here he joins many Americans of that time in an expansive argument from the British constitution against the policies of the current Grenville and post-Grenville administration. The constitutional documents, he believes, "exempt both our persons and property from the compleat jurisdiction of a British Parliament: for we neither have representation in Parliament, neither can we in any tolerable measure have it."

The two pamphleteers agree that colonial charters recognize a power of taxation by the colonial assemblies. Does that mean that the charters grant exemption from taxation by Parliament? They disagree.

Knox speeds on to a prior question. Can Parliament legally alter grants from the crown? Devotion, after citing some written law, summarizes, "It seems inconsistent to say that the king hath a right to grant charters, 'tis his prerogative, and that the parliament have right to vacate them without forfeiture. It is to suppose two opposite rights, one to give and the other to withhold the same thing at the same time." He thinks the implication of Knox's position is that English people have no other liberties "but such as lie in the breast of Parliament."

Then he presses an idea connected with his view of the structure of both church and state. If Parliament can modify charters, "does it not follow that the whole nexus, the band of union, is broken between Great Britain?" He had agreed, while sitting in the Connecticut House of Representatives, to the resolve, "That the constitution of this colony, being practiced upon as it has been ever since it existed, is the surest band of union, confidence, and mutual prosperity of our mother-country and us..." It "has been verified in fact, and by long experience found to produce... as many loyal, virtuous, industrious, and well governed subjects as any part of his Majesty's dominion."

Devotion felt a security in the tradition of Connecticut, verbalized in the Fundamental Orders of 1639 and largely woven into royal charter later. New departures now seemed to him wild and reckless risks. If the British government wanted a departure, he felt shock.

So he speaks in high rhetoric of "that right of jurisdiction which God and the king have given to the colonies and unto which the parliament have said, Amen; a right absolutely exclusive of all other rights under heaven; a right which could not be vacated by ten thousand violations of it."

As a New England Congregational clergyman, in his thoughts he would have linked the covenant theory of church with the compact theory of state. Both were rooted in Puritan tradition. John Locke, whose political theory was much used as an ideological guide in those days, derived a large amount of "the social contract" from his Calvinist heritage.

Devotion alludes to the movement of the pilgrims from England to Holland to New England, and to the later migration of Puritans. "I ask what determined these colonies to belong to Great Britain, before the charters were given, rather than to Holland?" To him, the answer to that question supports his arguments "For my own part I think of nothing which can with any propriety determine these colonies to belong to Great Britain but contract. This contract, on the part of the king...are the charters...on the part of the colonies, their acceptance and submission."

If the charters now are unsafe, he implies, the colonies' loyalty is unsafe. "They alone determine our relation to and connection with Great Britain." Subtly he enlarges on the threat: "I am far from wishing to have the American colonies disjoined from Great Britain." In those words, ten years before the Declaration of Independence, he speaks the unspeakable.

His second main dispute with Knox is over the latter's assertion "that the prosperity and security of the colonies has arisen from, and is connected with" Parliament's jurisdiction. When Knox argues that the large debt of Americans to the British merchants means that the creditors have confidence in the colonial system, Devotion's reply is like a hoot. "O prosperous colonists, to be in debt for their cloathing twice so much as their real property!"

In preparing to stand against the Stamp Act, the Connecticut legislature referred to Governor Fitch's reasoning when he wrote against it. Fitch's document included a whole section describing the economic situation of the colonies under British mercantilism. The colonies consumed British manufactures and products of other countries shipped in by British traders. The crown revenue as well as the British national wealth was thereby increased at the expense of the colonies. Profits from the whole trade cycle, said the document, "in general center in Great Britain."

Thus Devotion could not have given Knox's economic argument much weight. "The stating your argument is enough to refute it," he said.

———◆———

A copy of *The Examiner Examined* in the Benjamin Franklin Papers collection, Yale Library, bears manuscript notes by the Reverend Benjamin Throop attributing the authorship to Ebenezer Devotion. Throop was pastor at Bozrah, not far from Scotland.

———◆———

SNAKE'S NEST

"Cooler, men of Reason. Cooler.
Why do you rave? Your words flow hot.
Why so furious toward the king?'
Judge soberly. Does he wrong you?"

"Yes, wrongs! By small, yet steady acts
He makes us his nest to hatch out
Here a brood of legalized Snakes."

As did Cogswell, Ebenezer Devotion attended the September, 1767, meeting at New Haven of Connecticut clergy and clergy from the Presbyterian Synod of New York and Philadelphia. Like rivals trying to make a good impression on a new girl in school, Connecticut's Old Light and New Light factions jostled with each other at the meeting. The Presbyterian men attempted to promote harmony.

They debated whether the annual interchurch meetings should be continued and, if so, what the goals should he. Perhaps they felt somewhat less anxious than a year ago over the supposed threat of an Anglican bishop. They debated whether any persons who were not duly elected delegates should be seated and, if so, whether the New Light faction, with a grip on some Associations, should control the whole Connecticut delegation. They considered various methods of meeting, open convention, business by small committees, business by correspondence only. Joseph Bellamy advised keeping to the original plan of procedures. When Devotion concurred, they appointed him the Old Light member of a committee of three, with a New Light and a neutral, to plan continuation along the former lines.

Thus meetings continued to 1775, but neither Devotion nor Cogswell attended another. Enoch Huntington was present in 1768, Joseph Huntington, in 1775.

Meanwhile both Old Light clergymen like Devotion and New Lights drew together because of the disputes with Great Britain. The transition from political leadership by Governor Fitch and his allies to that of Governors Pitkin and Trumbull has often been interpreted as the result of New Light activism in eastern Connecticut. But actually the situation was scrambled. During the war, for instance, more than a thousand citizens voted for a western Connecticut Old Light clergyman patriot, the Reverend Elizur Goodrich, as a protest against Trumbull's supposed laxity in resisting trade in British goods via Connecticut ports.

Fitch was an Old Light, yet other Old Lights like Goodrich were pronounced resisters.

Furthermore, allegiances to Old Light and New Light church factions, prior to issues like the Stamp Act which opened a period of greater unity, were scattered statewide. Bethlehem, Connecticut, located in the western part of the colony, was where the most illustrious New Light of all, Joseph Bellamy, was pastor from 1738 until his death in 1789. But James Dana and John Hubbard, Jr., faced strong New Light opposition west of the Connecticut River, at Wallingford and Meriden. Most of the "Separate" Congregational churches, it is true, arose in the east. But if their presence suggests New Light strength, their inability to win a majority of the local church members to agreement with them suggests that Old Lights held a popular grip. Eastern Old Light clergymen Benjamin Lord (Samuel Huntington's pastor at Norwich, famous during the war for long prayers about current events) and George Beckwith (Hamburg) served on the Yale Corporation.

Besides owning a copy of *The Examiner Examined*, Samuel Huntington, then a lawyer at Norwich, gave other evidences of concern about the Stamp Act issue. He was one of the signers of a petition to the session of the General Assembly when Devotion was a member. The signers complained that the Stamp Act would bring "insupportable burdens" to Connecticut and the other colonies.

Also he associated himself with Jonathan Sturges, a leader in Fairfield of the militant "Sons of Liberty," through a letter in March, 1766, to Isaac Sears and the Sons of Liberty in New York. The letter acknowledged "most agreeable intelligence." Probably news had been relayed from London to New York to Fairfield concerning the likelihood that Parliament would repeal the Stamp Act.

He may or may not have attended the Sons of Liberty meeting about the same time, in Hartford, when people from various parts of Connecticut voted their approval of intercolonial joint resistance.

Samuel Huntington had five brothers and three sisters. The fourth brother, Eliphalet, remained on the farm to succeed their father. The eldest, Nathaniel, after graduating from Yale and ministering estimably to the Ellington church less than seven years, died of consumption at the age of 31 years.

Jonathan, the third son, was educated like Samuel, without benefit of college. Musician (composer of the round "Scotland's Burning"), then a "physician," he finally became pastor of the church in Worthington, Massachusetts, from 1771 to his death ten years later. A letter from Samuel to the Reverend Mr. Lyman, August 20, 1781, shows that these brothers had stayed in touch.

Enoch Huntington, eighth child in the family, is far better known. He graduated as a "Berkeley Scholar" at Yale.When he gave the master's valedictory and his elder brother Joseph the bachelor's salutatory at the same commencement exercise, in 1762, a hearer praised both, "excepting that they exceeded in length." Samuel's brevity of speech was not characteristic of those two.

Enoch went to Yale young. He earned his bachelor's degree before he was 20. (Joseph worked first as a clothier, the father's trade in addition to farming, and was 27 years old when he received his bachelor's degree).

Enoch stayed at Yale, tutoring and earning a master's, making life-long friendships with various Yale-oriented men. He was pastor at Middletown for nearly half a century and from 1780 a member of the Yale Corporation; from 1783 a member of its inner "prudential committee; 1788–93, its secretary. His name was one of several put forward to fill the vacant professorship of divinity in 1781 (Joseph's name, too, for the same vacancy), and, the college presidency itself in 1795.

In the election of the divinity professor, President Stiles called on Enoch to cast the first vote. It went to Abraham Baldwin. Probably this was a cue for others who intended merely to support the insiders' candidate, and the corporation elected Baldwin. Then when Baldwin declined, Enoch helped win the consent of Samuel Wales, second choice, to accept the position.

Upon Stiles' death in 1795, Enoch's name was put forward for the presidency of the college. His health was no longer adequate, however. Anyway, Timothy Dwight was too formidable. Dwight was one of a large number of preparatory students who had gone to Enoch for schooling before entering Yale; 30 years later, he sent his own son to be Enoch's pupil.

Enoch was generally rated an able, affable, and diligent pastor. Although his public speaking was flawed by a "hesitation" and his pleasant voice was strained during a cold, eventually, which shrivelled it to a whisper, his church persisted in admiring and liking him. He and his wife Mary had ten children.

During the political crisis with Great Britain, his attitude could not have been plainer. He preached a sermon at Middletown, for example, on the continental Fast Day, 1775. He compared America to Nehemiah and the workers who rebuilt Jerusualem's walls against the wishes of hostile chiefs nearby. "It is the duty of a people who are thus falsely and wickedly dealt with by their enemies, for their intimidation and hurt, to look to God by prayer to strengthen their hands." Sweepingly he charged Great Britain with "secret intrigue and open violence," presumably referring to measures in the colonies for enforcing the Stamp Act, then the Tea Act, finally the Intolerable Acts. And to the government from Grenville to North:

> We see, for a course of years, a long series of plans and schemes of subtle statesmen, and parliamentary debates and acts and resolutions, under ministerial influence, all evidently calculated to subdue this country. And if there has been a change of ministries, yet there hath been no essential change of measures.

In consonance with Whigs of past generations, he protested earlier conditions:

> The British constitution, heretofore so much the glory and happiness of our own nation and the envy and terror of foreigners, has from time to time been undermined till at length, under the hands of bribery and corruption, it seems rotten to the very core. Royal charters and the most valuable and essential rights of Englishmen have been unjustly and cruelly wrestled away, or most want only violated or sported with.

Instead of more epithets, he cited concrete offenses: "Whole fleets and armies, the *ultima ratio*, instead of sound reason and the principles of the British constitution, and of right and religion, made use of to convert us as a people." Also, "tortured language," probably an allusion to General Gage's June 12 proclamation of martial law, with its offer of pardon to rebels who turn and give allegiance to the crown ("particularly in a late proclamation set forth by him who has the infamy of being the chief ministerial tool of vengeance in this distressed country.") Again, the Quebec Bill, as if it were shame on "the dignitaries of the English Church in their places as members of Parliament" who voted for it.

> They are caressed as friends of government, while clergymen of different principles and conduct, of whatever church or particular Christian profession they be, who converse upon and preach up as occasion requires the duties, the privileges and liberty of the gospel and the friendly aspect it has upon the civil rights and happiness of mankind, and dare not attempt to press the religion taught by the Prince of Peace and most benevolent Saviour of men into the service of tyranny and oppression, and who show to the people the privileges and rights which they enjoy by divine revelation and how they ought to improve them so as to answer their duty and find their happiness, are called fanatical courting preachers, incendiaries, independents, enemies to government and order, and what not, and are marked out as objects deserving the severest chastisement.

After berating the dignitaries further and deploring molestations by Parliament, he reaches the point of defiance: "We have no alternative left us but to submit without conditions to all the demands of unjustly usurped and exorbitant power, or passively be knocked on the head and sacrificed in death, or make a noble, united and vigorous opposition. That the last is so universally the resolution of the country is matter of joy and thankfulness and an omen for good."

———————⟹⧫⟸———————

Samuel Huntington was the fourth child but the second son. Joseph was the fourth son.

Joseph described himself later as "much disposed to a studious life and always delighting greatly in books." He "spent much of his time in reading and enquiry, in the early periods of life."

He added: "Being also much favoured by a kind providence with regard to the best means of instruction, and a pious example from his parents in his early days, and afterwards with a more public education, the disposition of his heart inclined him, in great preference to all other employments, to the study of divinity."

When he and Enoch were students at Yale, the president of the college was a prounounced Calvinist, Thomas Clap. Holding that all Puritan colleges should adhere to the Westminster Catechism and the Savoy Confession of Faith, Clap shaped studies to tradition. So Joseph became a Calvinist. But he was inquisitive all his life and helped "New

Haven Theology" move onward from the strict Calvinism of Edwards' disciples toward the liberal Calvinism coming later under Nathaniel W. Taylor.

Joseph's years at Yale fell during a restless season. Clap was overly authoritarian. He attempted to regulate student life minutely beneath his own standards. Moreover, he attempted strenuously to enforce the regulations, authorizing himself even "to break down any college door" for the purpose of dealing with disorder. He contracted with a local tavern keeper, granting a monopoly on student liquor in exchange for an oath not to sell to students without written permission.

As a warning of dissatisfaction beyond the campus, the General Assembly stopped its habitual annuity to the college, explaining it merely as a means of cutting expenses. But an anonymous pamphlet, to which Clap replied anonymously, showed that the issue was Clap's style.

Two years before Joseph's graduation, Clap delayed the departure of graduates after commencement because they had spent time in "idleness and bickering." That was the year when no senior would consent to deliver the salutatory address in place of the classmate who had earned it by scholarship and Clap was denying the privilege to that student as a punishment. Someone had left a six-gallon barrel of rum in the college yard; all but five seniors confessed to being the culprit. When Clap threatened to deny them all their degrees, they wrote an apology which was read at commencement instead of the salutatory address.

Scribbled in books surviving from the college library of that period are comments such as "tyrant" and "old Tom Clap, you are quite wrong in your form of government."

Clap kept up the warfare until, fatigued in 1766, four years after Joseph's graduation, he quit.

Through all the turbulence the president and tutors were training Joseph in Bible, ancient languages, and Ames' theology and ethics. Also mathematics, geography, natural science, and Locke's philosophy. The books in the college library were supplemental. Clap advised students to read along "a regular course of academical studies" — first year, languages, arithmetic, and algebra; second year, logic, rhetoric, geometry; third year, mathematics, natural philosophy; fourth year, ethics and divinity.

In 1763, Joseph was ordained pastor at Coventry, not far from his home village. There he remained for 31 years, until he died. His own summary: he "soon took the pastoral charge of a kind and respectable people, from whom he has ever received…kindnesses.., living in a scene of harmony and love, excepting only with respect to a very few individuals, at one time and another, who yet have given him no great trouble."

He was credited with uniting the people of his church after they previously had become disheartened. Soon they built a new meeting-house.

The year after he settled in Coventry, he married Hannah Devotion, younger sister of Samuel's wife Martha. Young Sammy was born in 1765, Fanny in 1769. But in 1771, Hannah died, only 28; the two children went to live with Samuel and Martha.

As did Enoch and many other able clergymen, Joseph prepared a number of older boys for college. Among those he taught was Nathan Hale. Later Joseph remarried and fathered more children.

He sympathized with people who had problems, judging them charitably. For instance, he rather incautiously got into a pamphlet dispute, 1779–81, which grew out of his defense of a Mrs. Fisk, a woman who had been excommunicated by the Stockbridge church for marrying a "profane and immoral" man.

During that time he also wrote as follows to a clergyman at Springfield: She "had, when she left us, made full gospel satisfaction for the sin of fornication, which was the only visible and scandalous sin, so far as we know, which she had ever committed while resident with us. We therefore recommended her to all such gospel privileges as a visible gospel penitent may justly claim."

In 1777, when the Yale Corporation was electing a new president of the college, five on the first ballot voted for Ezra Stiles, four for Elizur Goodrich. Goodrich, who was too modest to vote for himself but unwilling to enlarge the majority for Stiles, cast a vote for Joseph Huntington.

Joseph was not really a contender at that election, but came closer to the presidency of another college. Some of his private pupils had entered Dartmouth College, and after 1769, when the king granted Dartmouth a charter, Joseph's ongoing sympathy had been welcome. President Eleazar Wheelock in his will named his friend Joseph to succeed to the presidency if his son, John Wheelock, chose not to take the office. Eleazar died in 1779, and there followed a time of suspense. John Wheelock was undecided. Ezra Stiles heard that eight out of ten Dartmouth trustees preferred Joseph. But John Wheelock eventually decided to accept, and Dartmouth awarded Joseph an honorary D.D.

degree in 1780 and elected him a trustee (1780–88). Young Sammy attended Dartmouth 1778–84, but transferred to Yale and graduated there in 1785 in the same class as that of his cousin, young Enoch.

Joseph's son Joseph Jr. also attended Dartmouth during those years, did not transfer to Yale, and Dartmouth in 1785 deferred granting his degree until a disciplinary question was resolved. An already separated Dartmouth student, Stephen Burroughs, who saw himself and young Joseph as "full of vivacity" and "almost perpetually prosecuting some scene of amusement or diversion," may have been involved in the discipline question. "My son was indeed much to blame," wrote Joseph, the worried parent, to John Wheelock. "I have been faithful with him by letter and shall add everything proper on my part."

Young Joseph soon married the sister of Lorenzo Dow, moved to Charleston, practiced law, and died in 1794—perhaps as the result of a duel.

At year end 1780, Ezra Stiles was reading "Dr. Huntington's letters on the New Divinity."

The two most notable of Joseph's several publications were *The Vanity and Mischief of Presuming on Things Beyond Our Measure*, which was a sermon delivered in 1774 and *The Gospel Improved, or, the Gospel Illustrated as a System of Real Grace, Issuing in the Salvation of All Men*, printed posthumously.

In the first of these he shows an interest in practical reason in preference to speculative reason. He seems to have accepted the concerns of "common sense" philosophy, such as John Witherspoon brought to Princeton with him from across the ocean, while aiming to harmonize those concerns with Calvinist tradition.

In the preface, he says he does not want to discourage inquiry. But he proposes tests for novel statements about truth,

1. Is it a point that is reducible to practice, for the promotion of vital piety and holy living?
2. Are our ideas in this point more sensible, clear, and distinct than they have been in many other cases in time past, in which we have afterward been abundantly convinced of our mistake?
3. What influence has our new discovery on those churches that we look upon the true churches of Christ? Does it promote harmony, peace, piety, and love among them? and mutuality between them?
4. How does it fit the minds of our Christian brethren? Those of them whom, without a compliment, we esteem at least as learned, as wise,

as sincere as ourselves, and as having made as honest and diligent inquiry into that very point as we have? Do most of these wise, learned, inquisitive persons agree with us and see the evidence much as we do?

5. Does our new supposed discovery promote our communion with the blessed God, increase our charity and goodwill to men, and really mend our hearts, our conversation, and our lives?

6. Does "the God of truth who rideth forth in the cause of truth" (Psalm 65:4) own and bless our new discovery and the arguments we advance in favor of it, for the general good of the human kind?

Joseph is aware of his place amidst the community of inquiring thinkers in religion, a way which resembles Samuel's awareness, among legislators and determiners of law.

The "things beyond our measure" which he has in mind, he is ready to illustrate:

> If we inquire how it was possible for holy creatures to become unholy...

> How unbodied spirits have access to, and operate upon our senses here in this world?... How is it that our words convey certain ideas to one another?... Our knowledge of these things lies mainly in facts; the ground and reason of these facts is a secret pertaining to the eternal mind...

> Fore-knowledge... It is only in regard to our way of conceiving that we call the knowledge of God, before Creation began, by the name of fore-knowledge... To inquire after our own election to everlasting life any otherwise than from the evidence of our sanctification is big with trouble and confusion to our minds...

> The doctrine of the Holy Trinity; we must indeed believe it, and a very glorious doctrine it is. But who can make plain to the human mind that divine mystery?

> Or should we ask why God suffered some angels to fall while he upheld others? Why the whole stock of humanity was plunged, so soon, in guilt and woe? Why a Savior was provided for our rebel world, in neglect of sinning angels? What our own lot will be in days to come? Why people who appear to be equally wicked or godly have such a different lot in this world? Why one nation in the world is favoured so highly above another? Why so few of mankind hear the sound of the glorious gospel? Why one soul

among the same people, and in the same assembly, is effectually called and another left to perish in his sins? It is beyond us to answer these questions, and thousands more.

He lists several dangers of perplexing our minds with such questions. "Never," he observes, "did the Christian people of this country see the time when the minds of the good, as well as others, were so much exercised about the nonessentials of religion, and curious to know things that relate neither to having faith nor to an holy and virtuous life."

In varying paragraphs, he draws applications such as: "Most say, the consent of the will is ever found in the act of saving faith, and the affections are also concerned in it. And whatever philosophy there may be to make the former sentiment plausible, the latter, I very humbly think, hath much more theology in favor of it."

Calvinism Improved is a carefully organized work of 331 pages, which Joseph said he had meditated for more than 20 years. On a basis of biblical-Calvinistic ideas, he contends against the orthodox conclusion that salvation is limited to only a part of humanity and that the remainder are eternally damned.

The biblical texts for his title page are I Timothy 2, 4, 5, 6. He gives the words of verse 6: "A ransom for all, to be testified in due time."

In his introduction, he recalls having preached "the limitarian plan" with satisfaction to others. But he could not finally feel satisfied.

> He preached, as did other divines, the atonement of Christ, a full and complete sacrifice for every sinner in the world, and the divine law wholly satisfied in the obedience of Christ unto death; that every sinner on earth was alike invited and most solemnly commanded to believe on Christ to the saving of his soul; that it was the greatest of all sin and rebellion against God not to believe unto salvation, and alike so in every sinner that heard the gospel; and that having faith did not create or in the least change the object or foundation of it, but was wholly grounded on an object and foundation forever immutable.

He states that he holds all those doctrines "more firmly now, if possible, than ever before, except only with regard to the limitation of the covenant of redemption, as not according to the eternal purpose of God."

In other words, he protests that he is still orthodox on the main points of Calvinism. He has investigated "neonomian" and "arminian" opinions and has found them "inconsistent with divine revelation."

He diverges at one point alone. In the Bible "I find a most glorious and astonishing system, and exhibitions of divine wisdom, power, and love, most harmoniously consistent with itself and with all the divine attributes, with pure reason, and with God's conduct in the universe; and in a most blessed way, accommodated and adapted to guilty, miserable man, in all the depth of his entire impotency and guilt; a complete Savior, undertaking to deliver him alike from both."

As a consequence of this intellectual find, "I can now preach the gospel to every creature, i.e. I can tell every human creature under heaven, Good news to him."

It leads to reflections:

> The more I have thought on these things, the more I am convinced of the utter inconsistency of the general preaching of Protestant divines, on any other ground than this...

> I am well aware that such an open advancing step to pour light into the minds of men, though it is no other, in the nature of it, than what has been many times done, may as in former times, in all probability, be an occasion of great alarms in the minds of many pious, good people. Among the rest (which is to me most disagreeable in prospect) several of my dearest and most valuable connections will probably be more wounded by this publication, or at least more aggrieved, than any other persons on my account.

At the time it came out, his book did shock New England. It was called "Calvinistic Universalist" doctrine. An alarmed clergyman published a defense of damnation. One of Joseph's daughters is said to have burned much of the printing as a sacrifice to orthodoxy.

He had faced the probable alarm calmly. "A spirit of enquiry, of light and liberty, does wonderfully increase," he believed.

Further, the second or third generation after his own may behold, he believed, the blessed millenial day. The "power of true religion in that day will not be brought on so much by the awful thunderings of divine wrath, and threatenings of hell and damnation, as by leading the blind, fearful minds and guilty souls of men to see and know the true character of God and the Savior... A sense and enjoyment of life eternal will abound, and the cords of love will effectually draw dead sinners to holiness and virtue."

At the same 1784 session of the Connecticut General Assembly which would elect Samuel Huntington, his presidency of Congress past, to the office of Deputy Governor (and this timing was probably no sheer coincidence), Joseph Huntington preached the election sermon. It was entitled, *God Ruling the Nations for the Most Glorious End.* Excitement over the occasion is suggested in what he said. He included a timely tribute to Governor Trumbull, retiring after his long public career, in particular his wartime leadership. And he included an appeal that Connecticut give "honorable support" to high government officials.

As if to heighten suspense until the moment of Samuel's rise from the upper house to the deputy governorship, with its possibility of succession to the top chair, Joseph touched on some memories: "When our tyrannical enemies first attacked us, it was with a force just enough to rouse and invigorate us, but by no means equal to a conquest. Had they fallen on us with all their might, unarmed, unprovided as we then were, what would have become of us? They pressed upon us with increasing force just fast enough to confirm our union and martial spirit..."

At the moment of pressure, of course, his hindsight was not available for the assurance of Samuel and other national leaders.

"The forming of the great council of our nation was indeed wonderful. Our Association, bill of rights, Articles of Confederation, and alliance, display divine wisdom and goodness. Our naval achievements, especially when we were weakest, have shown that God is might."

Even Samuel's intractable and bitter problem, "faithless, depreciating paper currency" is seen as a sign of Providence. "It has answered the end of a mighty tax upon us, and has made even filthy rags a cord for the necks of our enemies."

He detects the goodness of God "from the first effusion of blood at Lexington to the grand decisive scene at Gloucester and Yorktown."

The sermon was composed for the ear, easy and rhetorical. Only after delivery was it converted into print. It was not short. Printed, it comes to 42 pages. The first half is an exposition of Deuteronomy 32:8, which deals with a mythical, pre-memorial event: God "divided" the world's population, gave the nations their "inheritance," and "set the bounds."

It is largely a pageant-like recital of the emergence of nations, according to biblical and other classical sources, with the Calvinist view that all occurred by divine determination for a happy purpose.

Joseph is aware of tension between determinism and freedom. He voices the intellectual problem and confesses the inadequacy of an intellectual solution. Reasoning from "attributes" of God, as Thomas Clap had taught him to do, he asserts that God determines all things "in boundless wisdom and goodness." But "if any would thence infer that there is no freedom of will or moral agency in men, no desert of praise or blame, let them look into their own bosoms." He is content with the submission, "God is incomprehensible."

Diversity of languages, growth of nations to the point of political overweight, wars, tyrannies, religious persecutions, as well as valid ambitions leading the nations through adventure to social adulthood — these have served as "means" by which God has worked toward a chosen end. And the end? It is variously suggested throughout the sermon as universal brotherhood, immortal happiness, liberty, holiness, the kingdom of Christ, and summarized in the relic phrase, "that God may reign."

Although he celebrates the past of New England, he does not sigh for its return. Although he anticipates the Messianic Time in the near future, he does not hope away a careful attention to interim problems. The biblical framework and biblical detail which comprise much of his statement has been blended with the more philosophic religion of nature typical of his century. He quotes Milton, Shakespeare, Cicero. Congenial as he finds the emergent national feeling of America, and central as is his American standpoint as he surveys world history, yet he calls for universalism. "God wills," he says in the second part of the sermon, "that mankind should live on equal terms, as brethren."

Noting American experience along with the experiences of Old Testament Israel and of Greece, Rome, and young America's national contemporaries, all "sons of Adam," he reflects:

> As individuals and families are brethren and neighbors to each other, so are societies, towns, states, and nations, and should always act the fraternal part, and the neighbor...

> The horrors of wanton, offensive war appear in their proper colors. It is only Cain murdering Abel his brother.

God orders events "that all the nations of the earth shall be subservient to his own peculiar nation and kingdom." It is neither a special church nor a special nation which the preacher is stressing. It is covenant with God. God has acted "with a most tender regard to his own covenant people, in every age, wherever they might dwell, or whatever their number might be." Besides instances from past times, he would include "the great monarchy of France" (it would be five years before revolution there would sober and polarize American estimates of our wartime ally). The French monarch was honored for a purpose: "to protect the rights of mankind, to patronize liberty, and serve the cause of religion in such a day as this."

America was, of course, vivid in his message. He did not recite providential history without specifying a Whig version of the recent crisis, "How well-connected and quiet was the great British empire, from the accession of the Prince of Orange till after the death of George the Second? And how did every branch of the empire dread the thought of division? But when a British king became a tyrant and the parliament a band of despots, and would be content with nothing less than to bind a great part of the empire in chains of perpetual slavery... When they caused the sea and the waves along our coast to roar with their hostile thunder..."

Having begun his second part of the sermon with the words, "We have lately received our inheritance, as a distinct sovereign empire, from the great Disposer of all things," Joseph mentions the fertile land, but at greater length applauds the "civil constitution." He repeats an analogy which he had already suggested in 1781, when preaching at Hartford — "the body politic in similitude to that of the natural body." Again now he points out that Old Testament Israel "had thirteen free, independent states." An Israelite tribe, Joseph, when subdivided had made thirteen. (After the impending admissions of Vermont and Kentucky, the analogy would presumably become obsolete). "Out of these states their supreme council or general Congress was chosen, by delegates from each, often called their Sanhedrin." Further, "Each state managed its own internal police, each had a General Assembly composed of their best men, at the free election of the people, often called the elders of the tribe. Their government was theocratical. So for substance is our free, elective government."

Political philosophy had long been asking whether monarchy, aristocracy, democracy, or a mixture of those, was the best form of government. Mainline Calvinism had settled on aristocracy, checked and balanced by democracy. The aristocrats should especially be a community's "best men." Character counted most. Joseph was orthodox on that.

Logically enough, therefore, in the "jeremiad" which had become a stock component of election sermons, Joseph chooses only one social evil to treat at any length. "We are endangered by many vices — injustice and distortion, idleness and luxury, prophane swearing, the sure mark of a thoughtless sinner; a prophanation of the holy sabbath, intemperance, lasciviousness and wantonness, pride and extravagance." So far, it was a standard list for its time.

"But there is one abominable vice that is so pernicious to us every day, and so immediately threatens us with dissolution and anarchy, that I must bear my testimony more largely against it." (One understands that the revolutionary moment has new passed, and the task of national and state construction remains. More immediately, one interprets the threat he is about to describe in terms of the responsibilities his brother is about to assume).

"It is that unreasonable, raging spirit of jealousy pointing against all in power, especially against those in the most burdensome and important trusts."

Joseph does not name particular trusts and particular persons. Rather, his argument is twofold. "We elect all our rulers, and often enough in all reason. We choose such as we esteem men of the greatest wisdom and probity." He insists, "They are as good after in office as before."

The second point in the argument: jealousy destroys right judgment on the part of those who are jealous.

Still, the human nature of rulers bears our vigilance. "I would have all in power elective by and accountable to the people; and if in any case criminal, on fair trial, let them not be spared."

A clear sign of the adjustment to a new time is Joseph's concern for creditors, during his final remarks. The Assembly should pay debts owed to domestic lenders and foreign nations who aided the cause of American independence. Holders of loan office certificates, which helped finance the war, should be duly repaid. (Whether his family back on the home farm, along with other Connecticut farmers, were ready for the necessary taxes, Joseph seemed to expect the state to shift from the pattern of rural beginnings toward an economy of trade, cash, and paper forms. And had not brother Samuel pleaded from the chair of Congress to the states about sending money, whether from taxes or from loans? A profound financial settlement was necessarily underway).

In closing, Joseph addresses his fellow clergymen and the audience at large, previewing the hopeful time coming when Messiah reigns in visible glory over all the earth. "Great men shall mingle with common people... Mighty movements of providence in this world shall cease, and kingdoms, states, and empires be no more. Then shall we all know what is the true wisdom and happiness of mortal man." His premillenial belief was not elaborate nor lurid; he did not force it into the support of his thoughts about present practice. But it gave him joy and allowed him to face immediate facts buoyantly.

———⟫●⟪———

"There will be at the next election, as I think, uncommon unanimity with respect to the upper house; no alteration at all, your uncle has all the votes in this parish, and all in the town, except three Shayites, which is best read per syncopen. *This, so far as I can collect, is nearly a specimen for the other towns in the state. You must prepare for his succession at some distant period...*

"I hope to wait on the Governor, with you and his other attendants, on his way to the election, at my home."
—Joseph Huntington to young Samuel, April 8, 1788
(The elder Huntington served as
Governor of Connecticut, 1786–96).

———⟫●⟪———

The younger Samuel (Joseph's son, Samuel the elder's foster son) graduated from Yale, entered the Connecticut bar, aided his foster father's work in law and government. After the elder Samuel's death, the younger moved to Ohio, where he became Chief Justice of Ohio's Supreme court and the third Governor.

Sammy's manners were hail-fellow and free, but sister Fanny's far more subdued. She stayed with her widower-foster father till he died, then married the Rev. Edward Dorr Griffin, one of the founders of the American Bible Society, President of Williams College 1821–1836.

———⟫●⟪———

"Refused several invitations to dine out, that I might eat turkey with the Governor. Thanksgiving has not gone yet, for we had flip and pompion pies both. Drank several glasses of port, and was much pleased with several musical anecdotes from the Governor."
—Mason F. Cogswell,
travel journal, late 1788

———⟫●⟪———

THE PROPOSED MIXTURE

Which way is best for making societal policies? Monarchy? Aristocracy? Democracy?

America in the 18th Century said "no" to
monarchy. And they inquired, "Dear John Calvin.
Your fideist proposal of a mixture of aristocracy and
democracy is fascinating us. It seems an adequate
theory. Still, can it work out in practice?"

The First Presidential Year

"Congress have done no business these two days past on account of the state of Connecticut not being represented, the Prest. being from that state."

—Samuel Holten, diary,
November 3, 1779

"The President of Congress drank tea with us."

—Samuel Holten, diary,
December 3, 1779

"It is five years this day since the war commenced. I dined with the President of Congress."

—Samuel Holten, diary,
April 19, 1780

Huntington, whose eyes were said to be dark and piercing, engages in a warm personal exchange with his Connecticut colleague and friend, Oliver Wolcott:
"Had fortune favourd you with black eyes, it seems I might have still been more happy in being favourd with your personal conversation and company. However, it seems the matter is not yet so fully desired but that I may have some hopes that good gray eyes will possibly do."

—November 26, 1779

FOR FREEDOM

Imagine doubtful thoughts like:
"The thirteen states — concerted?"
For freedom. Yes.
"Pptt! Concede, my state is best!
The merchant and plowman — both?"
For freedom. Yes.
"Pptt! Concede, they always clash!
Allies — and independence?"
For freedom, Yes.
"Pptt! Concede, it can't happen.
Lawmaking by the people
And days of humble prayer — both?"

"My time is so incessantly employed in the indispensable engagements allotted to me at present, as obliges me to confide in my colleagues to transmit to your Excellency and the state we have the honour to represent most of the intelligence which is not official. And I doubt not my particular situation and confinement will plead an excuse for me."
    —Huntington to Governor Trumbull,
    April, 1780

Joy to great Congress, joy an hundredfold,
The grand cajolers are themselves cajol'd,
The farce of empire will be furnish'd soon,
And each mock monarch dwindle to a loon;
Mock money and mock States shall meet away,
Ana the mock troops disband for want of pay.
E'en now decisive ruin is prepar'd,
E'en now the heart of Huntington is scar'd.

    —Rivington's *Gazette*,
    loyalist newspaper,
    November 6, 1779

"When the procession arrived at the Roman Catholic chapel, the priest presented the holy water to Monsieur Luzerne, who, after sprinkling himself, presented it to Mr. Huntington, President of the Congress. The Calvinist paused a considerable time, (near a minute), but at length his affection for the great and good ally conquered all scruples of conscience, and he too besprinkled and sanctified himself with all the adroitness of a veteran Catholic."

—Rivington's *Gazette*
loyalist newspaper reporting the
funeral of Don Juan de Mirralles,
May 20, 1780

"I have the pleasure to inform you that the Chevalier de la Luzerne, the Minister of France, is in good health and much respected with us. I the rather mention this because Rivington, the British printer in New York, hath lately published an account that the people here were highly disgusted with him, which occasioned the Minister to repair to General Washington's camp, where he died by the hand of violence; than which nothing could be more false and scandalous and might give concern to the Minister's friends if not detected."

—Huntington to the Marquis de Bouillé,
governor in the Antilles,
May 27, 1780

Huntington was elected on September 28, 1779, taking the chair immediately.

Fourteen years after the Stamp Act seemed to Americans a long time.

"A free people," Huntington commented in a letter to Jonathan Trumbull, Jr., "must feel before they will unite in the necessary measures." The people had felt intent. Then they relaxed somewhat.

Boys who were infants at the time of the Stamp Act, unable to stand up or grasp a toy, now were working the hayfields, swinging their scythes for hours.

It was five years after the First Continental Congress. Four years after the shots at Lexington and Concord.

At first people thought they could rush to Boston and drive the British off North America. Now, 1779, the British occupied New York and Newport and Savannah. Howe had even spent a winter in Philadelphia.

Was this war costing too much time away from fields and trades and families?

King George was angry and firm. Was it wise to keep on defying him? He commanded great resources.

———

To Shovel Again, or Not

A man may want to change the channel of a creek running through his farm. Where he digs, the stones do not move unless the man works very hard. The stones mock his labor. The early mornings chill him. Noons scorch him and the flies know him by his sweat, crowding close. The timbers of a broken fence sass him when he passes by. "Every job tended costs other jobs neglected."

He keeps on digging, makes a new channel, turns water into it. Then he plans how to use the broader surface of the ground for the next seed time. Before then, however, spring thaw and big runoff. Floods seek out the old channel, mindless of his scolding and bellowing, his furious whacks with mattock and shovel. He ponders and starts to dig again. But how many more springs shall he dig again?

"I hope no man's heart will faint," declared Samuel Huntington. "If we continue firm and united, we must secure our rights and liberties." But that was back in 1776.

"From the best intelligence," he wrote in 1780, "it appears beyond a doubt that the British administration flatter themselves that such is the state of our finances, and the circumstances of this country, we cannot any longer keep up an army. Upon this they buoy up their hope and encourage their people that we shall soon submit to their terms."

Congress had just decided (September 1, 1779) not to print more paper money, once $200,000,000 had been printed.

That decision was like permitting a surgeon to cut off one's infected leg. Two hundred years later we forget the seriousness of it. If we remember its context at all, we may remember only Washington's waiting for Congress to send him an army and supplies so that he could join the soon-to-arrive or the now-arriving forces from France and go fight. Or that he waited mostly in vain.

The fact is that since June, 1775, they had been issuing the paper money, "bills of credit," thereby for a time paying the expenses of war and of forming a minimal federal government. They knew very well that they should not allow the supply of money increase faster than the young American economy needed it. To do so, they understood, would cause depreciation. But how else could they obtain a revenue?

In October, 1776, they offered four per cent interest on domestic loans; a few months later, six per cent. Loans were far from enough help. They began to issue "bills of exchange" on the credit of their commissioners in France. At last, before the states felt that their taxing procedures were sturdy enough to bear the strain, they requisitioned money from the state governments. According to Article VIII of the Articles of Confederation, federal expenses "shall be defrayed out of a common treasury, which shall be supplied by the several states." Taxes for such supply "shall be laid and levied by the authority and direction of the legislatures of the several states."

Revenue from those sources always lagged behind disbursement. So Congress printed more bills of credit, the value declined, and Congress could not retire old bills before new bills were circulating with them. Loans and taxes were not supplying treasury demand.

The awful chore facing Congress when Huntington became President was to govern without enough money. Whether on an infected leg or without the leg, America must struggle on.

———◦———

Congress conducted its business in fairly close accordance with the Articles of Confederation, having approved them nearly two years back, and sent them to the states for ratification.

Even after Thomas Burke's Article II ("Each state retains its sovereignty, freedom, and independence, and every power, juridsiction, and right which is not by this confederation expressly delegated to the United States, in Congress assembled"), some members feared that

Congress had too much power. At the same time, other members feared that they had too little.

They had power to make war and peace. Also, to exchange ambassadors, enter into treaties and alliances, set rules for captures on land and sea, settle disputes between states, regulate coinage, weights, and measures. Also, to manage Indian affairs, provide a postal system, appoint officers for army and navy, and direct operations of the armed forces.

They had no power to tax. Also, none to regulate trade. They could not enforce their requisitions. State legislatures selected delegates to Congress, perhaps opening the temptation for state legislators to feel senior. At least the state leaders felt that their claim on taxable wealth was more ancient and more proper than Congress' claim. After all, Congress had moved into the empty spot in government which previously had been filled by the British colonial administration. State leaders addressed Congress with respect, while assuming that issues of precedence had not yet been worked out.

In Congress, each state had one vote. State contributions to the common treasury were, by a formula which had been contested during the framing and which made nobody quite happy, proportionate to the value of the improved lands of each.

A few provisions in the Articles affected the manner of house business. A state must be represented by at least two, but not more than seven, delegates. Typically during Huntington's time in the presidency about 25 members were present and voting. States could recall delegates at any time and send others instead. Many delegates attended no longer than a few months, then were replaced. Therefore both stability and continuity of the body were problems.

Congress adopted additional working rules. Representation, from nine states made a quorum. The rules of May, 1778, provided:

"No member shall read any printed paper in the house during the sitting thereof, without leave of the Congress."

"No member shall speak to another" (former drafts of the rules had unsuccessfully proposed adding "or whisper" and "or otherwise interrupt the business of the house").

"No member shall speak more than twice in any one debate, without leave of the house."

A rule which slowed business and sometimes caused members discomfort was, "Each member present shall declare openly and without debate his assent or dissent to a question, ay or no, when required by motion of any one member, whose name shall be entered as having made such motion previous to the President's putting the question. The name and vote in such cases shall be entered upon the journal." Entries according to that rule did have the effect of rendering the members more accountable to their constituents, and now help us track the significant stands of the members and arrange them in groupings. But Samuel Huntington once wrote to Oliver Wolcott: "By a refind practice, we use a little too much Scripture language for my taste, i.e. ay and no; but 'tis a custom some are fond of as being useful." Doubtless it seemed often irksome.

Since March, 1778, Congress came to order once a day from 9 a.m. to 2 p.m. ("precisely"), instead of 10 a.m., after committee meetings, and again at 3 or 4 o'clock, as formerly.

Every morning, when the President assumed the chair, members were to take their seats. The minutes of the day before were read, then public letters, petitions, and memorials. Some of these were referred to special committees. Reports of the Board of Treasury and the Board of War were considered. Only then could members bring new business.

Huntington had signed his name in April, 1778, with fifteen other members, to the following engagement: "We the subscribers, members of Congress, pledge our honor to each other that we will meet punctually at the hour of adjournment, that on any subject in debate (except in committee of the whole house) we will not speak more than ten minutes, seldom more than once, never more than twice, and that we will unite in supporting order and preserving decency and politeness in debate."

But one of the signers, Samuel Chase, later struck his name off the list, "because violated by several of the contracting parties."

Thomas Burke wryly explained to the North Carolina Assembly (August, 1779) that Congress "cannot reject any business addressed to them by way of despatch through the President before it has undergone some consideration. When such application respects the interests of individuals, it too often happens that some member patronises the application, and a debate necessarily ensues, which consumes much time... Your delegates, with great pleasure, assisted in passing a resolution to correct this evil in some measure, vizt. that on a motion for postponing, no member should speak more than once."

During the internal quarrels, not long before Huntington began to preside, members of Congress supporting either Arthur Lee or Silas

Deane consumed too much time and energy. "If matters had been driven further," Elbridge Gerry was explaining to John Adams by letter, the day after Huntington was elected President, one subject of partisan disagreement having become Adams, too, "we should have been more deeply involved in animosities and dissentions."

In July, however, Huntington had written to Wolcott, "The state of our finances seems the only embarrassment in our public affairs." It is a remarkable assessment.

The word "embarrassment" in those days was not primarily a word for the feeling of chagrin, but for the situation which caused such a feeling; the difficulty itself. It signified an impediment and only secondarily the sense of being stymied by that impediment.

But, "the only embarrassment"! He was writing at the time when the peace ultima were under debate. Weren't there major difficulties? And how could the United States enter into any sort of peace treaty, or even into a proper alliance with foreign powers, so long as the confederation was not yet in effect? A year earlier, Huntington had signed the embossed copy of the Articles of Confederation, among signers for ten states. Since then, New Jersey and Delaware had authorized signatures. But while Maryland still held out, wasn't the authority to enter into treaties lacking?

There were plenty of additional concerns. Congress was hearing reports of irregularity in the purchasing departments of the armed forces. American prisoners of war, captured at the Battle of Long Island, or seized at sea or otherwise taken by the British, were living under miserable conditions off New York City. Vermonters were agitating for statehood, and both New Hampshire and New York thought the land was theirs.

But Huntington seems to have expected that those concerns, and several others almost as prickly, would somehow be dealt with. After you walk a long, hilly road all day in the heat, your priorities can be set. You know that above all you need a drink of water. Congress had been worrying and trying to cope until, we have to take Huntington's word, "the only embarrassment" was their baffling, vexing inability to pay.

Congress are determined, he wrote on, "by loans and taxation for the present at least to obtain the necessary supplies, should the states exert themselves." But he knew, and Wolcott knew, that the outcome was terribly unsure. They both regarded Connecticut as one test of the probability. Would Connecticut meet Congress' requisitions? Many people in their state probably lived whole days and weeks without often thinking of the war, the Continental Army, or the problems of Congress. Without thinking past their local acres and lanes. A young man from their town probably sent a letter now and then from camp. They saw a newspaper at times. Meanwhile they did not suppose that they could spare many of their resources for more taxes.

"Should the several states exert themselves..." Ah. And were enough people in the states in favor of independence? Tory sentiment and common apathy would have to be balanced by a considerable commitment to the war and to the process of forming a new nation. Closely tied to that question, whose answer would not emerge until a future day, was another question: would the people sustain a prolonged war? Would they endure the loss of New York, the aloofness of Canada.

Charles Lee's having failed to trap the British when they retreated from Philadelphia, Admiral d'Estaing's having disappeared to the West Indies, the army undermanned and underfed, soldiers dead and wounded and taken prisoner? How long would they keep on contributing?

Ah. Did the people trust Congress to apportion justly the number of recruits and the amount of money due from the states? During debate over the Articles, a heated disagreement over the basis of assessment nearly came to disaster. Should population, not land, have been made the basis, after all? If so, should not slaves have been counted as whole persons? If land and improvements were the right basis, still, who can judge the correct value of either? The people of each state tended to believe that other states were not so badly burdened as they.

And would the states attach special demands to their contributions? New Hampshire and New York, for examples, concerning their claims on Vermont? Connecticut, on the Susquehanna country?

Would a decade of popular speeches against taxation, of bonfires and tea-spilling, be surmounted and sublimated now that the Congress was in-charge? Would lately-constituted state governments prove capable of organizing an apparatus for systematic contribution?

"I hope," Huntington wrote further, "we may go thro' this campaign in that way." Hope.

On September 16, twelve days before Huntington became President, the Count d'Estaing had demanded the surrender of British-held

Savannah. After arriving from the West Indies, he communicated with General Benjamin Lincoln, who left Charleston at the head of American troops to join him.

Landing French troops and guns, the count began to prepare a siege. He was ready about October 3, and began to bombard. The British had refused to surrender. Bombardment continued a few days, according to plan, but then the count heard that the British fleet was coming. He also feared the possibility of a hurricane. So he cancelled the remainder of the bombardment and ordered a dawn attack on the city, October 9.

Continental troops fought well, including cavalry led by the Polish Count Pulaski, who was mortally wounded. When it ended, d'Estaing finally ordering retreat and later lifting the siege, Lincoln arguing in vain for fighting again, 300 American men may have died and 800 French.

The French troops and equipment went back to their ships and sailed off. Lincoln returned in discouragement to Charleston.

Congress never heard such news quickly. On November 10, Huntington sent General Washington copies of two letters from Lincoln, "which will give you the disagreeable intelligence of the failure of the expedition against Savannah, with the causes and circumstances attending the expedition and failure."

The British "southern strategy" having become clearer, Congress ordered three frigates to sail from Boston to Charleston, and named a committee to consider measures for the security and defense of the south.

———≫●≪———

"A part of Count d'Estaing's squadron... are arrived in the Chesapeake, but their future destination is yet unknown."

—Huntington to Wolcott,
November 26, 1779

———≫●≪———

When Congress decided in the summer of 1775 to issue paper money, they were careful to plan for the retirement of that money. Each state was to sink an assigned proportion by whatever mode of taxation it chose to apply. Congress asked for annual payments in each of the four years 1779–82. (Also, of 1783–86). The proportion of each state was determined by the number of its inhabitants of all ages, including blacks.

When the year for the first payment was about to begin, Congress called on the states for fifteen million dollars in 1779 and six million each year afterward. Inflation was toying with dollar values, however. So they called for forty-five million more in 1779. They needed it to offset new issues of bills for current expenses, reasoning that it would arrest the process of depreciation by drawing previous bills out of circulation.

They planned to punch a one-inch hole in each retired bill. It could never be exchanged again.

Soon after Huntington began to preside, Congress put forth an adjusted plan for revenues, anticipating no new money whatever from their own printing press. As a committee of the whole they constructed, then as a reconvened session of Congress they adopted, a plan calling on the states to send monthly payments from February 1 to October 1, 1780, each payment fifteen million dollars.

Then they worked on an apportionment. Generally members sparred to lower the amounts expected from their states. Virginia, they decided, should contribute $2.5 million per payment. Both Massachusetts and Pennsylvania, $2.3. Connecticut, $1.7. Delaware, $1.58. North and South Carolina, $1.0 each. New Hampshire, $.4. As for states where British control was effective, New York $.75, Rhode Island $.2. Georgia, being invaded, might pay "hereafter."

Congress assured the states that these apportionments would not necessarily serve as a precedent for future plans. In view of the small return from the states on previous requests for money, members of Congress privately were far from confident now. But they tried to seem stern. They agreed to "charge" the states a penalty of 6% annually on all deficient payments.

In their circular letter of October 9, drafted in the ways and means committee and signed by Huntington, Congress estimated that the last of the paper money already printed would be spent early in December. Then money must be sent by the states. The sums required were large, they conceded, but when new bills no longer swelled the total currency, and when taxes together with "other salutary measures" reduced it, they hoped the quotas might be lessened. For their part, Congress would endeavor to practice the strictest economy in spending.

"Other salutary measures" presumably included price-limitation laws, which they knew would be urged by a convention about to convene at Hartford. Five states just now were appointing commissioners to that convention.

———————————

Soon after taking the chair, Huntington presided over a vote touching on the title of his office. On October 4, two New Englanders moved to strike from John Jay's formal commission as diplomat to Spain, the words "late President of Congress and Chief Justice of the State of New York." Probably they acted both from republican manners, where distinctions of honor among citizens do not gain weight, and from ill will toward Jay after his part in the Lee-Deane feud.

Huntington voted with the majority in favor of retaining the words which connoted honor. True, his stands about Lee and Deane had differed from Jay's. His personal manners were equalitarian. But his background in the judiciary and his esteem for the office he now held prepared him, it seems, to favor the titles. As surely as he was not a presumptuous man, he was not demure. He took for granted the dignity of a presiding officer. The office, whether one liked its occupant or not, symbolized honor. And on the whole, Jay had earned credit in it.

———————————

Gouvernor Morris returned briefly to Congress after an absence of six weeks, although in the New York Assembly he had just lost his congressional seat to Ezra L'Hommedieu and, when nominated to fill the seat vacated by Jay, lost that to Philip Schuyler. He promptly seconded a motion by Witherspoon concerning the instructions on talking with Spain. The negotiator, they thought, should recede from the claim to free navigation of the Mississippi River if that claim was impeding a treaty of amity and commerce. Huntington, of course, joined the majority who defeated the motion.

Morris, however, busied himself as head of a valuable committee concerning another possible negotiation: to obtain a foreign loan. Congress adopted the committee's plan substantially and chose Henry Laurens to be their negotiator. He was to seek up to ten million dollars from Holland at an interest rate not to exceed 6%.

A trend toward mixed control of Congress' executive business was underway in the second half of 1799. In the past, committees of Congress sat as the directors of administration, although a small civil service did much of the work. But on July 30, as if admitting that executive duties in addition to legislative duties had proved an unrealistic burden, Congress had decided on a new Treasury Board composed of three persons who were not members with two who were members of Congress. And on October 28, Huntington presiding, they adopted the same distribution for a new Board of Admiralty. The board members who were not of Congress were called "commissioners" and, in the case of both boards, were paid $14,000 per year. "The salary, tho' it sounds high," Roger Sherman wrote to Governor Trumbull (when Jonathan, Jr., was elected to the Board of Treasury in December) "is really low as prices are at present." Commissioners' terms of office were to be "during pleasure" — so long as they pleased Congress.

When Huntington officially notified Thomas Waring of South Carolina (November 27) that he had been named a commissioner on the Board of Admiralty, he was careful to mention that another commissioner named (William Whipple) was from New Hampshire. The third, not yet named, "will probably be a gentleman from one of the more central states." Evidently Congress aimed to balance the boards sectionally. Early in December they appointed Francis Lewis of New York.

Like Whipple, Lewis was a former member of Congress. A little cronyism.

⟫◦⟪

Huntington had not been in attendance at Congress when the letter from General Philip Schuyler came (January, 1779) stating his decision to resign his army commission. Nor had Huntington been present in March when, against the votes of the New England delegates and the Pennsylvanians, a majority of Congress declined to accept the resignation. Nor, in April when a second message from Schuyler convinced Congress that Schuyler really wished to resign. They all then accepted what they took to be his "fixed" decision.

But after Huntington arrived in mid-1779, he probably heard frequent talk about Schuyler's sense of insult because Congress had believed his statements. His backers, apparently, were expected to have deciphered the idea behind his words. And, to have avenged his having suffered defamation earlier. They were expected to have refused steadfastly his request to depart from the army. James Duane had begged him not to resign. Then he wrote. "If you had communicated to me your wishes, instead of making the second absolute resignation, any reasonable vindication of your character — if any after the honourable acquittal by your peers, and confirmation by Congress, was necessary — cou'd have been obtained."

The New England delegates perhaps were amused by this phase of the difficult relationship between Congress and the General. Once the focus had been on them. Now it was on his close associates. But they kept quiet, after having failed to bring substance to their partisan charges against him at the time of his court-martial and exoneration, concerning the loss of Ticonderoga. Huntington could not foresee how intense his own struggle with Schuyler might become.

Huntington and Schuyler were not yet direct opponents, even though they represented adjacent regions of the continent whose rivalries already had produced bitterness. The cultural and commercial clashes of "Dutchman" *versus* "Yankee" were still capable of rousing angers. More immediately, the legal contest between New York and New Hampshire for jurisdiction over Vermont was complicated by passions of settlers from Connecticut and Massachusetts who held land grants from New Hampshire. Schuyler was a resolute supporter of his state's claims.

Dissimilarities between Huntington and Schuyler were obvious. Schuyler was the first child in a sibling series. Huntington the fourth, so they doubtless had learned some styles of interaction long ago which did not now accord. Schuyler grew up in a family owning thousands of acres of land; he thought of himself as one of the upper class. Huntington's father owned a couple of hundred acres and identified with the agrarian middle class. Schuyler was both soldier and entrepreneur. Huntington was a civilian and legal counsellor to entrepeneur. Schuyler worried and tended to fume at adversity. Huntington deliberated and waited for the opportune moment. Schuyler was a stronghanded achiever, Huntington a teamworker, far from being impatient with the conciliar process, valuing whatever time was required to develop applicable conclusions from the facts and the pertinent reasons contributed by a purposive team. His habitat was not the field tent of commanders devising strategy on the eve of battle; it was the town meeting, congregational meeting, legislative assembly, and court of law.

Both Schuyler and Huntington were described as men with piercing eyes. What happens when such men cross gazes?

Although his personal experience of facing Schuyler was still future, Huntington had heard a great deal about the onetime commander of the Northern Department. He had doubtless become wary through hearing of complaints and distrustful comments by New England troops in the northern command. The troops went so far in the fall of 1775 (Schuyler wrote Hancock) as to say they did not choose to move from Fort Toconderoga until General Wooster, whom they did trust, had arrived.

The Reverend Cotton Mather Smith, of Sharon, Connecticut, chaplain under Schuyler, wrote home during that period: "The Genl is somewhat haughty and overbearing. He has never been accustomed to seeing men that are reasonably well taught, and able to give a clear opinion and to state their grounds for it, who were not also persons of some wealth and rank." Smith tells of a blacksmith from the Connecticut regiment who "came up to the Genl without any preliminaries to offer him some information and advice, but withal not disrespectfully." Schuyler thereupon "spake very sharply to the poor man and bade him begone."

Huntington had become wary, also, because of an antagonism between Schuyler and Joseph Trumbull of Connecticut, son of the governor, over provisions for the Northern Department. Trumbull was Congress' appointee as Commissary-general of the Continental Army. Trumbull sent Elisha Avery, a Connecticut man, to take charge of the northern operation, where he clashed with Schuyler's man Walter Livingston, a New York man. Soon both Schuyler and Trumbull were taking the issue quite personally. During Huntington's first term in Congress, they managed to reassure Trumbull and to accept Walter Livingston's resignation, but seemingly not to end ill feeling. The Trumbulls easily resented abuse and the appearance of abuse. Soon Schuyler ran into twice the trouble. Joseph's brother John was named Deputy Adjutant-general of the Northern Department but somehow the commission paper was delayed or lost. John resented it — "as he ought to do," said Joseph. (But the fault was not really Schuyler's). When John finally received the paper, he sent it back to Congress with an indignant letter because it was dated three months late. Fortunately for American culture, he then devoted himself to painting instead.

Huntington had become wary, again, because of an antagonism between Schuyler and General David Wooster, of Connecticut, during the military expedition against Canada. Schuyler considered Wooster insubordinate, Wooster considered Schuyler vexatious. In that controversy, Schuyler had prevailed.

During Huntington's second term in Congress, they received reports by a congressional committee who were investigating Schuyler's role in the evacuation of Fort Ticonderoga. It was a step toward the court-martial.

But Huntington was not attending Congress during the drama of the Schuyler-Gates controversy of 1777, nor, during the period of Schuyler's court-martial. His knowledge of those events was by hearsay.

———❦———

In June a committee on which Huntington was serving had presented a progress report on its planning for a new system of expenditures by the Commissary-general's and Quartermaster-general's departments as well as the medical departments. The topic was receiving much attention inside Congress and out.

Huntington had written (July 3) to Jeremiah Wadsworth, his Connecticut friend who was then the Commissary-general, about "the two great departments' purchasing on commission," from which practice "general uneasiness" had arisen.

"In the present situation of our affairs," he remarked, it seems absolutely necessary to make some new regulations in those departments." Yet, "in this state of the campaign" — the annual season of accelerated purchases "it is exceedingly difficult if not dangerous to make alterations."

He included an assurance of personal trust: "I have the fullest confidence you will do every thing in your power for the good of the service."

The problem? In Huntington's few words: "The exorbitant price demanded for the necessary supplies for the army greatly embarrasses Congress as well as your department and the quartermaster's." Some people suspected that department agents, when earning commissions on purchases, did not try to keep prices down.

Six weeks later, Huntington again wrote to Wadsworth: "Am very sorry you think of quitting your department so soon. The risque is so great in appointing a new person to the office, which must be attended with serious consequences if he proves unequal to the business." He stayed on a few more weeks.

Meanwhile committees besides the one on which Huntington served had been studying the operations of the supply departments. Congress doubtless had been hearing, furthermore, about a business partnership which Wadsworth had formed with Nathaniel Greene, the quartermaster-general, and Barnabas Deane, brother of Silas Deane, although Greene wanted the partnership kept a secret. They doubtless had been hearing also that one other at least of Greene's business partners, Charles Pettit, was a deputy quartermaster-general, while certain contractors were dealing with both the business and the department. Greene had invested in shipping, privateering, iron, salt, grist mills, rum manufacturing, and real estate; in those ventures, he lost money. Wadworth's financial gains from the war derived mainly from his contracts, after he left his post as Commissary-general for the Continental Army to supply French forces for good pay.

Aware of public criticism, which wafted through Congress also, both Wadsworth and Greene felt like quitting their highly visible official stations.

Congress was about to put both departments under the direction of the Board of War — another move separating executive functions from the duties of legislators. In December, moreover, Congress would examine a proposal to pay agents of the departments fixed salaries rather than allowing them commissions.

<hr />

In mid-November, Philip Schuyler arrived to take his seat in Congress. The New York Assembly had elected him the month before and his New York colleagues had been urging him to come.

Huntington and Schuyler had never yet sat together in Congress. Probably they had never seen one another. Schuyler probably had heard of Huntington as a delegate from an uncongenial neighbor state, as a reputed Whig, and as President.

Now both David Wooster and Joseph Trumbull were dead. Connecticut considered both of them martyrs of the Revolution. Wooster was killed by a bullet at the defense of Danbury. Trumbull died from an illness to which fatigue, suffered during his official labors for his country, had contributed. But Huntington could remember being present when Congress received a report from the committee inquiring into derogations Schuyler had forwaded against Wooster during their Canada quarrels. "Upon the whole of the evidence," the committee had found, "nothing censurable or blameworthy appears against Brigadier General Wooster." On one of the issues between the generals the committee simply took into account Wooster's counter-complaints against Schuyler, without giving any judgment. Wooster, they noted, "from time to time, gave seasonable and due notice of the state of the army under his command, and what supplies were, in his opinion, necessary to render the enterprise successful."

Huntington also could remember being present when Congress defined Trumbull's authority as extending over "both armies ," Schuyler's and Washington's, against Schuyler's wish.

Now, however, a new atmosphere met Schuyler's arrival. He had been vindicated by a court-martial after the fall of Ticonderoga. Overcoming his own reluctance to appear in Congress, the scene of his loss of command to Horatio Gates and of his indictment leading to the court-martial, Schuyler manfully answered the urging of his colleagues. Reciprocating, members were ready to credit his past services and to appreciate his leadership skills.

On November 29, Congress accepted Wadsworth's resignation and named Ephraim Blaine to be his successor. The next day Schuyler was appointed to a committee of two (with Henry Marchant) whose task was to go to headquarters and consult with Washington.

"Nothing has yet been done," he had written Washington on November 18, "in the intended new arrangement of the Quartermaster-general and Commissary-general department. I fear the time which the latter has limitted for retiring from the business will expire before another is appointed, unless Congress is pushed to it both here and from your quarter."

When a letter from Washington was read in Congress, at the point during the daily agenda for official correspondence, Schuyler began the practice of commenting on the parts which he thought merited special attention. Sometimes he urged particular actions, writing about them to Washington and sharing his anxieties about them with the Commander-in-chief.

Schuyler did not like Congress' pace of work. He wanted more speed. His usefulness, he believed, would be to push and to cue Washington when to push.

Everyone knew that Schuyler and Washington were on good terms and that, for assessing the current military situation and the needs of the army, Schuyler was highly capable. Some members of Congress also, perhaps, felt more comfortable when Schuyler left his seat in the house to go to headquarters on his committee errand.

Before Schuyler left Philadelphia, his fellow delegate from New York, Robert R. Livingston, sounded him out on a proposition. Evidently what Livingston proposed was that Congress solve the problems of efficient management of military supports by appointing Schuyler to the top position on a reorganized Board of War.

"If the Board of War should be reorganized on your plan, and that appointment be offered as you wish," Schuyler wrote Livingston on December 7, "it will be necessary to give more ample powers than the board at present possesses." This comment probably reflects conversation between Schuyler and Washington. It discloses a drive for "more ample powers" in which Schuyler would figure for half a year.

On December 10, Schuyler wrote again: "If objection should be made to invest me solely with the power intended for the Board of War, and to let the gentlemen now on that board remain and be considered deputy-secretaries, Congress may if they please appoint me Secretary at War and President of the Board of War, deciding on what powers shall be invested in the Secretary and what he shall enjoy in conjunction with the board at which he is to preside."

Livingston may have begun quiet consultation with other members of Congress on his proposition before deciding that a more gradual approach to the envisioned role would be prudent. But to Schuyler he wrote (December 20): "Green has offered his resignation, which we have for the present refused." Then he added, "All eyes are fixed upon you. Wd to God you could be persuaded to take it with your former rank. Write to me on this subject as soon as possible."

———⟫●⟪———

Congress approved a warrant, payable to the President's steward, $1,000. October 30, 1779.

———⟫●⟪———

The "landless states" were continually edgy over the behavior of "landed states." At issue were claims to jurisdiction over land west of the presently recognized state boundaries. After a debate on Virginia's desire to open a land office, Congress succeeded in approving (late October) at least the preamble to a proposed act: "Whereas the appropriation of vacant land by the several states during the continuance of the war will, in the opinion of Congress, be attended with great mischiefs..." the vote was eight aye, two no, one state divided.

Congress gave a considerable amount of time in November to receiving the new French Minister, the Chevalier de la Luzerne.

Gerard, after waiting until his successor arrived in Philadelphia, had come to Congress in September to make a formal address and receive a formal response. Huntington, although present, had not then been a ceremonial figure. And in August, 1778, Huntington was not attending on the occasion of Gerard's formal presentation to Congress. He may have felt a little of the excited anticipation before he went away.

Now, in any case, he would be a prominent participant in the welcome for Luzerne. Congress planned that the President would sit two feet above the delegates, the honored guest, one foot and a half above. They would repeat the forms of address and the procedures they had adopted for Gerard. Luzerne sent a copy of his proposed address. Congress named Gouvernor Morris, with Dickinson and Houston, to compose a reply, later voting to accept the composition. They named two of their best-mannered members, Morris and John Mathews, to accompany the French Minister to the State House and into the chamber. Three others were named to direct the entertainment following the ceremony. The hour would be twelve-noon on Wednesday, November 17.

So at the agreed hour, they gathered. Luzerne entered and presented a letter of credence. Then he addressed Congress and Huntington read the prepared reply.

Huntington got along well with the French embassy. They understood that he was not oriented to French culture and grimly watched his freedom in voting against the French position at times. But they sensed in him a sincere esteem and support for the alliance and personal goodwill toward themselves. Also his shrewd insight into the political motives beneath French policy led him to hope more of French performance than many of his colleagues were ready to hope. And after all, the alliance was providential.

Late in November, Congress debated a new "self-denying motion" like one adopted in 1776. New Englanders Gerry and Sherman wanted Congress not to appoint to public office any member during the time he was sitting. New York countered with a motion to postpone, which lost, then with a motion to except a member if deprived of his seat by the legislature of his state, which lost, and finally a motion to except a candidate for an ambassadorship or other foreign service, which lost. Philip Schuyler offered the latter two motions. Huntington voted against all three.

Possibly opinions on the question were affected by members' feelings about a particular office or candidate for it. Gouvernor Morris, for instance, was being mentioned for certain foreign posts. But more profoundly the question touched on two principles. One was the prevention of a possible conflict of interest if a member were to participate in appointments. The other was preservation of the dignity of membership in Congress against its belittlement if a member used it as a means to obtain another office. Henry Laurens thought it would be degrading if a member of Congress became a foreign minister. It would send that member "from sovereignty into servitude."

Possibly some members were thinking of Schuyler's recent reluctance to take his seat in Congress. Possibly they also were thinking of his markedly greater desire, not long before, to be reinstated as a top general of the army. After Laurens' resignation from the President's office, the New York delegation spoke of Schuyler for President. But James Duane, thinking it over, probably wishing to avoid a contest between Jay and Schuyler for the chair, it being New York's turn, played down the honor. He compared the honor of becoming President unfavorably with "your high station in the army, where you may be long and so eminently serviceable to the United States and to your own in particular." Did Schuyler then agree with such an evaluation?

(Maybe Duane's comparison should be taken at face, not as an attempt to reach Schuyler's own bias. Yet Duane took pleasure from his own service in Congress: his usual subtlety invites speculation about his aim in this case. Possibly he entertained doubts whether Schuyler's temperament and style were suited to the delicate usages of the continent's infant deliberative assembly. He seems to have taken for granted that a President would hold office "a single year" and that "in the chair of Congress your lips will be sealed"' — but those assumptions had not leashed either Hancock or Laurens).

———

In late December, Nathaniel Peabody described Congress' difficulty in making a punctual morning quorum:

"What makes it very difficult, a number of us generally attend from one to two hours in the morning before we can make a Congress, and then are obliged to set till near sunset before we adjourn, and by the time we have dined and done a little committee business, it is near honnest bed time."

———

In early November, William Sharpe wrote to Governor Caswell: *"I momentarily look for Messrs. Burke, Penn, and Jones, to deliver Mr. Harnett and myself from the house of bondage."*

———

"Mr. Ellsworth arrived here last Wednesday. Mr. Huntington and he are well."

—Roger Sherman to Governor Trumbull,
December 20, 1779

———

Concerning a matter which was not urgent. Henry Laurens sent a letter to Governor Trumbull by Connecticut's courier, Jesse Brown: *"I gave notice to Congress that I had received…dispatches from your Excellency and should beg leave to present them the next day. When that day arrived. I found it impracticable to obtain a reading and patient hearing, and so the next and the next …I then judged it necessary to consult the Honorable Mr. Huntington on the expediency of detaining Mr. Brown. He was with me clearly of opinion he ought to be dispatched because we could discern no prospect of getting the papers properly before the house in any certain reasonable time… Yesterday I returned from Congress at half past 4 o'clock. I rose this morning an hour before day and am now writing by candle light in order that he may begin his journey early."*

(September, 1779)

———

On November 29, Congress authorized the last issue of paper money. When that paper was used up, they would have to devise another way to pay expenses.

After several days of discussion in December, they decided to adopt a new requisition policy which by-passed the need for any money. They began asking the states for supplies in kind. So Huntington sent messages like the following message to Governor William Livingston of New Jersey, requesting specific quantities of flour grain for the use of the army, "The pressing necessity," he wrote, "admit of no delay." He informed Governor Livingston that Congress was considering measures to compensate a state which furnished specific supplies at a lower price than others.

In a second letter three days later, he increased the request and clarified the procedure. Supplies furnished by the states "will be credited to their quotas of the monies they are called upon to raise for the United States, at equal prices for articles of the same kind and quality, and for others in due proportion." Furthermore, states' accounts are to be "finally compared and adjusted so as to do equity."

Congress had thought carefully about the policy. They first had talked of income from foreign and domestic loans, from a lottery, and from the possible sale of western lands if the states deeded over those lands. Allen Jones thought that checking expenses of the Commissary's and Quartermaster's operations might prove a "cure," and that, "until we do this, I shall think all other schemes useless." Robert R. Livingston saw "some advantage" from a policy of requisitions in kind, as a method of fixing a standard for money. Thomas Burke hoped it was a "radical remedy." It would be Burke's task soon to frame a more thorough plan along similar lines.

<hr />

Congress meanwhile recommended to the states (November 19) that the states enact laws to limit prices and to prohibit engrossing and other devices for withholding goods. Acting on a communication from the legislative council of New Jersey and on a message from the convention held at Hartford on October 20, they supposed that neither state taxation nor market operation would quickly abate the general rise of prices. But fluctuating prices thwarted Congress' attempts to estimate future expenses and to set salaries. Something had to be done.

Huntington, in a comment he wrote to Wolcott soon after this vote, was not hopeful about its effect. "You will know," he wrote, "that every individual in Congress is not so wise as always to judge conformable to their resolves, and this in particular is a subject on which time and experience only, and the latter repeated, will bring all men to agree in judgment."

Although he was not attending Congress in January and February, 1777, when price limitation was the subject of an important debate, he was present the following April when the debate was resumed. By the time they then recommended laws against speculating, engrossing, and forstalling, he had departed.

The recent Hartford convention, however, had been comprised of thirteen fit persons from five states. Of the thirteen, five had attended

Congress during 1779, and two had been elected to Congress but did not attend. Two had attended in former years and three would attend in future years. Thus their message was received seriously.

They were convinced that prices had risen "much beyond what could naturally arise from the quantity of circulating medium." One cause, they suggested, was "the artfull designs" of enemies, aimed at ruining the credit of federal money.

They saw several reasons why previous laws to limit prices had proved abortive, too many continental bills in circulation, too low prices at first, diversity in the laws, and the absence of laws in some states.

If Congress recommended taxation rather than stabilization of prices, they thought, "the engrosser, monopolizer, the opulent farmer and trader" (as distinct from the poor) anticipating, probably would increase prices in proportion to the expected taxes. "Too great a burden will be cast on the poor or middling farmer" and the currency will be further depreciated.

They favored price limitation, therefore, as far westward as Virginia, "in aid of the measures Congress have so wisely adopted." (Everybody, was in favor of stopping more printed money, unless he was a debtor who wished to pay off in cheaper bills).

On January 27, 1780, Washington wrote to Huntington and through him to Congress, that the army was "comfortable" after having long suffered a serious shortage of supplies. Probably the Commander-in-chief chose his phrases even more carefully than usual for this letter. It was a letter notifying Congress that he had by-passed their supply procedures and had successfully carried out an extraordinary procedure of his own.

"We were reduced at last to such an extremity and without any prospect of being relieved in the ordinary way," wrote Washington, "that I was obliged to call upon the magistrates of every county in the state for specific quantities to be supplied in a limited number of days."

Doubtless Congress had already heard of this supply operation in the counties of New Jersey. For one thing, John Witherspoon, their member, was party to it. And news of it probably came to Philadelphia by various channels after Washington communicated his plan to the magistrates on January 8.

Dealing directly with the magistrates was feasible and, in the event, effective. Yet it was politically novel, even dubious. Ordinarily state governments were the intermediaries between continental government and local communities. State governments sifted Congress' recommendations and sent down to localities whichever they chose. Washington had ignored such state prerogatives, yet Washington was commissioned by Congress and Congress were appointed by state governments.

As it happened, Washington had occasioned a debate three years back, over the question whether Americans were citizens of the United States or citizens only of the thirteen separate states.

He had attempted by proclamation to require everyone who had taken an oath of allegiance to Great Britain to renounce it, in effect, by taking a new oath of allegiance to the United States. Members of Congress disagreed over whether the proclamation amounted to an unwarranted assumption of federal sovereignty. That disagreement helped prepare the way for the adoption, oversoon as later developments in American political thought would show, of Thomas Burke's states rights Article II in the Articles of Confederation. That article reserved to the states all powers not expressly delegated to Congress, and no power was delegated expressly by which Congress could deal with states who defied the powers which were delegated.

The citizenship issue may well have risen in the minds of Congress when they received Washington's letter about the New Jersey magistrates. But for the moment they did not object. Washington clearly was responding to an emergency, and they could offer no better method. Furthermore, he wisely connected his plan with the power of impressment which Congress had granted him late in 1777. (Huntington was not in Congress at the time of that grant. It was a low time for Washington's reputation, and some congressional critics had grumbled about "a delicacy in exerting military authority on the citizens of these states." Others deemed emergency powers of impressment to be necessary).

"I have been well aware of the prevalent jealousy of military power," Washington had stated in 1777. "I have been cautious and wished to avoid as much as possible any act that might improve it." The local millers of flour, he had observed then, were "unwilling to grind, either from their disaffection or from motives of fear."

Now, in 1780, Washington fared well with the New Jersey magistrates. "I should be wanting in justice to their zeal and attachment, and to that of the inhabitants of the state in general, were I not to inform Congress that they gave the earliest and most chearful attention to my requisitions and exerted themselves for the army's relief."

What he had done was to write them, describing the shortages. "The distress we feel is chiefly owing to the early commencement and uncommon vigor of the winter," he judged, "which have greatly obstructed the transportation of our supplies." He asked the magistrates' help in calling on the people for grain and cattle. "As you are well acquainted with the circumstances of individuals, you will be able to apportion the quantity required to the ability of each." So it was a fair method.

He sent them a list of delivery places, with a table of needed quantities and a statement of the time allowed for collection. "The weight of the cattle to be estimated by the magistrates, or any two of them, in conjunction with the commissary." The commissary would make out certificates, specifying each deliverer's quantity of supply, and the terms of payment.

Washington expressed his confidence that the magistrates and the people would cooperate. If they did not cooperate, he would have to use a different mode — meaning, he would have to impress, "which will be disagreeable to me on every account, on none more than on the probability of its having an operation less equal and less convenient to the inhabitants."

Washington's report to Congress about the assessment in nearby counties was briefer and more guarded than his January 30 description to Philip Schuyler, with whom he felt an affinity not only from army leadership but of social class and landholder interest. To Schuyler he stressed the trying conditions which the method was designed to relieve. He more exactly detailed his procedure. "Nothing but this great exertion could have saved the army from dissolution, or starving."

I don't find any comment by Huntington on Washington's plan, but of course he knew a lot about "the prevalent jealousy of military power." The years of Thomas Gage were not far past, and the effects of Britain's Mutiny Act and Quartering Act, which had occasioned excitement in Huntington's community, not to mention the words to which he gave his signature in 1776: "He has affected to render the military independent of, and superior to, the civil power."

The Fast Day resolve for early 1777 had been drafted in Congress by Samuel Adams, with John Witherspoon and Richard Henry Lee. Recommending repentance and reformation "to all the members of the United States," it significantly mentioned in particular "the officers civil and military under them." In the new republic, a citizen was seen to rank above an officer.

Although Huntington probably knew that the aristocratic Virginian who had attended the First Congress wearing a military uniform, soon afterward expressed a low opinion of New England troops during the siege of Boston, he seems never to have joined those New Englanders who had tried to dislodge Washington from the top command. Instead, throughout their extensive correspondence during his term as President of Congress, his attitude was altogether respectful. It began soon after he took the chair, "I...am happy in the first exercise of that important trust with which Congress have been pleased to honour me, to have the opportunity of conveying to you the thanks of Congress for ordering with so much wisdom the late attack on the enemy's works at Paulus Hook." Not many days later. "Be assured, sir, it is with pleasure I have the honour of communicating to your Excellency the continued approbation of Congress on your eminent and unremitting service to the cause of your country."

Later in his letters, Huntington subsided into a more routine manner, with fewer compliments, but the tone of respect continued. When, on a few roll calls, he voted against measures which Washington had been urging, he did not alter that tone in the least.

His whole view of events differed slightly from Washington's. Their principal goals were identical, win the war in order to build a free republic. The longrun work of each furthered those goals, Washington's pre-eminently. But their different responsibilities of the moment and their different training impelled Washington more toward winning the war, Huntington toward charting and building. Huntington's first thoughts were about consent and constitutional propriety, Washington's about performance of necessary tasks. Those thoughts were not incompatible but the emphases differed.

Washington never really neglected the concerns which Huntington symbolized; thus he instructed the collectors of emergency provisions: "As we are compelled by necessity to take the property of citizens for the support of the army on whom their safety depends, we should be careful to manifest that we have a reverence for their rights and wish not to do any thing which that necessity and even their own good do not absolutely require."

On October 27, as we have seen, the committee "to report a plan for establishing one or more courts of appeals, for finally determining captures on water" had submitted its proposal. A copy of the report is extant, written by William Paca, who apparently succeeded Huntington as the committee's chairman after Huntington became President.

By January, 1780, the proposal had gone through considerable debate and resultant change. Huntington doubtless found the debate extremely interesting, guiding its progress from the chair. The Huntington-Paca committee's version was a plan for two sets of judges, each set to hear cases in two of the proposed four districts. An "eastern district would consist of the four New England states; a "northern" of New York, New Jersey, and Pennsylvania. The first set of judges would work in those districts. Likewise, a "middle" district would consist of Delaware, Maryland, and Virginia; a "southern" of the Carolinas and Georgia. Those would share the second set of judges.

It was a plan which would allow judges to travel into all of those states when necessary, without being drawn too far from home and ordinary professional commitments. The judges, furthermore, would not have to familiarize themselves with varying particulars in the admiralty laws of all thirteen states.

But after debate, Congress preferred a plan with only one set of judges. To meet the problem of extensive travel, they decided that the court might sit either in Philadelphia or eastward to Hartford and southward to Williamsburg. The proposed "eastern" and "southern" states would never be host to court sessions. On the other hand, "finality" of judgment needed a single court. Two courts might develop uneven standards of equity, one part of the country thus seeing itself treated better or worse than the other.

Most other features of the Huntington-Paca plan were preserved in a version which Congress considered early in January. After mid-November debate, Charles Thompson, secretary of Congress, had written a report incorporating agreements so far. It had been utilized December 4–7. Preserved from the original were the proposed number of judges — three. Any two judges, when appointed and commissioned by Congress, were competent to try cases. Judges were to appoint a register and a marshal and to exercise the power of a court of record, including the power to fine or imprison for contempt or disobedience. The admiralty courts of the states were expected to carry out decrees of the appeals court.

Besides the features preserved from the original plan, Congress added others. The most important, in light of the *Active* case, which had caused tension between Congress and the state of Pennsylvania: "that the trials in the courts of admiralty, in cases of capture, be according to the usage of nations and not by jury." The *Active* case had highlighted the problem of assuring a fair trial when a jury was deciding cases between local parties and out-of-state parties. Regardless of the legal issues, juries tended to favor their neighbors. Yet, the principle of trial by jury continued to be cherished in the ideology of the Revolution. So should jury decisions be removed from this plan?

Other new features included a method for funding the expenses of the court. A duty of one per cent would be levied on the contested prizes. Any surplus received, after expenses, would be used for the support of seamen disabled in the service of the United States.

Appeals had to be initiated within five days after a verdict by a state court of admiralty, and lodged with the register of the court of appeals within forty days afterward. The party appealing must give surety to prosecute and, be answerable for costs and charges if the sentence is confirmed.

Congress was not yet ready to adopt the plan. On December 4, they divided 4-4. January 8, they divided 6-6, Huntington voting for the proposal. Congress then appointed a new committee, headed by the President's young colleague from Connecticut, Oliver Ellsworth, later to be Chief Justice of the United States Supreme Court. The committee worked quickly and in one week offered a plan for consideration.

Those who opposed previous versions of the plan were not ready to assert a federal power over the judicial procedures of states. A basis for just such a power had been explicitly put into the Articles of Confederation, but the Articles were not yet in effect and some states evidently paused before making the concept an actuality.

The Ellsworth committee plan omitted old phrases about state courts and about the appointment of a marshal. It concluded instead with a recommendation to the states "to make laws authorizing and directing the courts of admiralty therein established, pursuant to the recommendation of Congress, to carry into full and speedy execution the final decrees of the court of appeals." Federal power to fine or imprison state judges and court officials had vanished.

On January 14, Congress heard the report. The next day they considered it. They voted on it bit by bit, accepting a court of three judges, appointed and commissioned by Congress; accepting the appointment of a register. When they came to "usage of nations and not by jury,"

New Hampshire moved to amend by providing for trial by jury. Huntington voted against the amendment, for the committee's wording. So did nineteen delegates from ten states. The two delegates from New Hampshire had support by two from Massachusetts. Even the three from Pennsylvania, Searle, McLene, and Shippen, all radical Whigs, voted against trial by jury. (In fact, soon afterward the Pennsylvania legislature eliminated trial by jury from their state admiralty law; their adamant support of their own court in the *Active* case apparently was not based on that principle, even though the specification of that mode had seemed pivotal in Judge Ross' argument against federal intervention. Ross himself was said to have sympathized personally with the appellants as to justice, but thought himself bound by the legal terms then in effect.)

New Hampshire and Massachusetts also voted in opposition to the paragraph about holding court sessions no farther eastward than Hartford, but Huntington with sixteen other members from nine states sustained the paragraph. But when a Massachusetts delegates, Elbridge Gerry, moved to amend, eliminating support of disabled seamen if there were surplus money from the one per cent duty on prizes, Huntington voted for it. So did the majority: Ellsworth and two of the three others on his committee voted for the original paragraph. Presumably Huntington found this a nonessential and possibly he wished to placate his fellow easterners, from whom he had been differing on some points.

When the bit by bit voting ended on January 15, Congress at last had established an appeals court. It would be the first permanent court to exercise federal jurisdiction: the beginning of a United States judicial branch of government. Huntington had to be pleased. His name was suggested as a possible judge on the court, but he did not wish it.

On January 22, Congress named Paca of Maryland, Titus Hosmer of Connecticut, and George Wythe of Virginia to the judgeships. Later Wythe declined, and they named Cyrus Griffin of Virginia. When Huntington notified them of their election, he wrote: "I hope the business may not employ so much of your time as to interfere with your other engagements and deprive the public of your service in this important station."

With the summer military campaign in prospect, Congress in February agreed on goals for recruiting troops. They asked the states to bring strength up to 35,211 men, exclusive of commissioned officers.

Later the same month they adopted a plan more fully developed than in December for the quotas of specific supplies which they were requesting from the states. Beef, rum, salt, hay, flour, corn, forage, tobacco, rice — these materials were requested in various specific quantities, according to the estimated resources of twelve states. Georgia again was excepted.

The report of the committee for estimating these supplies was written by Thomas Burke. He wrote a thoughtful letter to Governor Caswell a few days later, restating Congress' recognition of the fact that after the stop to bills of credit, "the only resources are the contributions of the states, and what may be obtained by loans." More explicitly, "It is not in the power of Congress to call them forth otherwise than by requisitions to the several states; and if the states fail to comply, it will be utterly impossible to carry on the war." Congress was concerned, as this statement shows, about the limits on their ability to meet urgent needs. Burke believed that the limits, while awkward, were politically proper. Other critics, both in Congress and out, fretted about those limits as if Congress needed principally to become aware of them and, once aware, would do better at their tasks. Few critics, however, concretely recommended a course of allowable action.

What Congress was doing, at least, was using the restricted power which their constituents had thus far allowed them in a manner so conspicuous that the insufficient enlistments and provisions could not be blamed on their neglect. They did not agree amongst themselves on the next question: whether sufficient power was allowed them.

Burke listed several reasons why, he thought, Congress could not simply ask for money. It would be unfair to people distant from the location of army camps. Perhaps he had brooded over the fact that people near the camps, unlike the people of his state, sold produce and received money for it, thereby paying their money quotas more easily.

Another reason he listed was that a sellers' market was operating. Burke believed that prices would therefore rise in excess of revenues. He spoke for everyone in Congress who was shocked by the high price level, especially as it frustrated their wish to be thrifty in public purchasing. Congress tended also to feel shock over the irregularities in their agents' dealing with suppliers, favoritism, kickbacks, conflicts of interest, "the evil of a numerous staff department, established in such a manner as to enhance the most ruinous abuses."

Accordingly he saw the method of specific supplies as promising to accomplish its aim "without incurring heavy public debts, without giving political advantages, without causing partial burthens, without having us exposed to the abuses of peculation or danger to our affairs from the precarious subsistence of the army." The last benefit he mentioned, however, would not be realized: the states never responded sufficiently. Therefore the other benefits could not be gained for long.

Burke imagined three techniques by which the states might procure the specific commodities needed. The first was by certificates, redeemed by taxes. "A tax can be calculated because the purchase is previously made and the price known," whereas experience had shown that when the sequence is the reverse, a calculation would be impossible. "The urgency of the public demands, and the avarice of individuals, would raise the prices to so enormous an height, before it could be collected, that they money would go but a very little way in purchasing supplies." (Certificates were an element, as we have seen, in the method which Washington tried out).

Another mode, Burke thought, was by collecting specific contributions in each state by direct requirement. The third mode, by contract — "that most desirable mode."

After Congress voted for a procurement scheme, Huntington allowed himself to state his personal concern over the want suffered by Continental troops. "It is most earnestly to be desired," he wrote to Washington, four days after the act of the 25th, "that the several states may exert themselves and procure such supplies and magazines, and may relieve the Quartermaster and Commissary-general from their embarrassments and prevent any further distress in the army for want of provisions."

Everybody seems to have taken it for granted that the states would not feel enthusiastic about these askings.

Burke, for instance, had tried to anticipate the thoughts of Gaswell, "You will find the quotas assigned to North and South Carolina far beyond what is their supposed proportion, but the prospect of a vigorous campaign in the southern states, the probability of great armaments being there employed, the impossibility of supplying them with provisions from any other states, with other reasons which will occur to you, determined the delegates of these states to assume the quotas as they now are."

Congress preferred not to formulate a set of quotas. They decided not to hear out arguments about what would be the "just" proportion for their respective states. Instead, they made a rough assignment for the time being, pledging an adjusted settlement later. This evasion seemed necessary for legislative progress, and they repeated it with regard to troops, too.

Their tactic did not win unanimous support. In mid-February, they were feeling nervous about debate over the supplies plan, when the able and articulate delegate from Massachusetts, Elbridge Gerry, convinced that his state's assigned proportion was oversize, moved to recommit a section of the plan fixing the price of beef. He had in mind another pricing measurement. Congress found his motion out of order.

He then asked for a roll call vote on whether the motion was out of order. Huntington finally ruled that it was the sense of the house that his request for the roll call vote was also out of order. The whole point of their tactic, after all, was not to attach their approval either to the price which Gerry disliked or to any other price. "As it is not in the power of Congress at present," Huntington soon explained in his circular to the states, "to determine the just quota of each state, they have made provision in this as in former acts that justice shall be done to each state in the final settlement of the accounts."

Gerry, however, took offense at being ruled out of order. He left the chamber angrily. The next day he wrote Huntington a letter defending his motions, citing house rules, and renewing his request that the sense of the house be taken by a record of "yeas and nays." A polite correspondence between the two men followed.

Gerry had isolated himself on this issue. James Lovell, a Massachusetts delegate, wrote to Samuel Adams, who then was in Boston, urging him to support Congress' specific supplies act, entreating "that you would use your utmost eloquence to promote this business and every other essential to a vigorous campaign."

Gerry remained in Philadelphia for a time, not coming to sessions of Congress, however. Soon he went to Massachussets and sought support for his stand, from the state legislature among others. Congress' former President, John Hancock, gave him no comfort, he held that Congress "must certainly have a right to establish their own rules." In August, 1783, having dropped the protest, Gerry returned to Congress.

=⟫●⟪=

A British expedition under Clinton had sailed from New York toward Charleston. Congress tried to keep informed about it.

On their voyage, the British came into rough seas, which slowed them down and cost them the loss of equipment. They eventually disembarked 30 miles below Charleston. They began a slow movement closer.

Congress tensely called on Virginia, North Carolina, and South Carolina to fill up their quotas in the Continental Army and to raise a body of militia for the defense of Charleston. To the governor of South Carolina, Huntington wrote, March 6: "It is to be hoped that the enemy have been so scattered and disabled in their passage from New York that, before they are able to take the field, you will have received such reinforcements from the main Army, Virginia, and North Carolina, as shall enable Genl Lincoln with what assistance your state can afford to defend Charlestown and frustrate the designs of the enemy in that quarter."

Nor did that hope limit his hoping. "Should the enemy be again defeated in the southland, there is reason to hope it will be their last effort." Presumably he was thinking of a possible second Saratoga, this time in the south. If the British experienced such a defeat, their logistic difficulties, their desire to restore normal transocean trade, and their worsening relations with the European powers, probably would prompt a somber policy review so he could have supposed.

———————

On March 5, Philip Schuyler arrived back in Philadelphia, having lately attended the New York legislature and used his influence wisely toward their cession of western land claims.

Congress had named him, January 21, with Thomas Mifflin and Timothy Pickering, to a commission for reorganizing the support departments of the army. Huntington had written him of the appointment; his reply was that he could not, consistently with his honor and reputation, accept a "station either less honorable or less important" than his former position in the army. He was not asking to be reinstated to that former position, and he was willing as a member of Congress now to serve on a committee of Congress to consult with the Commander-in-chief and heads of the civil departments of the army. In such a way he could further the goals of the January 21 resolution.

Huntington instructed Mifflin and Pickering to proceed as commissioned. A congressional committee, he told them, was appointed to confer with them. Schuyler was named to that committee, but he found the appointment still insufficient; his personal dislike for Mifflin and

Pickering and his professional disagreement with their army politics led him to consider Congress' new offer "indelicate." Two other members of Congress, however, accepted places on the committee.

Desiring to use his abilities wherever he was ready to exercise them, Congress next appointed Schuyler, with others, to a committee on finance. He accepted.

"My object," he wrote on March 11, "is a fixture of the present circulating medium at a given ratio, calling it in, speedily destroying it, a new emission quoted to states and sent forth on permanent funds, the quantum to be emitted to be proportioned to the periodic destruction of the present bills, the new ones to bear a specie interest payable at their redemption or in bills on France, at the option of the holders." This was a weighty proposal. It aimed, in other words, at an obliteration of the old currency and an issue of new.

"I believe the reports will bear this complexion," he commented, referring to the thinking of his committee. "What transformation it will undergo in the house is impossible to determine, as every man wishes to be thought a financier and must have his ideas."

The committee discussed and honed his idea, and Oliver Ellsworth wrote it up for report and house action. March 18, Congress adopted it, 6 states to 4, one state divided. The eastern and middle states voted yes. The southern, no. Huntington agreed with Schuyler on this bold measure. Principal features of the plan were:

1. The states were asked to send the continental treasury in the course of one year all of the old bills of credit issued by Congress which were circulating as paper money.
2. The old bills would be devalued at the rate of one dollar in silver and gold for 40 dollars of the bills. This rate was higher than the going rate in common exchange.
3. The old bills would be destroyed when received.
4. New bills would be issued to replace the old, not to exceed one new bill for 20 old bills.
5. The new bills would be redeemable in specie within six years, and would bear 5% interest per year; or if the holders preferred, they would be redeemable in bills of exchange on the United States commissioners in Europe.
6. The new bills would be credited by state funds and, as well, endorsed by the United States.

7. States would receive six-tenths of the new bills for their use — use such as paying for the specific supplies Congress had requisitioned. Congress would receive four-tenths, receivable in payment of the states' monthly money quotas.

Copies of this act were to be dispatched to the states with a letter from the President requesting the legislatures to adopt the plan promptly and send copies of their acts to Congress.

Congress believed that the reduced money supply, the plan for redemption, and the payment of interest would secure the new bills against depreciation. "This act is the result of much labour and deliberation," Huntington wrote the states, "as the happiest expedient that could be adopted to extricate these states from the embarrassments of a fluctuating medium, and at the same time and in some measure afford the necessary means for supporting the ensuing campaign."

Very explicitly, he continued: "You will readily perceive the importance of this measure and the indispensable necessity of unanimity in the states in conforming thereto."

⸺⟫●⟪⸺

Huntington's style of correspondence with the states, and particularly of appealing to the states, itself seems to have become an issue. Schuyler and others seem to have felt some irritation over it.

Was the President too polite, too calm, too temperate in his official letters? Did his note of hopefulness muffle the note of urgency which he also sounded?

For example, when describing the wants of the army and the straits of the treasury, he wrote not only: "The aid of the states is absolutely necessary to afford supplies." He added a typical phrases "…until such time as matters are put in a proper train, which I trust will not be long."

Not merely: "The importance and necessity of a substantial compliance with this act of Congress" are obvious. But this typical modifier: "…so obvious that nothing further seems necessary to be added to excite the most vigorous exertions on the part of the several states."

Not merely, "As this provision is wanted to supply the fleet of our ally in America." Further: "It is not doubted the several states will readily comply with the request of Congress."

The states, in fact, were not complying. By March 28, Schuyler could not stand it. He moved that a committee of three be appointed to prepare and report "a letter to the executive powers of the several states, stating the necessity of procuring and forwarding immediate supplies."

Congress agreed to the motion. They named Muhlenberg, Ellsworth, and Schuyler to the committee. On April 4, the draft letter was before Congress, worded by Ellsworth yet expressing Schuyler's feelings.

"Congress are obliged to call on the executive powers..." No. Those words, carried over from Schuyler's motion, were eliminated. They decided it was enough to say: "Congress are obliged to call on the several states to use every possible exertion to expedite the public supplies." Whether Schuyler was satisfied by this change in the direction of Huntington's style (or, of genteel 18th Century style), he himself doubtless continued thinking that "the executive powers" were exactly those called on for exertion.

"The states are greatly difficient (sic) in the quotas of money they have been called on for," went the draft letter. "More than fifty millions of dollars of the quotas that have become due to this time remain unpaid." After suggesting the "fatal" consequences of the deficiency, the letter indicated what was the duty of the states:

"The making provision to feed the army, tho' an object of the most serious and immediate importance, is not all that is essential to be done at this time. The arrears of the quotas that have become due must be brought in... The treasury must also be supplied."

"And these means must be furnished fully and in season."

"The case calls for plainness and decision."

"The recruits also raising in the several states should be forwarded to the army with the greatest dispatch."

The peremptory tone of this letter was the new element. After debate, Congress committed the letter to a new committee of three. "Some gentlemen," Schuyler wrote to Washington the next day, "were averse at the decisive plainness with which we intended Congress should address the states, whilst others contended that we should speak still more pointedly."

A few weeks later (May 31), Washington let Congress know of his own leaning, he desired Congress, among other things, to "speak in a more decisive tone."

The spokesman of the new committee, however, was Thomas Burke, champion of states' supremacy. On April 7, Congress debated his new draft and sent it back for more work. On April 10, they debated it further. Rather than starting abruptly with the current "deficiency," as in the Ellsworth-Schuyler version, Burke's contained a long opening which reviewed the aims of the war and the success gained to date. Arriving at the problem of deficient conveyances of money, the draft said: "Your representatives in Congress are apprehensive that their constituents are not duly sensible of the difficulties under which all our affairs are laboring." Not "executive powers," but "constituents."

"We are now constrained by our anxieties for your welfare, and by the adoption of new means, to press you in the most urgent manner to give the most serious attention to our representations."

After reciting stark facts and stating "hopes that by means of the exertions which the states are expected to make, the operations of the next campaign will be crowned with such decisive success as to insure peace upon terms honorable and advantageous," the drafters ended the letter with a paragraph detailing the "opportunity" of the moment. It began, "Most respected friends and fellow citizens, we cannot close this address without once more pressing you to avail yourselves of this happy opportunity..."

On April 20, after more debate. Congress decided to refer the drafts to still a third committee. Ellsworth went back on, with two others. The next day they debated the third draft by paragraphs and committed it for final phrasing by William Churchill Houston.

A letter was agreed upon, April 24. Shorter and less deferential than the second, but less imperious than the first draft, it began with a statement of confidence "that the citizens of these states are not more desirous to be informed of their affairs than they are ready and willing to afford the most vigorous assistance." After another summary of the present deficiency, the letter came to the point: "Urge, therefore, the instant execution of every measure which has been adopted, and the speedy adoption of such as yet remain to be taken."

The final letter described the situation of the moment, if not as a "happy opportunity," at least as a "promising occasion" and a "conjuncture...favorable to great and deciding efforts." Yet "the crisis calls for exertion." By contrast, the first draft had bluntly called the situation an "emergency."

The final letter toned down the words characterizing states' noncompliance, from the first draft's "dilatory or parsimonious" to "through languor and inattention." The result of noncompliance was no longer "disgraceful" but "disappointment."

———≈⟫●⟨≈———

Their inability to agree readily on the text of a letter to the states was an education to the members of Congress. They realized that they were really disagreeing over the deep question of the constitution. Although they might speak more often of prosecuting practical aims, a profound question was emerging. What powers belonged properly to Congress and the government which Congress authorized, including the military? What powers belonged to the states?

Huntington's letters show clear awareness of the problems they faced to make government efficient. He wanted to solve those problems and was willing to act boldly, as in the case of the March 18 act for new currency, to meet certain of them. As for the most bothersome question, he would confess in 1781, "I have long since been convinced that the present method of supplying the army with provisions, by requisitions on the several states, a method dictated merely by necessity, is and will be attended with great difficulties and embarrassments." So he did not differ from critics of that method concerning its efficiency or inefficiency. "Yet Congress have no other means in their power at present to obtain the necessary supplies."

Wholesale impressment seems to have been the only alternative method seriously considered. It was considered quietly, however. Few people cared to follow the lead of the roaming armies of Europe. As a result of his experience in New Jersey, Washington concluded: "Military coercion is no longer of any avail."

Nathaniel Greene, assessing the possible use of military force as a means of obtaining carriages and forage in July, mused, "Even this would be precarious and uncertain, as well as unequal and distressing to those who lay most within reach of the army."

Having concluded that Congress' existing powers were limited, Huntington rather often hinted at the need for more thinking about the question. For instance (July 15): "Congress will press every measure in their power," implying that certain measures which might be conceived were nonetheless outside Congress' authority. Without indicating whether he felt privately happy or unhappy under the limits, an indication which he probably felt was irrelevant for the moment, he accepted the limits as circumstantial and unavoidable. They were explicit in the Articles of Confederation, which Congress was still trying to induce holdout states to ratify. Weren't they also defined by the viewpoint of most state legislators and their local associates in the towns of America? He felt there was nothing for him to do except point out to the states, "Congress have no resources but in your spirit and virtue." To him, the words "spirit" and "virtue" were not abstract. He learned their actuality from the steady constitutional habits of Connecticut. Until spirit and virtue predominated again in the decisions and actions of the Revolution, attempting measures beyond Congress' given authority would be futile as well as dangerous.

Other members of Congress, meanwhile, wished grimly "to assume powers." This issue came nearer the surface after Congress, April 6, decided to send a committee of three members to headquarters of the Commander-in-chief. Such a committee, many members believed, could assist in the final re-arrangement of the military departments, the task on which Mifflin and Pickering were working, with members Roger Sherman and Allen Jones. The committee might assist, furthermore, in noting the many grievances of enlisted men and officers of the army. Washington had suggested that among the causes of army discontent were the states' uneven terms of enlistment, unequal rewards, and disparate provisions for their troops.

On April 12, Congress voted instructions to the committee. The vote was 7-3: 16-8 by individual members, Huntington "no." Huntington did not explain his negative vote but, in May, writing to the states, he included an "apology" for "the demand and the warmth with which they intreat you" (the committee would be sending their own letters to the states). The issue of a peremptory tone of address, it seems, had not been settled. It had been relocated. The committee supposed "that the states will impute to our zeal, and affection for the interest and weal of our country, the liberty we take, and not to a spirit of dictating, which would be equally improper as presumptious."

Beyond the issue of how to address the states, however, lay a more significant disagreement: whether the army should increase control over its operations. Huntington and other civilian leaders shared the old distrust of a powerful military establishment which had prompted passionate protest against British colonial rule.

Washington himself alluded to such a sentiment when he wrote an appeal to the states for supplies (August). "It has been no inconsiderable support of our cause to have had it in our power to contrast the conduct of our army with that of the enemy, and to convince the inhabitants that while their rights were wantonly violated by the British troops, by our own they were respected. This distinction must unhappily now cease, and we must assume the odious character of the plunderers instead of the protectors of the people, the direct consequence of which must be to alienate their minds from the army and insensibly from the cause."

Philip Schuyler led the drive for more control by the military. Having bypassed Livingston's suggestion that he accept the position of quartermaster-general, which Greene was ready to vacate, Schuyler hoped still to be appointed to a more autonomous office. On April 8, while Livingston and two others were drafting the instructions for the committee at headquarters, Schuyler described his view of the committee's role in a letter to Alexander Hamilton, "A committee... invested conjointly with the General with a kind of dictatorial power, in order to afford satisfaction to the army."

He thought "some good may result" if the committee members were persons who "are not jealous of the army." Also he seems to have discovered a third phase of his longtime tension with Connecticut (after David Wooster's and Joseph Trumbull's phases). If Sherman should end up "at the head of the triumvirate," he wrote, weighing the chance, "the General will be tormented with a thousand little propositions which Roger has thrown together, and which he entitles system." At the moment, Sherman was advocating reforms in the administration of military departments, to eliminate waste and abuse. It may have been Sherman who stood as an adversary against Schuyler's appointment to the committees: someone, unnamed, had suggested "it would not be proper to send a person who, as he has been in the army, will probably have a bias in its favor."

Sherman voted with Huntington, as did Oliver Ellsworth, the other Connecticut delegate, although the latter had served with Livingston in drafting them, against adopting the instructions on April 12. Seven states "yes," three "no."

On April 13, Congress decided whom to place on the committee. First they dealt with the procedural question whether, because they were delegating powers of Congress, this election required agreement by seven states, a majority of states, rather than a simple majority of those states who were present. The Connecticut members all favored seven. Schuyler himself favored seven, but Livingston and Scott, his fellow New Yorkers, made it safer for him by voting, as did the house, for a majority of those states present. Then they filled the committee. Schuyler was elected. John Mathews of South Carolina, a volatile and outspoken critic of Congress' restraints on the army, was elected. The third member was Nathaniel Peabody of New Hampshire.

The three committee men moved later in April from Philadelphia to Morristown, where Washington was headquartered. The constitutional question of army powers was beginning to take shape.

———>●<———

LaFayette, on May 10, came to Morristown and gave the news to Washington that Count Rochambeau, commander of the French expeditionary force in America, could be expected soon with his force. The news soon reached Philadelphia.

"I do myself the honour through you, sir, to communicate to his most Christian Majesty, our illustrious ally, the grateful sense Congress entertain of his unremitted attention to the interest of these United States," Huntington wrote to Luzerne.

But to the states he wrote more nervously: "This force, generously calculated either to produce a diversion in our favour or to forward the operation of our arms by being directed to the same object, may either by our exertions be made the happy means of delivering our country in the course of the campaign from the ravages of war or, being rendered ineffectual thro' our supineness, serve only to sully the reputation of our arms, to defeat the benevolent intention of our great ally, and to disgrace our confederacy in the eyes of all Europe." He used the word "confederacy" where often he had said, "these states."

Then he said bluntly "The military departments are at a stand for the want of money to put them in motion." He asked for money by June 15; also, "your quota of supplies, which the present exigency renders more requisite than ever."

His own past experience in sessions of the governor's council in Connecticut enabled him to guess the troubled thoughts of many hard-pressed state leaders, upon receiving his letter. So he sought gently but staunchly to block their exits by adding "it may not be improper to suggest to you that if a strict and immediate collection of taxes should be insufficient to procure the necessary sums within the time limited, it may perhaps be more speedily obtained by loans."

———>●<———

On the same day when he wrote to the states for support of the arrival of the French force, Huntington presided when Congress directed the committee at headquarters to expedite the income of supplies which they had requisitioned from the states by their resolution of February 25. They empowered the committee, with Washington's advice to increase the amounts of those requisitions or to add further items within them. Also they authorized the committee "to give assurance, where any of the aforesaid articles shall be purchased or otherwise procured on the credit of the United States, that the just value of the same shall be paid, with interest at six per cent, as fast as money can be raised for that purpose." The committee was to report their proceedings to Congress, and these special powers were conferred for sixty days, not longer.

"The committee had lobbied for an even greater delegation of powers to them. When they heard of the French expedition, they asked Congress to yield "to a small committee or other persons to be appointed, with advice of the Commander-in-chief, ample powers for drawing forth the resources of the country on this interesting occasion." What powers which Congress could have yielded would have proved "ample"?

They furthermore agreed that it would be necessary to ask the states "to invest for a limited time in Congress, or such persons as Congress may appoint, dictatorial powers, to pass laws authorizing Congress or such persons to impress carpenters, caulkers, teamsters, waggoners, batteau men, horses, carriages, vessels, materials for building, and in general whatever may be necessary to enable our military force and that of our ally to operate with vigour."

They did not state whether they had candidates in mind when mentioning "such persons as Congress may appoint" to exercise dictatorial powers.

Congress did not delegate powers to that extent. Nor did they entreat state legislatures, as the committee had advised them to do, to assure payment for purchased goods and services "if continental officers should not be able to make immediate payment."

The committee sent John Mathews to Philadelphia to lobby for the augmented powers. Was there a trace of mockery in Huntington's explanation to the committee, after this visitor had concluded his errand, of not sending them a copy of the act which augmented their powers slightly? He would have forwarded it, he wrote them, "had I not understood that the Hon'ble Mr. Mathews was possessed of it before he left the city."

Washington had let his desire be known in a letter to Duane (May 14) that a small committee residing near headquarters be allowed to act for

Congress "with despatch" to enable cooperation with the French. Thus on May 19, Huntington informed the states: "Congress for the greater dispatch have thought it expedient to appoint a committee to assist the Commander-in-chief in drawing out supplies." This was the letter when he tried to prepare them for "the demand and the warmth" of the committee's approaches. Soon the committee began to write letters to the states with all the fervor which Huntington had anticipated.

In June, Congress discussed, modified, and approved an address to the states, drafted by Livingston, as re-inforcement of the committee's letters. "We trust," they said, using a couple of bolder words than before, "that at this critical emergency no present ease or convenience of individuals will be put in competition with the lasting happiness of millions."

Congress was expecting momentous results from the newly heightened French involvement. Actually, when Rochambeau and around 6,000 French troops arrived at Newport in June, the British responded by instituting an effective blockade of Narragansett Bay. It immobilized the French troops during the remainder of 1780. Huntington shared in the general disappointment. "The season is so far advanced," he wrote to Governor Trumbull in mid-September, "that I begin to fear nothing capital can be attempted against New York this campaign, unless we should soon obtain the dominion of the seas by a superior naval force on this coast."

The American cause was in poor shape.

"It is painful," Huntington owned more openly than was usual for him, "to reflect upon the distresses and difficulties" suffered by the army — lack of meat and depreciated pay, for examples. He was reflecting in that mood, May 31.

Two regiments of the Connecticut line had just marched mutinously at headquarters, demanding a full ration and prompt pay. Their ration had been cut, their pay was five months overdue.

June 18, Huntington wrote about British threats in New Jersey, in a letter to Governor Trumbull. "It is mortifying to find Genl Washington hath not an army sufficient to remove them."

The fall of Charleston already had happened. During early June, news began trickling into Philadelphia which patriots tried not to credit until they could be certain. Huntington wrote to Washington on June

5: "I have received no official intelligence from the southward of the surrender of Charles Town." Governor Nash, from whom he had received a letter, "takes the liberty to doubt whether Charles Town has surrendered; that the account still wants explanation, though I fear it may eventually prove true."

June 12. "We are still held in suspense, having no certain accounts respecting the fate of Charles Town, but a variety of reports in contradiction to each other."

June 13. General Gates had now been ordered to take command of the southern department "in consequence of intelligence received via New York, that Charles Town surrendered the 12th ulto and the garrison are made prisoners."

June 15. "The last evening, Colo. Ternant arrived with despatches from Genl Lincoln, containing a particular account of the siege and surrender of Charlestown, which will soon be forwarded to your Excellency."

In time, what had happened became clear. The unseasoned, outnumbered American forces had decided to try a defense of Charleston. They were almost sure to lose. Clinton, the British commander, moved slowly but expertly, after disembarking at John's Island. Deliberately he inched toward Charleston, waiting for re-inforcements from Savannah. During early April, he fortified his positions for siege, under American fire. He received re-inforcements from New York; the British fleet arrived off Fort Moultrie.

May 8, an abortive truce, but the next day, firing again. The disastrous surrender soon became inevitable. Lincoln was among about 5,000 Americans taken prisoner. Huge stocks of supplies went to the British. Clinton quickly sent expeditions to occupy all of South Carolina. Leaving Cornwallis to try winning North Carolina, he led 4,500 men back to New York to resume the faceoff against Washington.

THE DAY BEFORE PLANTING CORN

A corn farmer, hands weary,
Scratched rocky ground with his hoe.
"I want a mightier blade!
I want a big earth-grinder!"

The seed waited in the shed.
Air masses shifted about.

Quietly the sky opened.
At a corner of the field
Apple trees forgave the soil
Its hostility, and grew.

A congressional vote on August 2 shows Huntington's misgivings about pressure for military solutions of the problem of inadequate American battle readiness.

According to Ezekiel Cornell (Cornell to Governor Greene, August 1), there was current talk about the "necessity" of appointing Washington "sole dictator of America."

Meanwhile, Washington and the committee at headquarters asked Congress to lift restrictions on the authority of the Commander-in-chief to act outside the territorial limits of the United States. Perhaps joint operations with the French could be hindered by those old restrictions. Huntington thought not. And given the talk of a dictator, he felt skittish about seeming to increase the General's authority in any particular. Although Congress lifted the restriction. Huntington was among a few who voted no.

Excited by Washington's tentative plan for some sort of campaign against Clinton, Philip Schuyler submitted in late June a draft proposal for reorganizing the Quartermaster department. His proposal was agreeable to the committee at headquarters and to Generals Washington and Greene. Schuyler left Morristown and came to Philadelphia to lay the document before Congress.

The committee, he wrote to Huntington and Congress on June 17, "would have ventured on it without a reference to Congress" — on the basis, presumably, of Congress' original instructions to them — "had they conceived themselves authorized to have determined on the pay to the officers."

On June 19, Congress referred his proposal to a committee of five, to which Schuyler himself was named. So was General Ezekiel Cornell, a Rhode Island friend of Greene's. But the other three members named were known to be critics of Greene's methods. They were Roger Sherman, whose participation in the drafting of Mifflin's and Pickering's plan Schuyler had derided; General Artemas Ward, Pickering's compatriot from Massachusetts, often Sam Adams' ally; and General John Armstrong of Pennsylvania, who had written Washington in January about retrenching expenses of the civil staff of the army.

Schuyler argued for his plan, the essence of which was to spare Greene from "petitess" — his word for the Mifflin-Pickering-Sherman-Jones system of regulation. But criticism of the costs and abuses of the department had become too strong to be stemmed.

Wooster had once believed that Schuyler over-regulated his conduct of the campaign to Canada. Now Schuyler was scorning an attempt to regulate the work of the Quartermaster, which he thought better left to the administrator's resourceful best work under test of many hundreds of dissimilar and unpredictable circumstances.

The more basic question, it seemed to New Englanders like Sherman and Ward, Pickering and Huntington, was whether corrupt practices could ever be necessary for practical success. They had heard a din of accusations for too long. Quartermaster's employes were accused of marking up prices to gain higher commissions. Of filing false returns. Of making deals with vendors to take poor goods or underweight goods.

Less than a week after the debate ended, and before its passions had subsided, a committee report written by Timothy Matlack came to Congress. It expressed a concern that "no adequate provision hath been made for the just punishment of delinquents" in supply departments. Those were persons who embezzle or misapply, damage, or spoil provisions, horses, forage, arms, clothing, ammunition, or other military or hospital stores or property belonging to the United States. Such persons, if convicted, said the report, "shall suffer death, or such other punishment as shall be directed." Congress agreed to consider the report in a few days but, presumably wishing to allow time for a cooling off, waited a month. Then it was briefly recommitted and appeared with a new ending in the writing of Samuel Huntington; "shall suffer such punishment as the said court shall, in their discretion, direct according to the degree of the offence." This form of the resolution passed.

Gerry wrote Lovell (August 14) about a complaint which came to his attention. Instead of buying when they received public money, some officers of staff invested the money in articles of merchandise, which they stored until prices rose. They were allowed to spend money without strict accounting as to the dates when the money was advanced to them.

On June 26, Schuyler left Philadelphia. He gave Greene his opinion that his plan, now that the five-man redraft was nearly complete, was "mutilated... in such a way as will in great measure destroy its utility."

On June 30, the redraft committee reported. Congress debated the first paragraph. Should they appoint two more assistants to the Quartermaster-general? Cornell and Ward voted "ay," Sherman "no." Huntington, "no." The proposition was defeated, 9-3.

Debate resumed on July 6. Shall the Quartermaster-general be paid $166 per month in addition to his pay as an army officer? Thomas McKean wanted it lowered to $100. But, to encourage reliance on salary instead of commissions, eight New Englanders including Huntington voted "ay" and one, "no." Congress, "ay" 9-2.

So the debate continued. "It is proposed that only one Assistant Qr. M-gl will be allowed, John Armstrong wrote on July 8, "and he to reside near Congress." After describing methods for deputy quartermasters in the states, Armstrong brought up the question whether Nathaniel Greene would be willing to serve under the developing new plan. "It is not yet known whether he will serve, but as the system is only designed for the campaign, it's thought he will."

After the report was recommitted for some changes, its bulk was read and enacted on June 15. "All the officers employed will be on salary and not commissions," Sherman wrote to Governor Trumbull. "Issuing posts in the country are to be discontinued."

The effect was to eliminate Greene's two principal assistants, Col. John Cox and Charles Pettit. Also, to deprive the whole department of their gains from the commissions. Greene was furious. He felt that a conspiracy against him was to blame.

And he objected to other features of the plan. For instance, locating the one authorized assistant quartermaster near Congress, where he must keep careful accounts, receiving quarterly returns from all the departments and reporting those as soon as possible to the Commander-in-chief and to the Board of War. And, withholding pay from officers who would not take an oath of allegiance and an oath of office; requiring certificates of officers when they received issues of forage; and so on.

Greene said he could not be held responsible for the conduct of all his subordinates. Congress insisted that he be held responsible. He also argued against the timing; introduction of a new system in the middle of a campaign.

On July 26, Greene resigned. ("Administration," he wrote, choosing that word because it was a revolutionary word usually saved for throwing at the British royal government, "seem to think it far less important to the public interest to have this department well filled and properly arranged than it really is, and as they will find it by future experience.")

Greene seems to have thought that taking commissions, even when open to abuse, and other practices which might be counted fraudulent under normal conditions, were necessary evils under conditions of war: tangled supply lines, depreciated pay, arduous work.

His harsh words chafed a number in Congress. They reacted angrily, some feeling he should be discharged from the army. So when the committee at headquarters attempted to salvage the plan which they had sent to Congress and by that means dissuade Greene from quitting, it was malapropos. They wrote a message to Congress one morning at 3 a.m., urging the total repeal of the new plan and a plea to Greene, Cox and Pettit that they remain on duty under the old procedures. "Aware, sir," they told Huntington and Congress through him, "of the delicacy of giving an opinion on a subject were (sic) the feelings of Congress are so evidently concerned, nothing could induce us to it but the clearest conviction, founded on the most minute observations and meeting with the concurrance (sic) with the Commander-in-chief, that a change of officers in the Quartermaster-genl's department, in this stage of the campaign and under the embarrassments of our affairs, must be absolutely productive of ruin."

Congress already had referred some earlier letters from the committee concerning their dealings with Greene to five prestigious members:

Samuel Adams, Thomas McKean, Roger Sherman, Henry Laurens, and Abraham Clark. In due course they adopted a resolution, drafted in the writing of Adams. As the committee at headquarters knew that the Quartermaster-general had requested the sense of Congress on so important a subject as his responsibility for the conduct of his subordinates, "they ought not to have interfered therein."

During the first week in August, Schuyler left Morristown to go on private business to Albany. His aspiration to direct the military affairs of the confederation had come to nothing. Months before, the New York delegates would have proposed his name as Greene's successor. Now Timothy Pickering was being appointed the new Quartermaster-general, determined to make the plan work which Shuyler had scorned. In February of the next year, Schuyler's aspiration would brighten a little again, then dim out for ever. Meanwhile, he would serve his country as an able vigilante on the New York frontier, the British continually attempting to win cooperation from Indian tribes there. Probably the letters he had joined the committee at headquarters in sending to the states had slightly quickened the efforts of some recipients. And Washington had taken comfort from his confidence and sympathy.

<hr />

In July, General William McDougall, while assigned to West Point, visited headquarters on business. He discovered an agreement between himself and several officers, Congress had wronged them by past decisions about rank and promotion. Presently their main grievances were financial. The depreciation of currency had seriously diminished the value of their pay, which had been fixed in 1775. Nearly a year ago, officers had signed a memorial, asking depreciation adjustments. The meager results of that initiative upset them.

While at camp, McDougall signed a second memorial (July 11) and agreed to take it personally to Congress and lobby for it. From July 31 into September, he was in Philadelphia on that mission.

Henry Laurens felt worried. Not only was it an "unlucky moment" for Congress because of Greene's resignation. Now, also, the officers "remonstrate for means which shall enable them to dress purpose better. So when the memorial was laid before Congress, August 3, Laurens and Adams, Sherman and Clark, and Joseph Jones were appointed the committee to report on it. They began the same day to meet with McDougall.

He told them that the officers wanted depreciation adjustments in pay, increased allowances for living expenses, and a pension for widows and orphans of officers killed in the war. Excepting Robert Howe, all of the officers, including Greene and Knox, had signed the memorial. Their basic concern was loss of time from private occupations, as well as hardships of the field.

A significant discussion about the philosophy of government took place. McDougall was ready, having already modified his own beliefs after having formerly been an enthusiastic Son of Liberty. He now thought the people of America expected Spartan virtues of the army, but lapsed themselves into a love of luxury. Sam Adams, not surprisingly, held fast to the early principles of the Revolution. So they talked of classical history, philosophy, and types of government. The armies of Athens and Sparta, said McDougall, lived as the citizens did; their condition therefore was "easy and happy." But the condition of the American army was different.

He told Adams, "Our army no longer consider themselves as fighting the battle of republics in principle, but for empire and liberty to a people whose object is property." The army wanted a share of "that property which the citizen seeks, and which the army protects for him." (The word "empire" was a word which Philip Schuyler used in those days to characterize the aims of America).

Adams, who personally practiced a Spartan lifestyle, was not convinced by the discourse. He wrote out the following draft of a resolution, "Patience and self-denial, fortitude and perseverance, and the cheerful sacrifice of time, health, and fortune, are necessary virtues which both the citizen and the soldier are called to exercise while struggling for the liberties of their country." Also, "Moderation, frugality, and temperance must be among the chief supports, as well as the brightest ornaments, of that kind of civil government which is wisely instituted by the several states in this union."

McDougall felt, after his conferences with men of the committee, that he had "dealt very plainly with them, but with prudence and decorum." He had let them know what were the opinions which some "judicious" people entertained about Congress. "This will no doubt give me a place with others in their black list." Yet the committee, too, must have spoken plainly. "Something will be done," he concluded, "but their means for present relief are small."

Adams' resolution, along with more functional phrases written by Sherman, were adopted August 12. Congress would adjust for depreciation in cases of officers who were not in the quota of any state. (Congress had already requested the states to compensate the officers and soldiers they were contributing). The officers would be paid in new bills, per the currency act of March 18. Moreover, Congress granted 1,100 acres of land to major-generals, 850 acres to brigadier-generals. And officers soon would be furnished with two months' pay "on account" to relieve present wants.

Huntington sent an official copy of this act to McDougall. "Some further matters were under consideration for the benefit of the general officers, their widows and children, which are in committee and I trust will be speedily determined." The letter closed with words which Huntington reserved for a few chosen addressees: "With sentiments of esteem and respect."

The President did not mention a motion, put by Livingston, of which McDougall doubtless was aware. It was a recommendation to the states that they provide a pension of "half pay for life" to officers of the army, their widows or, if none, their orphaned children until 14 years of age. The motion lost, 3-6, one divided. The vote of individual members was closer, 10 aye, 11 no. Huntington voted, no. On August 25, Congress ordered that the record of this voting be struck. It was a question on which people, in Congress and out, were differing passionately.

On August 24, they had voted the remaining actions to which Huntington had referred. Their pay, which Sherman could not resist saying had been set originally by the four eastern states, was deemed still in the right ratio to that of other officers. Because money had depreciated, states ought to grant half pay pensions to widows and orphans — if they were indigent. Congress would allow officers rations heretofore withheld: if subsistence money in lieu of rations withheld did not equal the cost of those rations, the deficiency would be made up. Finally, a clause was repealed in the act of May 15, 1778, regarding pensions: recipients of the pensions would not be forbidden to hold any public office or to profit from services to the United States or any state.

When Huntington sent copies of the two acts to Washington, August 12 and 24, he described them as "making farther provision for the army in their present difficult situation." He remarked that Congress was still considering "the subject of depreciation, in order to settle a just scale of depreciation for the army with as much accuracy as the nature of the case will admit."

McDougall, after appraising what Congress had enacted, wrote them that the measures were not adequate. But four days afterward, he left Philadelphia.

The smallness of Congress' means for relief, which he had conceded, was visible from time to time in the following months. For instance, they provided that officers entitled to keep horses could, if the horses were wounded or disabled in action, receive pay for them, "provided," in the words of Huntington's summary, "the horses so wounded and disabled are delivered to the department of the Quartermaster-general."

——————

On August 25, Congress received a report, which was read September 7, written by Thomas McKean for a committee dealing with claims by Francis Hopkinson.

Hopkinson was not only a lawyer, a satirical poet, and the continent's Treasurer of Loans. He was also an artist, interested in heraldry. He had designed the seal of the College of Philadelphia, and participated in designing seals for the American Philosophical Society and the State of New Jersey. Lately he had been working up a design for the "Great Seal" of the United States.

McKean found that there was animosity in the Treasury Board. The board usually went into secret session from 9 a.m. to noon, and one day had shut the door in Hopkinson's face when he appeared on business, and "also treated him with unmerited indignity on other occasions." They were now opposing payment for his work on the Great Seal and other such work. The behavior of the board, McKean judged, "is very reprehensible, extremely disgusting, and has destroyed all friendly communications of councils and harmony in the execution of public affairs." His report included the recommendation that the secretary, Charles Lee, and Commissioners Ezekiel Foreman and John Gibson all be replaced.

But in the aftermath, Hopkinson was never paid for his design.

The proposed design, according to an earlier report on the seal itself, written May 17 by William Churchill Houston, was three inches in diameter. One side showed the arms of the United States, a striped shield beneath a constellation of thirteen stars, the shield supported by a warrior holding a sword and by a goddess of peace holding an olive branch. The Latin motto was *bello vel paci*, "war or peace."

The reverse side of the shield showed another feminine figure, Liberty, seated in a chair and holding a staff and cap. The motto was first intended to include the title *Libertas*; but that word was struck, and the proposed motto was *virtute perennis*, meaning freely, "moral quality enables liberty to endure."

The symbolism of staff and cap interested Hopkinson. In one of his verses, the figure Britannia says:

> "A magic wand I once possessed,
>   A cap aloft it bore;
> Of all my treasures this the best,
>   And none I valued more."

Congress did not hurry about adopting a Great Seal. The 1780 proposal followed congressional inaction on some ideas developed in 1776 by Franklin, John Adams, and Jefferson. Their ideas included the shield and the goddess of liberty supporting it, the eye of Providence, the motto *e pluribus unum*, and also, at Franklin's suggestion, the figure of Moses passing through the Red Sea, with the motto "resistance to tyranny is obedience to God." Adams favored featuring Hercules, choosing Virtue rather than Pleasure while outlasting his great labors.

Congress adopted no seal until 1782, when Charles Thompson, aided by William Barton, proposed the design which was approved and still is in use.

———————

In mid-August, Washington summed up the results of all the applications to the states by Congress, the committee at headquarters, and himself: "We have every reason to apprehend we shall not be in a condition at all to undertake anything decisive." They had fallen short of the required 504 continental battalions. Further, "We are now fed by a precarious supply day to day... As to forage and transportation, our prospects are still worse."

Speaking to the states in a tone of firm command had not, it seems, solved the problems it was expected to solve.

Alone at Morristown, without Schuyler or Peabody, feeling thwarted but by no means subdued, John Mathews wrote a long, "private" letter to his fellow members of Congress about their acceptance of Greene's resignation. He thought there would follow "a total derangement of this department."

One passage especially proved provocative: "It may be asked whether Congress are to be dictated to by their officers? I answer without hesitation that, on the present occasion, they must. Necessity compels them to it, and it is a duty they owe their constituents not to suffer punctilio to militate against their essential interests. If there are men in the great council of this nation capable of such a conduct, I will not say what I think are their deserts."

Congress ordered, August 11, that the committee at headquarters be discharged from further attendance there. Huntington and Sherman, Adams and Ward, voted "aye" with nineteen other members. Five, "no." The vote by states was 10-2-one divided. Schuyler's and Mathews' states were the two which voted "no."

Ezekiel Cornell, who voted "aye," wrote to Nathaniel Greene two days later, that it was "necessary for several reasons" to recall the committee. (In the same letter he assured Greene that Roger Sherman had been, Greene's fast friend in Congress throughout the recent trouble, "as well as every other member from that state.")

Cornell's reasons: "to keep harmony, among ourselves." He himself had no charge against the committee, "some of their letters were in a style rather warm, but that I imputed to Schuyler's zeal and the warm climate of Mathews' nativity."

Whitmill Hill interpreted the recall, to Burke: "Experience convinced Congress that they daily engaged them in quarrels with the army, instead of correcting any of the abuses they were intended to inspect... Congress have for once had firmness enough to persist."

———※※———

While Schuyler was withdrawing from the continental scene, his old rival Horatio Gates was again becoming prominent. Many members of Congress, although studiously polite to Schuyler, were positively fond of Gates. His sentiments and manners seemed more "republican." And after Saratoga, he was the symbol of success against British arms by state militia.

The chronic reluctance of the states to support a regular central army to the extent wanted by Washington, and by most men in Congress was a result of their citizens' dislike of all taxes including taxes for army upkeep. They thought that when the British threatened to attack, their militia could be warned, rapidly mustered, and led as at Saratoga to defend them. A long-term army, by contrast, remained idle for long intervals, wasting tax money for their food, quarters, and staff organization. They regretted time off from ordinary work on the farms and in the trades.

June 13, Huntington informed Washington and the states' executives that Gates had been appointed to command the southern department. His letters were, as usual, concise and businesslike. Then to Oliver Woolcott, however, he added a personal word: "I most devoutly wish his former good fortune may still attend him."

He sent Washington news of Congress' acts (June 17 and 19) to bolster the southern army, adding a restrained comment, "Congress cannot but hope that the measures they have recommended, if executed with punctuality and despatch, will change the face of affairs in that country."

Gates took command at Coxe's Mill, North Carolina, on July 25. Lincoln's former southern army being now largely in British prisons, Gates' troops were those whom Washington had started southward in April with the aim of relieving Charleston. Moving on south, their specific mission dissolved, they at least attracted some militia and seized some supplies. On August 3 Gates led them across the Peedee River in South Carolina.

"We have received by this day's post, just arrived," Huntington wrote Washington on August 28, "intelligence from the southward that General Gates has formed a junction with a body of troops under General Caswell (sic) within the state of South Carolina, and also various accounts of some advantages gained by our troops in several encounters with detachments of the enemy."

Three days later, he received Gates' chilling report: on August 16, the southern army had been defeated. Huntington to Washington: "A most unhappy event, and unexpected immediately after the intelligence we had just received of several advantages gained by our troops in that area."

"It is said," he wrote to Governor Trumbull, one of Gates' cordial friends, "the militia fled at the beginning of the action. Genl Gates in vain attempted to rally them, and finally escaped himself with his aids by the fleetness of their horses."

Gates had been advised (John Rutledge to Gates, August 14, 1782) that the British were weak at Camden. At one time, there had in fact been a weakness, but Cornwallis had received additional forces.

Both Gates and Cornwallis planned to surprise each other. Their advance contingents happened to meet by night at the same spot of ground, August 15. They skirmished and disengaged. After a council of war with his top officers, Gates decided to fight, still underestimating Cornwallis' strength. They set up a battle arrangement. Cornwallis with 2,400 experienced and well-disciplined troops attacked; Gates'

2,000 militia fled, his regulars under DeKalb, at the right wing, held their stations for a time, but DeKalb was killed and the wing was overpowered. Unable to rally the militia, Gates rode to Hillsborough, North Carolina, to attempt a regrouping.

In his letter to Trumbull, Huntington had declared: "I am yet in doubt what judgment to form as to the cause of this disaster, and how far it might have been prevented, but am fearful our troops were too much flushed with their various successes and the advantages they had lately gained, and were too rapid in advancing without sufficient strength and caution. It is said they had not magazines of provision and were obliged to move to get their daily subsistence. This unfortunate event at present engrosses the attention of Congress to adopt measures for the defence of the southern states and prevent the further ravages of the enemy in that quarter."

He wrote Gates about information "that a part of the continental troops made good their retreat, and an army are again collecting." If the information was correct, Congress intended to lay up magazines for a southern army of 15,000 men. "It is to be hoped that the panick which it seems had seised the militia will wear off, and that you may yet be able to check the progress of the enemy until more effectual measures may be taken to expel them from South Carolina and Georgia." That was early September.

Gates' critics in some sections of the army and in Congress changed his forecast. In October, he had to direct Washington to order a court of inquiry into Gates' conduct as commander of the southern army, and to appoint another commander until the inquiry was finished.

An event more shocking even than the disaster at Camden began to engross everybody's attention.

———⟫●⟪———

Washington, riding back from Hartford, where he had conferred about military plans with Count Rochambeau, stopped on the Hudson to visit Benedict and Peggy Arnold, September 25. Instead of a pleasant visit, he discovered with horror a treasonous plot to betray West Point. The next day, he notified Huntington and Congress.

"We had before received intelligence from General Greene," Huntington replied by letter, "that General Arnold was gone over to the enemy. Immediately orders were given to search and seize his papers and effects to be found here, which was speedily executed, but I am not yet advised of what particular discoveries have been made."

Then, descending from the extraordinary to the nearer ordinary, he seems to have recalled the importance of Washington's meeting with the French commander, and to have supposed that Washington had avoided possible foul play at the hands of Arnold or Arnold's accomplices, "With congratulations on your return to the army."

Years ago, Huntington probably had heard tales about the enigmatic past of the traitor about whom everybody was gossiping. All his life, evidently, Arnold had wanted people to notice him, like him, approve and praise him. As a teen-ager he used to show off and win attention. It was said that he once impressed friends by jumping on a paddle wheel at a mill in Norwich, Huntington's adopted city, holding to a paddle while the wheel lifted him up and over and into the water of the mill stream. That another time, when a crowd had gathered in Norwich to watch a burning house and the fire fighters had decided they could not save the house, people had gasped to see a figure walking along the ridge pole, near the flames; it was Arnold, who had stayed up on the roof until moments before its collapse.

Arnold moved to New Haven, where he ran a drug store and a shipping business and became captain of the local militia. He left for Lexington as soon as he heard of the shooting there, led some fighting, and proceeded to the siege of Quebec. There, at the forefront of an attack on the Palace Gate, he was wounded in the left leg. Later, on Lake Champlain, he led a naval fight; under his direction Americans built and equipped some small ships and went out to meet a unit of the British Navy. Their ships were destroyed, but the fighters escaped.

At Saratoga, although he had given up his command, irked at Gates, he could not restrain himself from entering the action and leading men in frenzied attacks which helped gain the victory. Gates gave him credit. Again, however, he was wounded in the left leg, this time becoming a cripple for life.

Huntington had missed much of the tension which built up between Congress and Arnold, absent by the accidents of rotating terms when Congress ranked Arnold Brigadier General after Quebec, Major General after the defense of Danbury, 1777. Arnold was furious in 1776 over not being ranked Major General. Again Huntington was absent when, in 1777, Congress investigated Arnold's expense accounts concerning money advanced him in Canada. In renewed anger, he had attempted to resign from the army, but Washington intervened with a request that he go north to oppose Burgoyne's march toward the Hudson. Arnold quickly withdrew his resignation, taking the chance to fight.

In June, 1778, Huntington was concluding a term of attendance when Washington ordered Arnold to Philadelphia as the city's military commander. There, Arnold lived in one of the best mansions, with housekeeper, coachman, groom, and various other servants; his splendid carriage was drawn by four horses. He entertained the wealthy elite of the city, including some whose sympathy for the cause of Independence was dubious. By then, besides social approval, he craved money: his first wife having died, he married Peggy Shippen, a young Philadelphia woman of wealth and social prominence.

His part in the affair of *The Charming Nancy* did not seem wrong to him. He had sent twelve military wagons belonging to the state of Pennsylvania on an eight-day trip to get a cargo of dry goods off *The Charming Nancy*, a schooner. The facts that he had entered into a business understanding with the owners of the schooner and that, consequently, he made half the profit when the goods were sold in Philadelphia, seemed to him to be inoffensive. He could not understand why the Executive Council of Pennsylvania objected and why, later, he was brought to court-martial. He had acted, he explained, to save the cargo from British capture. Congress received charges against him from the Pennsylvania Council, and ordered a court-martial, Huntington not yet attending. Arnold indignantly resigned his command; soon he established contacts with the British.

Huntington was told, when he arrived at Congress in 1779, that Arnold was impatient for trial and acquittal. And on March 31, 1780, Huntington presided when the verdict was released, guilty on two of eight counts. Washington, who liked Arnold's ardor as a leader of fighting, executed the sentence by a gentle reprimand. Arnold soon wrote to Schuyler, asking help in obtaining the command at West Point. Schuyler supported the appointment, as did Livingston, and in August, Washington ordered it.

"There has long subsisted a jealousy between Congress and the army," Arnold reported to Lord Germain, October 7, after his flight from arrest. "The former have been jealous of the power of the latter" and "have excluded the army from every appointment of honour or profit in the civil line." In the same report he included facts about Washington's army.

He received from Clinton a British appointment as Brigadier General.

"The treason of Benedict Arnold," Huntington wrote Governor Trumbull in mid-October, "hath been the topic of much conversation, and many of his scandalous transactions are brought to light that were before concealed." Early that month, Congress ordered the Board of War to erase Arnold's name from the register of names of continental officers; Huntington reported that decision to Washington. In Norwich, a mob destroyed the tombstone of Arnold's father.

——————⇒➤●⇐←——————

Resigning himself to no effective 1780 campaign in the north, Washington on August 20 urged Congress to plan for the recruitment and supply of an army for the year starting next January 1. The sobering news of Camden, after Charleston, readied Congress for prompt response.

On September 21, they sent a plan to Washington for comment. On October 3, they enacted it. This act was in time for the states to try, if they would, meeting a January 1 enlistment date. (The acts for 1779 had not been completed until March of that year. For 1780, not until January — the enlistment date being pushed to February 1.) Washington's "returns and deficiencies" in the enlistment quotas of the states, Huntington wrote him, may be laid before their respective assemblies, "most of which meet before the end of this month."

One of Washington's recommendations had been as in years before, to provide continental officers with a postwar pension, "half pay for life." Huntington, with most delegates from New England, had maneuvered and voted against such a measure in 1778 and 1779. They were mistrustful of any move toward a standing army. "I was not a little surprized," Huntington wrote to Governor Trumbull after Congress enacted the measure this time (on October 21), "as the question had so often been discussed before, and as often negatived."

As an economy, Congress had decided to reduce the number of regiments, with their officers. Yet, Huntington pointed out to Trumbull, the unforeseen pension was allowed to those officers, "as well those who shall be reduced by the new arrangement of the army as those who shall continue in service."

Connecticut's delegates, having been instructed by their state assembly to oppose the measure, "looked upon themselves as bound" by those instructions. The comment shows his alertness to political sentiments back home. Probably it also expresses his view of the structural reliance of Congress on the states. Whether or not the private convictions of the delegates differed from their instructions, the instructions were seen as binding.

But, "I confess for myself ever to have opposed the measure and take that to have been the sentiments of all the delegates from Connecticut who have been present when the question has been debated." Presumably he was including General Joseph Spencer, whose stake as a continental Army officer distinguished him from the civilian delegates. (Spencer's votes on the question, 1779, supports that inclusion).

"Though I am as willing as others generously to reward the officers of the army," Huntington affirmed, as if the particulars of the debate were fresh in his mind, "and think they merit much from their country, yet I have ever been opposed to pensions for life as a reward for their services, as inconsistent with the genious (sic) and spirit of our constitution."

He said he was concerned about its consequences among the people. Probably he was thinking of the problem of factions. What would happen in communities where pension-takers were set apart from civilian taxpayers who had no pension? "What effects it will have with them, time will best discover: hope it may be better than my fears."

During the season of shock over Camden and Arnold's defection and Congress' reactions, Huntington tried to end his term as President. On or before September 28, he told Congress that one year had elapsed since his election. Doubtless he assumed that the stipulation in Article IX of the Articles of Confederation applied: "The United States in Congress assembled shall have authority... to appoint one of their number to preside, provided that no person be allowed to serve in the office of President more than one year in any term of three years."

Although the Articles were not yet officially in effect, Congress had approved them for ratification in November, 1777, and since that date Laurens had presided a little more than one year; Jay, less than ten months.

Besides his assumption about the one-year rule, Huntington felt that he had put concentrated work into the office. It was from that feeling that he had written Governor Trumbull: "The period that confines me to my present painful situation is almost expired and, as I have been long absent from my private affairs, and my health somewhat impaired with the burthen and fatigue of business, I hope to obtain leave of absence."

A friendly motion, put to the house on September 28, that the one-year rule be observed "henceforward" was blocked when Sam Adams moved to postpone, seconded by Timothy Matlack. The four New England states voted unanimously for postponement. So did New York, Pennsylvania, and North Carolina. Among individuals voting "aye" was Madison. They evidently wanted to keep Huntington in the chair. But according to John Mathews, the decision required "four hours of hard struggle."

Mathews thought that Huntington "seemed to be highly pleased with the opinions" of those who wanted him to remain. Perhaps there had been few occasions in the past when support and gratitude for his conduct of the presidency were expressed. His own polite style perhaps had seldom evoked such expression. During the discussion, one delegate whom Mathews identified with sarcasm as "the greatest republican in America" (probably Adams) stated in support of keeping Huntington "that he had a right to set there for life." Mathews' appraisal: "Damnation seize such sycophants!"

Finally Livingston moved "that no rule or practice of the house limits the term for which the President is elected." Lovell seconded. All 23 votes were "aye" — a courtesy. So they kept Huntington. It was an honor he had not expected nor wished. Although Congress provided him with suitable lodging in the Pemberton house at Third and Chestnut, as well as supply of the presidential table and an able steward, Richard Philips, his absence from law practice in Norwich caused him a net financial privation. The journals of Congress and the President's letterbook, furthermore, attest that he was busy. The work demanded of him by his office was heavy.

Mathews, however, had wished for a different outcome. He wrote to Peabody that "an elevated station had made a man forget himself, who from being a very modest one had so strongly imbibed the sweets of power as to become a very conceited and ambitious one." A fact which could have entered into that bitter assessment; usually, if Huntington had left the chair, it would have been the south's turn to fill it; Mathews could have felt thwarted.

What did the contest really mean? Did either Congress or the presidency of Congress matter? Was the Congress of 1780 a gaggle of second-rate men fated by puny abilities to fail at tasks which the great members of 1775 and 1776 might have done better? Washington had departed to the army; Franklin, John Adams, and Jay, to diplomacy; Jefferson to the governorship of Virginia.

Although drained of such men, Congress during 1780 was not weak. With Huntington that year sat a future President of the United States (Madison), a future Vice-President (Gerry), a future Chief justice of the Supreme Court (Ellsworth), and a future Speaker of the House of Representatives (Muhlenberg). Also twelve future state Governors besides Huntington himself (Sam Adams, Burke, Mathews, Gerry, Collins of Rhode Island, John Henry of Maryland, Johnston of North Carolina, Plater of Maryland, Sullivan of New Hampshire, Telfair of Georgia, VanDyke of Delaware, Walton of Georgia). Livingston was Chancellor of New York, 1777–1801, afterward aiding in the Louisiana Purchase. Besides Muhlenberg, Madison, and Ellsworth, eight would serve in the United States House (Bland of Virginia, Clark of New Jersey, Clymer of Pennsylvania, Few of Georgia, Floyd of New York, Benjamin Huntington of Connecticut, Livermore of New Hampshire, Sherman of Connecticut). Few, Henry, Johnston, Walton, Ellsworth and Sherman would serve in the United States Senate, as would Schuyler. Among others, Joseph Jones, Thomas McKean, and Jesse Root would distinguish themselves as jurists in their states. John Witherspoon would continue as President of Princeton.

LORD NORTH AND THE LADY LIBERTAS

Imagine a pen and ink caricature of Lord North, approaching the seated Lady with her staff and cap.

North: "My Lady Libertas, pardon me, but I notice that you have taken the place which Dr. Franklin had desired for Moses, who was bringing down the Red Sea upon Pharaoh. Does it annoy you to be a substitute figure?

Libertas; "Hardly. Moses and I are frequent cohorts, even if his shaff and mine are not identical. He was a suitable nominee."

North: "And I notice also that Mr. John Adams at first nominated Hercules. Since you are now in his place, too, I am curious whether you resemble Zeus or Yahweh; which one?"

Libertas; "We resemble each other, all three of us, more than you may have noticed."

North: "Not to pause at your riddle, I must inquire: Were you pleased with Hercules when he killed those lions, those centaurs, and many humans?"

Libertas: "I am pleased by life, not by death and killing. Yet I am displeased by every forced tribute, including the one to Erginus which Hercules opposed."

North: "Another riddle, I fear. Or if not, I decline to follow your implication."

The Second Presidential Year

"I find the post was robbed of my official letters of the 6. ulto, addressed to the four eastern states, covering dispatches relating to recruiting the army, as your Excellency had conjectured; but presume the intelligence the enemy obtained thereby must be very disagreeable to them."

—Huntington to Governor Trumbull,
November 9, 1780

"Colonel John Trumbull was in London the 25th of October last, and had been there some time in company with Mr. West, the celebrated painter. This intelligence I have received from a gentleman just arrived in this city from London, who tells me he saw Mr. Trumbull and conversed with him and a number of other Americans who had taken an active part in the war in America, and appeared openly in the city and no notice taken of them by authority."

—Huntington to Governor Trumbull,
father of the painter, December 29, 1780

"We waited on Mr. Huntington, President of Congress. We found him in his cabinet, lighted by a single candle. This simplicity reminded me of that of the Fabriciuses and the Philopemens. Mr. Huntington is an upright man, who espouses no party, and may be relied on. He is a native of Connecticut, and was delegate for that state when chosen President."

—The Marquis de Chastellux,
Travels in North America,
London: 1787
The interview described, November, 1780

"His Excellency Samuel Huntington, President, is a man of mild, steady, and firm conduct and of sound and methodical judgment, tho' not a man of many words or very shining abilities. But upon the whole, is better suited to preside than any other member now in Congress. In his dress and manners he is very plain, very gentlemanly, and truely republican. He is from Connecticut."

—Thomas Rodney, diary,
March 10, 1781

"I have had great anxiety lest the flame of faction, which on a former occasion proved so injurious, should be kindled anew. But so far as I can judge, the temper of Congress is in general by no means prone to it, although there may be individuals on both sides who would both wish and endeavor it."

—James Madison to Edmund Pendleton,
November 7, 1780

NOT YET READY AT SEA

They meet and bow. One coughs and speaks:
"Hello, sir... I should say, 'Monsieur.'
Tell me, are you a true ally?"
Startled face: "We are, sir. Lead on!"
Gasp, nodding of head: "We shall. Yes.
I mean, when we get set. We shall."
Smile, twirling of brass fob, "Just so.
When you get set, we shall assist."

Like two hawks who surely know
How to circle and swoop down
On the cackling prey below.
A large hound sleeps near the prey.
Each hawk, perched, waits for the other.

*"The Author of nature has given mankind a certain degree
of insight into futurity. As far as we can see a probability that
certain events will happen, so far we do well to provide and
guard. But we may attempt to go too far. It is vain to think
of providing against every possible contingency."*

—**Huntington to Connecticut convention**
debating the Constitution, January 4, 1788

Although a large amount of Huntington's time was needed, after he
was kept in office, for attention to military affairs, he would preside during the next three-quarters of a year over four enactments of
importance for the civil government. Already he had presided over the
decision to start a federal judiciary. Now similarly he would help enable the beginnings of a plan for the national domain, the establishment of executive departments separate from Congress, the final
ratification and first implementation of the Articles of Confederation,
and the revision of instructions to the peace commissioners.

Land outside the borders of the thirteen states had become the
object of several anxious competitions. The states knew they must not
allow competitions to harm their united effort toward Independence.
But several states were firmly, if courteously, asserting claims to large
amounts of territory. Many claims were based on royal charter grants,
some of them overlapping. Private land companies often based claims
on formal agreements with Indian tribes. Venturesome settlers were
thinking their own thoughts about title to the land they broke.

New York, New Hampshire, and Massachusetts each claimed rights
to Vermont land. The Vermonters, who were mostly settlers from Connecticut, muddied the legal problem further, in 1777, by declaring
themselves a new and independent state.

Kentuckians, too, soon would take an interest in home rule at
Virginia's western settlements.

Huntington early saw the value of confederation as the cardinal value
at stake in the land disputes. During debates over contents of the
Articles of Confederation in July and August of 1776, he warned that
if Congress assumed power to set Virginia's western boundary, "the
consequence is, not to enter the confederation." He did not deny the
worries of the landless states: "Admit that there is danger from Virginia,"
he proposed. If any state became vastly larger and richer than others,
it would be a danger. But the main object was for the states to unite.

"A man's right does not cease to be a right because it is large," he also said. Evidently he was thinking of land from the viewpoint of individual rights: for instance, a Connecticut farm owner's. He was not thinking of a community's right, for instance, when Massachusetts had once claimed the Connecticut town of Enfield; and Rhode Island, the Connecticut town of Stonington. Governor Andros had once claimed for New York all of Connecticut west of the Connecticut River. Economic needs, political capabilities, social loyalties complicate a land dispute between communities.

Land has size. Does a right have size? Landless people may feel, rather, that property rights are secondary to equity rights. Soon Maryland made clear that the value of confederation was endangered by the grievance of landless states.

Congress imagined a map of the original thirteen states in a way which the 20th Century does not copy easily. To the delegates of Massachusetts, Connecticut, Virginia, and the Carolinas, a map showed their land reaching from east coast to west coast. Their charter grants included land "to the South Sea," meaning the Pacific Ocean. If some delegates adjusted their image to the 1763 treaty with France, it went merely to the Mississippi River.

Delegates from New York and Georgia, even before 1763, imagined from the east coast to the Mississippi.

Those seven extensions from the Atlantic coast were interpreted variously. As the outcome of hot disputes, some boundaries had been agreed. Some overlapping claims remained to be settled, such as the Wyoming Valley, claimed by both Connecticut and Pennsylvania; later Congress awarded it to Pennsylvania.

But Rhode Island, New Jersey, Pennsylvania, Delaware, and Maryland were confined. Their map had no imaginary extensions westward. John Dickinson was not teasing when he proposed in his draft of the Articles that Congress be empowered to limit boundaries of states "which by charter or proclamation or under any pretence are said to extend to the South Sea."

The approved form of the Articles did not include Dickinson's proposal. Congress was not empowered to set boundaries, except as the last resort on appeal of boundary disputes between states. A wary proviso was put into the final draft: "that no state shall be deprived of territory for the benefit of the United States." Therefore, state acts of cession would be a necessary step toward national domain.

Whether a common desire for confederation might have moved the states to resolve their clashing interests in western land, the fall of paper currency helped to do so. United States land sales, if the states ceded the territories they were claiming, could bring in revenue which the continental treasury urgently needed. Members of Congress talked more and more about such a revenue source as the financial system sagged.

On February 19, 1780, Philip Schuyler, with the cooperation of Livingston, persuaded the New York legislature to make the first move. He desired both confederation and a well-financed central government. While arguing for the projected revenue from federal land sales, he gained support also from New Yorkers who believed Congress would more readily help them prevail in Vermont if they relinquished title to western territory. Landless states would like the new chance to participate in the development of Congress' domain. At the same time, landed states would like New York's withdrawal from any overlapping claims, and would like the precedent of one state's giving up a part but not the whole of their claimed lands. New York was able to separate their claims cleanly, still contending for the eastern part while unconditionally ceding the west. Other states would have to try the device of placing conditions when they ceded.

The duel between Maryland and Virginia was slow to moderate. Delegates from those states had received strong policy instructions from their legislatures back home, climaxing with Virginia's "Remonstrance" late in 1779. Influencing the legislatures to a significant degree were the investors in Virginia's Ohio Company, and in the middle states' Illinois-Wabash Company and Indiana Company.

In late June, 1780, Congress referred the problem of states' western boundaries to a five-man committee, one member from Maryland and four from landed states including Virginia. Its report, written by Duane of New York, came to Congress quickly but was not discussed on the floor until September. By then Virginia's Joseph Jones and James Madison had agreed to Jefferson's earlier vision of the west as a place for new states.

Congress adopted their committee's proposal, which recommended that landed states make "a liberal surrender of a portion of their territorial claims" to the United States, cited the New York act with approval, and urged the one state still holding out, Maryland, now to subscribe to the Articles of Confederation. Then the Virginia delegates moved that if the states were to cede, as recommended, "the territory so ceded shall be laid out in separate and distinct states" under Congress' direction. No state should be more than about 150 miles square. This motion was referred to committee.

Huntington wrote a presidential letter to the states, enclosing a copy of the recommendation together with copies of a "declaration" by Maryland's legislature, Virginia's "Remonstrance," and New York's act of cession. In deliberating, Congress was "impressed with a sense of the vast importance of the subject," he wrote, "it is to be hoped and most earnestly desired that the wisdom, generosity, and candour of the legislatures of the several states... may direct them to such measures... as shall speedily accomplish an event so important and desirable as the final ratification of the Confederation by all the states."

Jones left Philadelphia and went home to Virginia, hoping to encourage the legislature to vote for cession. On October 10, Congress turned to the Jones motion about laying out new states, revised now by committee and reported in Sherman's writing. Ceded land would be disposed of for the common benefit of the United States. Future new states formed in western territory would be "distinct republican states" which shall become members of the federal union, and have the same rights of sovereignty, freedom and independence as the other states. Expenses incurred by existing states while fighting off the British in the ceded areas were to be reimbursed.

One proposed paragraph, invalidating the legal basis for certain land company titles, was struck out. It had read: "Purchases made of the Indians of any said lands by private persons, without the approbation of the legislature of the state to whom the right of pre-emption belonged..." Instead, the wording, "Purchases and deeds from any Indians of Indian nations...which shall not have been ratified by legal authority..."

Virginians felt uneasy about addresses to Congress by the private land companies. Later, Theodorick Bland, for one, asked that the members of Congress be polled previous to any vote on state cessions, whether they were personally interested in the claims of a company or companies which had petitioned Congress. It was, apparently, an early attempt at setting standards for lobbying.

On Jones' revised motion, Huntington voted "aye" with the majority. On the same day he transmitted a copy of it to Jefferson: he was eager for Virginia to hear that it was passed. Days later he transmitted it to the other states.

In October, the Connecticut assembly guardedly surrendered the state's right or pre-emption of soil, but not of jurisdiction, and only "in just proportion of what shall be ceded and relinquished by the other states," as its cession of vacant and unappropriated lands to the United States "for their use and benefit." Although guarded, the cession was intended as a positive measure to cement the union and to establish an estate for the public by encouraging immigration of "industrious forcigners": so Oliver Wolcott assured John Laurens (December, 1780). The Connecticut cession, however, probably because it seemed overly qualified, was not much advertised at the time.

On January 2, 1781, the Virginia assembly also voted a conditional cession. It gave up land north of the Ohio River, if Congress created at least two new states there and if Congress excepted a tract already promised to Virginia soldiers (particularly soldiers who fought in the west under George Rogers Clark) and if Congress voided private purchases and deeds from Indians.

Soon after Virginia acted, Maryland ratified the confederation.

———————

The question of Vermont was still open.

Although "the king in council" heard claims from both New York and New Hampshire and decided, in 1764, for New York, the contest went on. New Hampshire refined its argument; Massachusetts entered a claim; the settlers challenged them all.

The settlers, who were mainly from New England, combined to resist the civil power of New York under the colorful leadership of Ethan and Ira Allen, Seth Warner, Remember Baker, and the "Green Mountain Boys." In 1777, they declared themselves an independent state and petitioned for admission to the United States. New York considered their actions a "revolt," turning to Congress for vindication. And for its part. Congress felt even less eager to deal with this three-way dispute than with the complaint of Maryland against Virginia.

In 1775, the Green Mountain Boys had participated in the American capture of Fort Ticonderoga and Crown Point; and in 1777, joined forces with New Hampshire's militia against Burgoyne's army. Should the thirteen states disown the aspirations of such comrades? Yet "common defense" was one of the bases of the confederation, logically they were committed to suppress a revolt in any state.

Adding to the dilemma, the Articles described a way for Canada to join the union. Other colonies could join, too, if nine states agreed. But the case of Vermont was not foreseen. No way was stipulated for people within a state's territory to turn themselves into a new state, however ready they were to pledge allegiance. So for two years after Vermonters applied for statehood, Congress stalled.

Just before Huntington's first year as President, Congress finally began to consider the problem. First, they listened to New York's thesis. Huntington was one of five members named at that time to a committee on the question. Governor George Clinton addressed them vigorously, demanding support particularly after the Green Mountain Boys — Vermont's militia — dispersed New York's militia in Cumberland County. John Jay himself drafted a committee report which recommended that New York, New Hampshire, and Massachusetts pass laws authorizing Congress to hear and determine the differences among them relative to boundaries, also referring to the decision of Congress their differences with the people of Vermont. Congress adopted those provisions and set February 1, 1780, as the date for a hearing. Grantees of the three states should bring disputes over land titles "to be heard and determined in the mode prescribed for such cases by the Articles of Confederation."

Also, a sort of internal truce was recommended. Congress resolved that until the determination, Vermonters "abstain" from governing any citizen loyal to any of the states; that the states "suspend" executing their laws over inhabitants loyal to Vermont. No unappropriated lands should be granted or sold.

Jay departed, Huntington took the chair. In a few days, the business was back. Members had discovered that the Articles of Confederation contained, really, no provision for handling disputes about land titles, if brought, not by states but by would-be states, or by private persons of unclear citizenship status. So the paragraph recently voted with that reference was repealed.

As for recommending to the three states to pass laws authorizing Congress to hear and determine the disputes, they now stipulated hearing and determining by commissioners or judges appointed in the mode of the 9th Article of Confederation. The whole Congress would not determine the disputes.

On February 1, the brothers Ethan and Ira Allen, who had been lobbying in several states for Vermont's cause, came to Philadelphia with Jonas Fay, Stephen R. Bradley, and Moses Robinson. Bradley had written a lengthy "Appeal to the Candid and Impartial World" which included a section on "The Right the State of Vermont Has to

Independence" and "An Address to the Honorable American Congress." In his words to Congress, after assailing New Yorkers passionately, he explained why Vermont did not comply with the congressional resolutions of September 24. The liberties and privileges of his state were "too sacred" for arbitration. Referring to the Articles of Confederation, he noted that Congress had no power to meddle with internal police and civil government. Further, Vermont as a body politic was older than the confederation. Not being represented in Congress, Vermont could not submit to resolutions passed without their consent. By asking three states to pass laws authorizing Congress to act on the question, Congress admitted it had no right to act. And if only one state voted such an authorization, Congress was giving to that state power to pledge the faith of the union, even of states who refused. Yet, he assured Congress, Vermont remained willing to agree with equitable proposals and to bear a proportion of the burden of the war against Great Britain.

Stephen R. Bradley, like Seth Warner and the Allens, was a native of Huntington's state. A Yale graduate, he now was a young apprentice lawyer. One may guess that he sought out the Connecticut delegates in particular whenever he came from Vermont to visit Congress.

Otherwise, on February l, the scheduled hearing was postponed. New York and New Hampshire had voted to accept the procedure recommended by Congress. Vermont had agreed to present again their application for statehood, and not to submit the question of their independence. But nine states, exclusive of the parties to the disputes, were required to be represented in Congress for the procedure. Too few were present. Most delegates felt reluctant.

In May, John Morin Scott of New York moved a resolution, noting that Vermont, with the intent of supporting their right to independence, had proceeded to grant unappropriated lands and to exercise civil and military authority over the persons and estates of New York citizens. Therefore, they were "guilty of a breach of peace of the confederacy." The United States were "bound to protect every of the said states in the full enjoyment of their rights and property against every usurpation." Grants of land after September 24 by either Vermont or the states were null and void. Moreover, as soon as a sufficient representation was present in Congress, they would proceed to the hearing without delay.

William Ellery of Rhode Island moved to postpone a decision on Scott's proposal, and postponement carried 7-2 (Huntington "aye" with

twelve other members; Scott "no" with four others; the states "no" were
New York and Virginia). Thomas Burke, who had voted to postpone,
then moved a resolution: "That the lands contained within the limits
of the United States are, and of right ought to be, under the jurisdiction of some one or other of the thirteen United States" and so under
federal protection. Whenever jurisdiction was infringed, Congress was
bound to employ "the common forces." This motion was referred to
committee (Huntington voted with New York and Virginia this time,
against Rhode Island and Massachusetts, for referral). May 29, June 1
and 2, the committee report was debated. Congress then resolved that
Vermont's recent land disposals were "unwarrantable, and subversive
of the peace and welfare of the United States," they should abstain.
And Congress would hear and determine the disputes "in the mode
prescribed" as soon as the required nine states were represented. Eight
states "aye." (Huntington "aye" with nineteen others; Ellery of Rhode
Island and Holten of Massachusetts "no" with two others).

A week later, Congress set September 24, as the hearing date. Huntington wrote a brief presidential letter to Vermont's Governor Thomas Chittenden, enclosing the two pertinent acts, addressing them
merely to "Thomas Chittenden, Esquire." He did not use the words
"state of Vermont" but, "the people inhabiting the New Hampshire
Grants (so called)." His closing sentence: "It is expected that due
notice will be taken of these acts by all persons and parties concerned
in conforming themselves thereto." Congress was holding fast to the
procedure for adjudication which it had laid down.

The Vermonters took due notice. They authorized Chittenden to
prepare a letter of reply, and sent Ira Allen and Stephen R. Bradley to
Philadelphia with the letter. Echoing Congress' word "subversive," the
letter began by stating that the people of Chittenden's state considered Congress' resolutions "subversive of the natural rights which they
have to liberty and independence," and incompatible with the principles on which the United States grounded their right to independence. It referred to Bradley's "Appeal" of a few months previous,
stating as to Vermont's view that it was independent: "It appears that
Congress, by their resolutions...have determined that they have power
to judge the cause, which has, already, determined the essence of the
dispute, for if Vermont does not belong to one of the United States,
Congress could have no such power, without their consent." An independent state is not subject, that is, to an arbiter it has not accepted.

Nor does the letter rest with logic. It proceeds to hard warnings. Vermont must either submit or "continue their appeal to heaven and to arms," it hints significantly of "connexions." Vermont's posts on the northern frontier, for instance, afforded security to neighbor states, which in turn had won "friendship of part of the private gentlemen and yeomanry." Too, Vermont had "the general approbation of disinterested states." But if Vermonters were "deceived in such connexions, yet as they are not included in the thirteen states," they are "if necessitated to it, at liberty to offer, or accept, terms of cessation of hostilities with Great Britain."

This bold hint shocked Congress into a new wariness. Not even the New Yorkers who had most adamantly pressed their state's claim wanted to force a major disaffection by Vermont. Loyalist strength in the states was already a serious concern. So when James Madison moved some resolutions contrary to the Vermont viewpoint soon after Congress received Chittenden's letter, debate lasted three weeks and closed without a decision.

In making his motion, Madison was thinking of the parallel between the three states' interest in Vermont and Virginia's in its western lands. For the sake of confederation, he was prepared to cede the western lands — conditionally. For one thing, Virginia wanted to keep jurisdiction south of the Ohio River, where the number of settlers was growing. For another thing, Virginia had always taken a serious view of the basis in the 1609 royal charter for its jurisdiction; thus it made a point of formally acknowledging the legitimacy of four states' occupying parts of the chartered area (Pennsylvania, Maryland, the Carolinas). Now they were engaged in an intense, although orderly, struggle with land companies based in Pennsylvania, Maryland, and elsewhere, who sought to bypass the old charter in claiming title to land acquired from Indian tribes. Virginia's insistence on keeping jurisdiction in the course of that struggle affected its attitude toward New York's and New Hampshire's claims to jurisdiction over the territory which Thomas Chittenden was tentatively governing.

Even the cession of western land, carefully tended by Madison and Jones, now delicately advancing in Congress, made sense only if it was a truly jurisdictional act.

So intent was Madison on safeguarding the legality of Virginia's claims that he rejected Vermont's declaration of independence, neglecting the analogy with the declaration which Virginians Richard Henry

Lee and Thomas Jefferson had fostered. One Virginian, Theodorick Bland, noticed the analogy. But Madison's motion began, "It appears to Congress that the territory commonly called the New Hampshire Grants is within the limits of some one or more of the United States," it was an attempt to nudge Congress off the balance they had been keeping.

Further: "That every attempt by force to set up a seperate (sic) and independent jurisdiction within the limits of any one of the United States is a direct violation of the rights of such state, and subversive of the union of the whole, under the superintending authority of Congress."

This motion was still under consideration by Congress when, on September 19 and 20, New York delegates presented the legal case for their claim of jurisdiction. James Duane had spent profuse time and work preparing the case. If Congress listened to him with awareness that as a land owner in the disputed territory he was an interested party, they also knew that Chittenden and the Allens were interested similarly.

Ira Allen, Stephen Bradley, and representatives of areas desiring to join Vermont, attended New York's presentation in silence. They had decided not to be drawn into formal debate, which could be interpreted as a departure from their refusal to submit the independence of Vermont for arbitrament. In a "Remonstrance" to Congress, September 22, they stated: "By the mode of trial now adopted, the state of Vermont can have no hearing without denying itself." Authorization of the trial by the claiming shares *ex parte*, they held, signified that the dispute over Vermont's independent status already had been judged. They offered to furnish troops against the British in equal proportion to the quotas of Congress for other states, and to submit their dispute at the close of the war to the mediation of "sovereign powers." Or else, to submit the dispute to the mediation of one or more legislatures of disinterested states, or to Congress — but not if Congress' authority to decide were given by a state or states "that make but one party."

Even less distinctly, they repeated the threat which Chittenden had hinted: "We stand ready to appeal to God and the world, who must be accountable for the awful consequences that may ensue."

September 27, when New Hampshire presented its legal statement, Allen and Bradley declined to attend even as silent listeners. By letter to Congress, addressed to Huntington as President, they requested that Congress postpone the inquiry. Then they left Philadelphia for home.

Ethan Allen's first contact with the British officer Beverly Robinson, as he told Congress via Huntington by letter the next March, occurred six months before Congress' hearing. Congress suspected it enough to worry.

John Sullivan, delegate of New Hampshire, was among those who worried. He told the Vermonters he would much rather that Vermont became a separate state than joined to New York. He also assured them that New Hampshire "did not wish to persecute the people of the Grants with that violence that the people of New York had done." But privately he did not think Vermont could be judged a separate state. He favored appointment of a commission to adjudicate, as provided in the Articles of Confederation, as a means of concluding all disputed points. He assumed that the determination could not favor Vermont's independence but would make an award to New Hampshire or New York. He opposed the suggestion that Congress might divide the disputed points, deciding first the single question whether Vermont should be independent. New York, he thought, favored that procedure for a tactical reason: if Vermont's independence were rejected, the area would at least temporarily revert to its status following the royal edict of 1764, and go to New York. Then New York could delay a final judgment between its claims and New Hampshire's, while working to conciliate the settlers.

Madison's proposals of September 16, besides rejecting Vermont's independence, stipulated that a commission decide between New Hampshire and New York, but temporarily that the inhabitants decide by an election to which state they would be subject.

Debate in Congress resumed October 6. The first to speak was Huntington, beginning his second presidential year. He opposed finding that the disputed territory was within one or more of the existing states, because it would deprive the inhabitants of a chance to support their claims. He understood that they had arguments to present in favor of their being recognized as independent. Allen and Bradley had written him on October 2: "We have many papers more authentic than those that have been exhibited to Congress." Those "will show our right to sovereignty, over the claims of all our adversaries, which we have not here at present." Huntington thought that an *ex parte* hearing would be unjust to Vermont.

Allen and Bradley, in their "Remonstrance," had protested against "partial modes pursued, plans adopted, *ex parte* evidence exhibited."

Huntington's background as a judge made him sensitive to objections of the sort. He wanted to heed Vermont's case.

True, he admitted, Vermont had received due notice. He wished, frankly, that they had submitted their cause to Congress when notified. But they had stated procedural reasons for their not accepting Congress' authority. "We ought not to decide against them." Commissioners ought to be appointed by Congress, agreeable to the authorizing acts of New York and New Hampshire. Thus Congress would be in a position to determine the issue.

Theodorick Bland agreed with Huntington's premise. The resolution had in view an indirect and unfair manner of deciding. It would deprive the Vermont spokesmen of all future opportunity to vindicate their own independence. New York and New Hampshire each had proved, he said, that the other had no title.

However, instead of supporting Huntington's preference for a commission, he made a drastic substitute motion: that the people of Vermont be made an independent state. Nobody seconded the motion.

Madison disagreed about the arguments offered by New York and New Hampshire; he thought they had proved that the territory lay within the boundaries of one or the other.

Richard Howly of Georgia suggested that it was an inexpedient time to make any decision. They should devote the time to opposing their common enemy.

As the debate went on, James Duane, the foremost advocate for New York, grew discouraged. "The debates took a turn most injurious to New York," he jotted in his notes. Later, writing to Governor Clinton, he said, "Several states were disposed to support the independence of our revolted citizens."

Congress reached no decision and, for the time being, set no date to try again.

"You will see by the enclosed paper, the enemy have landed in Virginia."

—**Huntington to Washington,**
November 1, 1780

"I am informed by letter from Governor Jefferson that the British have reimbarked and left the Chesapeake."
—Huntington to Washington,
December 4, 1780

Slowly Huntington realized that the plan of March 18, for replacing the old paper currency with a new had not gained enough compliance from the states. They did turn in a large volume of the old bills, but at the same time left many in circulation. Meanwhile, states' paper money, a cascade of certificates issued by the supply departments, and the new currency also circulated. All of these instruments of exchange continued to depreciate; prices continued to climb.

In the summer of 1780, when Pennsylvania joined in approval of the plan, Huntington informed Council President Reed that most states now were complying. But they complied incompletely, and Congress searched for another assurance of revenue. At the time when the March 18 act was under consideration, Burke and others had favored asking the states for authority to levy a small duty on imports. Livingston spoke for the idea on August 22. Congress' inquisitive committee on ways and means, whose dreams included rounding up a significant amount of the citizens' precious metals and depositing it in a bank, talked of the duty on imports frequently in November and December.

On the last day of January, 1781, the proposal had ripened to the degree that Congress met as a committee of the whole and reported out a bill for seeking the needed authority. It was an innovative project. Congress had been trying to operate within the terms of the Articles of Confederation, but to a majority of them those terms did not seem realistic for war financing. Even before the Articles had been permitted to become officially effective, now they were designing a major change.

The next day, Burke moved to strike words recommending that states "pass laws granting" the authority to Congress, and to substitute "vest power in" Congress. The word "power" still frightened several members. Although Sam Adams decided to vote with the majority for the substitution, Huntington did not.

Neither Huntington nor a majority of the Congress favored a motion by Witherspoon to seek even more power: over interstate commerce.

But Huntington and a majority voted for the new impost. Providing that the states allowed it, Congress could levy a duty of 5% *ad valorem* on most imported articles. Money raised from this source would be used to discharge war debts of the United States, principal and interest. But first, all the states (except South Carolina and Georgia, then occupied by the British) would have to pass laws vesting the power.

Thomas McKean, who voted "aye," counseled the speaker of the Delaware council that the duty would "be vastly short of the like duties" such as the poundage imposed by England and other countries.

Huntington sent a circular letter to the heads of state governments, more fervent than most of his circulars. Vesting the requested power in Congress would be "indispensably necessary." After summarizing the details of the proposal, he remarked: "The necessity of the duties and imposts being raised under one general and uniform direction, is an idea that will readily suggest itself." Had he said no more, he would have held to his usual confidence that his knowledgeable readers needed no long explanations or strong urgings. Whether he himself felt, in this case, that more needed to be said, or others prompted him, he did not end the letter there. Somewhat indirectly but unmistakably, he expressed feelings which had built up during his one and one-third years in the chair. "Although it may be improbable any person not particularly acquainted with the daily business in Congress should have an adequate conception of the difficulties and embarrassments that arise from want of some permanent fund to support the national credit and cement more effectually the common interest of the United States," he began, "yet I doubt not the wisdom, knowledge, and penetration of the respective legislatures will view those embarrassments as very great." A fund to repay interest, at least, was necessary to attract loans. Support of the army by states was precarious and unequal so that "a train of embarrassments too tedious to need enumeration must ensue." These had already been "felt to a degree."

His understatement could not quite cover the fervor of his desire that, after all, they might cure their chronic anxiety over public privation and debt.

Soon state legislatures began sending him the news he wanted from them. They had passed laws, vesting the power. But Rhode Island would not.

Resolved by Congress: "that John Laurens, aid-de-camp to General Washington, be presented with a continental commission of lieutenant-colonel, in testimony of the sense which Congress entertain of his patriotic and spirited services as a volunteer in the American army, and of his brave conduct in several actions, particularly in that of Rhode Island on the 29th of August last; and that General Washington be directed, whenever an opportunity shall offer, to give Lieutenant-Colonel Laurens a command agreeable to his rank."

—November 5, 1778

John Laurens was taken captive at Charleston, and soon exchanged. He returned to the army. (1779.)

—————————

Income from a duty on imports, if it came at all, would come too late for the needs of the 1781 military campaign. Was there another source, besides contributions from the states?

Huntington chose the word "anxious" in writing to Washington (October): "Congress are extremely anxious not only to avoid the embarrassments heretofore experienced by delays in recruiting the army until the opening of the campaign, but also to establish a permanent army."

Three days after he wrote that letter, Congress appointed a committee to draft a memorial to Versailles. Its purpose was to promote aids and supplies from France "for a vigorous prosecution of the war."

Earlier France had provided financial aid. Wasn't it time to ask for more?

The hope which Huntington had placed in results of the French alliance had, so far, proved oversize. He had hoped in 1778 and 1779 more of d'Estaing than the brief spurts of activity off Newport and Savannah, followed by withdrawals. In July of 1780, when Rochambeau arrived at Newport, Huntington hoped to begin "the intended cooperation with rigour and efficiency." But the American component was inadequate and the British held the French inside a blockade. By autumn, the opinion had become ordinary that America should trim down the original high expectation of France's role. Yet, LaFayette had come back with assurances of larger French support after a year's visit to his homeland; when Congress from dire need had again and again drawn bills of credit in their minister at the French court, Benjamin Franklin was able to obtain payment; and Huntington continued to hope.

The memorial to the French king, after discussion and revision, came before Congress November 17. They decided to say that the United States needed 25 million livres. On November 22, they agreed to a letter in the writing of James Duane: "We ought not to conceal from your Majesty the embarrassments which have attended our national affairs and rendered the last campaign unsuccessful." They therefore mentioned the loss of Charleston, British superiority at sea, frontier raids, British penetration through South Carolina into North Carolina and preparation to seek control of the four southern states. Referring to their appeal to France in June, 1779, they acknowledged the king's friendly disposition, although "through unfortunate events" the proportion of needed supplies which actually arrived was very small. (Congress struck out a more subjective statement on this point from the draft: "While we return our thanks for this proof of your distinguished regard, your Majesty ought not to be unapprised that a very small portion hath hitherto arrived.")

They mentioned the British decision to prolong the war. Then: "Apprised of the necessity of foreign aids of money to support us in a contest with a nation so rich and powerful, we have long since authorized our minister to borrow a sufficient sum in your Majesty's dominions, and in Spain, and in Holland." Now, with internal resources impaired, they asked "a foreign loan of specie at least to the amount of 25 millions of livres." The loan "will be indispensably necessary for a vigorous prosecution of the war." They pledged to repay it.

Concluding with a prayer to "the Supreme Disposer of events" to protect King Louis and continue to France "the blessings arising from the administration of a prince who nobly asserts the rights of mankind," the letter was to be signed by Huntington and attested by Secretary Thompson.

In the same session, Duane, Madison, and Houston were appointed to prepare instructions accompanying the letter. The delegates from Georgia had recently suggested sending an "envoy extraordinary" to carry the letter to the king. Such an envoy would be expected to argue forcefully the case for aid.

A problem which Congress discussed, largely outside their formal sessions, was whether such a move seemed, in Oliver Wolcott's word, "unfavorable" to Franklin, the resident minister. Perhaps a few critics were willing but the majority of members were unwilling to downgrade the celebrated "doctor" whose accomplishments in publishing and essay writing, practical science and cultural organization, statesmanship and genial sociability were a credit to his country. Furthermore, his success in persuading the king's circle to contract the treaties of alliance, amity, and commerce, and his status of affection and respect with the French generally, suggested that he might be the ablest spokesman for the project at hand.

Still, Franklin's growing distaste for asking the French for money had become known. He objected to "the storm of bills" sent for him to redeem over there by arrangement with the officials. Those bills "terrified and vexed" him, he wrote to Jay. And his popularity itself might hinder him from risking tough talk on the subject of a large new application.

Besides, he was 75 years old. It was a question whether he had the stamina necessary. Congress accordingly had decided to send someone as a consul, to help the movement of supplies from France.

On December 8, they decided to create an envoy extraordinary. The next day, Sullivan nominated Alexander Hamilton; Wolcott nominated Jonathan Trumbull, Jr; Georgia's Rich and Howly, who had figured influentially in the entire project, nominated John Laurens, son of the onetime President of Congress. All three nominees were members of Washington's staff. Sam Adams nominated McDougall. In two days they chose Laurens.

"The appointment of an envoy on this occasion," wrote Thomas McKean to John Adams, "seems to imply a want of confidence in our minister's attention, abilities, or something else. However, I hope it may not be construed in that light, but rather considered as an evidence of earnestness in this business."

On December 21, Congress voted changes in language. Laurens would not be called "envoy" but "minister." The phrase, "in conjunction with our minister plenopotentiary" was removed, presumably to avoid any need for its interpretation. Soon the instructions, commission, and letter of credence for Laurens were reported and adopted. The Board of Admiralty was ordered to fit out a frigate to transport him.

The outcome of the mission was perhaps foregone. John Sullivan informed Washington in late November that he had "long since, without the knowledge of Congress, solicited the French minister and Mr. Marbois to favor the application, which they have already done by writing the French court warmly in favour of it." Sullivan and LaLuzerne had a close, mutually useful relationship.

LaLuzerne wrote to Vergennes in December, while watching the application mature, that the loan was necessary, whether requested by Franklin or Laurens, it would enable participation by the American army in the next campaign.

Meanwhile, on December 4, Vergennes was encouraging LaLuzerne to rely on the good judgment of Congress. He himself did not suppose "that they will judge us from any other facts than the generous proceedings of his Majesty." He commented on Franklin: "The method he pursues is much more efficacious than it would be if he were to assume a tone of importunity in multiplying his demands, and above all in supporting them by menaces, to which we should give neither credence nor value, and which would only tend to render it personally disagreeable."

It would turn out that a candid John Laurens, like Arthur Lee first, then John Adams, would make himself disagreeable at the French court. Did it matter? Vergennes was saying that Congress "ought to rely much more on our goodwill than on the importunity of Dr. Franklin." And he said that the French already had "promised him a million of livres to put him in a condition to meet the demands made on him from this time till the end of the year" and were "occupied in providing for him new resources for the year coming."

But on January 1, Huntington wrote to Franklin, enclosing copies of the letter to the king and the instructions for Laurens. "Colonel Laurens is coming to France," he said, "charged with a special commission, to solicit with your advice and influence the aids in money and other articles referred to in his instructions."

By mentioning "your advice and influence" Huntington, for himself and for Congress, was trying to prod gently, "it is the pleasure and expectation of Congress you should not delay any measure for obtaining the aids requested, or wait for the arrival of Mr. Laurens."

Franklin did not wait. On February 13, he wrote Vergennes, "I have just received from Congress their letter for the king." He summarized the request, referring to America's military preparations and hoping for French "aid of their own exertions." He added information which he had received from other sources. Then he came to his own appeal: "I am grown old. I feel myself enfeebled by my late long illness, and it is probable I shall not long have any more concern in these affairs. I therefore take this occasion to express my opinion to your Excellency, that the present conjuncture is critical; that there is some danger lest the Congress should lose its influence over the people, if it is found unable to procure the aids that are wanted; and that the whole system of the new government in America may thereby be shaken; that, if the English are suffer'd once to recover that country, such an opportunity of effectual separation may not occur again in the course of ages."

On March 10, the day before Laurens landed at a French port, the king wrote to "our very dear great friends and allies, the President and members of the General Congress of the United States of North America," acknowledging their letter of November 22. "We have resolved," he said, "to assist you as much as our necessities, and the extraordinary and very great expenses required on our part by the war which we are carrying on for your defense, will permit. We have ordered the Chevalier de la Luzerne to acquaint you more particularly with our intentions." France had decided to grant six million livres, a part to be used for the purchase of arms, clothing, and other supplies needed by America, the remainder to be drawn by General Washington. Franklin reported this communication to Congress on March 12.

In the letter reporting it to Congress, Franklin offered to resign his position.

Late in May, Luzerne also informed Congress of the grant.

At his first interview with Vergennes, Laurens expressed thanks but stated that the amount of the grant was insufficient.

Huntington had written Laurens in January, at the same time he wrote to Franklin, enclosing the commission, instructions, and letter to the king. "My warmest wishes for your safety, prosperity, and success attend you," were the closing words. They were a slight variation from the less personal style of Huntington's usual official letters.

Huntington also had written to Governor John Hancock, asking his help for fitting *The Alliance* to transport Laurens from Boston. Laurens had worked with others besides Hancock to speed preparations of the frigate. He then had embarked in early February, arriving in France March 11. First he conferred with the Marquis de Castries, minister of marine, whom he kept pressing throughout his stay in France for a greater French naval commitment. He wanted France to take control of the American coastal waters.

After his first audience with Vergennes, he sent a lengthy memorial to the foreign ministry, listing points he deemed persuasive and extracting a letter from Washington. He also sent a reduced estimate of the supplies needed. "The grant of six millions which his Majesty is pleased to make under the title of a donation to the United States will be acknowledged with the liveliest emotions of gradtude by affectionate allies. At the same time, it would be frustrating the gracious intentions of his Majesty toward his allies, and betraying the common cause of France and America, to encourage a belief that the above mentioned aid will enable the United States to surmount the present perilous juncture of our affairs." He called the sum "inadequate," and asked for a loan in addition.

April 8th, Vergennes told Laurens that France would guarantee a loan to be negotiated with Holland, 10 million livres. Laurens promptly sought to obtain the amount of that loan from France as an advance, plus a further credit for supplies. He soon sent a new memorial to support those requests and to accentuate the wish for French naval superiority along the American coasts.

Later in April, he discussed with French officials how to ship the six million granted in March. They agreed that the total would be divided among several ships, for safety, two million on his frigate. He began to expect no result from his request for further credit on purchases.

In May, Vergennes wrote Luzerne that Laurens' "demands" and "threats" had become "unfit importunity." With a tone of finality, the foreign minister wrote Laurens a synopsis of the aid agreed to. Laurens also learned that Spain would not facilitate shipment of the granted livres and that Holland had decided not to loan the ten million in addition. But he hoped that, at least, the French navy would order detachments from the West Indies to the American coasts.

On June 1, Laurens sailed from Brest, carrying the 2.5 million livres, which Robert Morris would later receive and rapidly convey to pay Washington's troops heading for Yorktown. Before Laurens' return, Huntington finished his term in Congress and went home to Connecticut.

Throughout the period of Laurens' stay in France, Huntington's correspondence with Franklin was, as ever, respectful and unruffled, sounding a note of normalcy between them. Vergennes and others knew that Franklin had felt offended by Congress' resort to a special minister. Huntington's attitude probably diminished that feeling. (Congress did not accept the resignation Franklin had offered.) In June, Huntington added to an ordinary, unvaried message about business: "Mr. Secretary Thompson desires you would be so good as to send him the machine, with proper directions, to be used for striking copies of letters, as mentioned in yours of the 12th of March." Probably it was a significant response by its selectivity; the offer to resign, likewise mentioned the 12th of March, was causing no flap.

Laurens' mission was successful in at least one result: it signified both to Franklin and to the French court that American leadership was intent on meaningful action during 1781.

———————

"I do myself the pleasure to transmit you the enclosed copy of an act of Congress of the first instant, by which you will be informed that they approve of your retaining the picture of his most Christian Majesty which was presented to you by that monarch.

"That there is no charge against you before Congress, properly supported, and you may be assured your recall was not intended to fix any kind of censure on your character or conduct abroad."

Huntington to Arthur Lee
December 4, 1780. (Commissioned
to France 1776, also Spain 1777,
Lee was recalled 1779).

———————

"Toryism is triumphant here. They have replaced every Whig, except the President."

—Arthur Lee to Elbridge Gerry
Philadelphia, November 6, 1780

———————

"The partial successes against Lord Cornwallis, and the rising spirit of the militia in that quarter, it is to be hoped, will much disconcert the British in their intended operations."

"Should the intelligence from Holland and Portugal prove true respecting the Armed Neutrality, it cannot fail to have a powerful influence in our favour."

—Huntington to Washington
December 9, 1780

———————

On August 21, 1780, Congress received from the Board of War a report on Americans held captive by the British. Congress learned that 245 officers and 2,326 non-commissioned officers and privates had been captured at Charleston. At New York and Long Island 270 officers and 350 non-commissioned officers and privates were being held. The fact that the largest of these numbers was not a rounded number suggests that a careful analysis was behind the report. But it would have been impossible for the Board to account accurately for all personnel listed in May who now were missing in action, paroled, escaped, or dead while in prison. Nevertheless, the number was large.

Congress' immediate concern was to plan adequate rations and clothing for those in prison, as well as hospital stores and expenses for those sick while in prison. They decided to send provisions to make up any deficiencies of one-third ration per day for the n.c.o.s and privates. The officers received a little more of the bad prison food than others.

Even though four to five hundred prisoners were taken at Savannah, during 1779 (the year when Huntington went into office) fewer Americans had been captured than during 1776 (when four to five thousand had been captured at Long Island and New York), 1777, and 1778. But New York's prisons were confirming several hundred at the time of Huntington's election.

While Huntington was attending Congress during a part of 1778, they appointed Elias Boudinot the first Commissary-general of Prisoners. He worked up a system for sending money and supplies to sustain the prisoners, spending large sums of his own money. When he resigned, they replaced him first with John Beatty, then with Abraham Skinner.

At first both the Americans and the British expected the war to last only a short time, in which case the problem of prisoners would face them briefly. British facilities to keep prisoners were unready.

A political problem accompanied the problem of few facilities. Were captive Americans to be treated as rebel criminals or as prisoners of war to whom the law of nations applied? So long as American independence was the issue at arms, it was politically important to maintain, formally anyhow, that the captives were rebels. Yet the British in fact treated them as prisoners of war and their suffering was due far less to vindictive than to inept administration.

Both sides, of course, held each other's captured fighters. Soon a procedure for exchange went into *de facto* operation. But Congress noticed that the British gained more from exchanges than the Americans, to offset the remoteness and unsureness of British manpower.

From the start, therefore, Congress fretted over terms of exchange. For instance, as lately as August 7 a committee of Congress had concurred with Washington's opinion that a general exchange of prisoners, although strongly urged by motives of humanity, would be "highly impolitic."

Congress set a policy aimed at regaining personnel in equal numbers from both sides: soldier for soldier, sailor for sailor, in the order of their captivity. That aimed also at recovering money spent to keep British prisoners. But those aims were not easy to achieve.

Congress' lack of control over prisoners taken by state forces — on land, by state militia, and at sea, by privateers — became one more sign of delicacy in the confederation. Congress sent advice about policy to the states, but could not assure compliance.

Huntington felt for the captives. Late in 1779, he wrote to Beatty on behalf of a petitioner. "What the poor woman means to petition for," he explained, "is that her husband might be permitted to come home on parole. I understand he is a 2d lieutenant and now a prisoner on Long Island. Congress have referred this petition to you. If it be in your power to get the man released on parole or by exchange, I wish it may be done."

In January, 1780, Congress was in the mood to be flexible for the sake of the captives. They wanted to ease negotiation procedures for exchanges. Thus they voted Washington discretionary authority. Also they wanted to obtain enough British seamen to exchange for American seamen. Thus they assumed custody of all prisoners taken either by continental or by state forces. They even suspended a requisition on the British for arrears of payment toward the keep of British prisoners in American custody.

For their part, the British asked "hard" money when Americans paid them for prisoner keep. Continental currency was too depreciated, and furthermore, British hesitated to legitimate it by accepting it. But Huntington cannily suggested an argument for Washington to use, Congress had "relied" on British payments due for the keep of "Convention troops" — troops held since Saratoga — to defray expenses for the keep of American officers. Yet Congress was not demanding those payments as a pre-condition of exchange.

In April, Congress authorized Washington to permit a British official for the care of captured British to reside in the territory of the United States, with functions similar to a like official on behalf of the

United States behind British lines. So the problem gradually seemed to lessen.

The total number of prisoners in captivity dwindled. A comprehensive continental concern gradually seemed to gain priority over the states' separatism in this task. Huntington welcomed the concern, and lest the states feel any alarm about it, he voted "no" with the 3-8 majority when Congress voted whether to charge the states with the expense of securing and supporting British prisoners captured by them and later exchanged for their inhabitants.

Huntington's appreciation of the subleties of exchange policy had surfaced in 1778 on the occasion of a very different issue. It came up while the British were occupying Philadelphia. Loyalist Pennsylvanians in the vicinity apparently were capturing civilian patriots indiscriminately — not only patriot military personnel — and conveying them to the British. The British apparently offered the civilians in exchange for their captured military men. Congress was angry and passed a resolution which soon was prominently advertized, proclaiming death to those seizing any loyal citizen of the United States within seventy miles of the headquarters of any army where a general was in command; the death sentence was to be imposed by court-martial. Nine states' delegations voted "aye." Only Connecticut voted "no." The delegation split, at that: Dyer "aye," Huntington and Wolcott "no." Abraham Clark of New Jersey and Jonathan Bayard Smith of Pennsylvania also voted "no." Probably Huntington was not thinking about the death penalty as such, but about a novel assertion of power in a case of abduction of citizens by citizens, where state law otherwise would control. (The proclamation did not have much effect. Two and a half years later, Washington was writing to Council President Reed about a problem: states' exchange of British prisoners for captured civilians — ahead of captured military personnel, and out of the order of their captivity.)

Although the overall situation concerning prisoners eased in early 1780, it worsened terribly, upon the fall of Charleston. At the same time, new information was coming about the treatment of prisoners in the British prison ships on the Hudson River. At year's end, Abraham Skinner wrote a letter to his deputy, Thomas Bradford. Congress received a copy of the letter, along with other papers on the subject, on January 4. They referred it to committee. Skinner was upset by a recent frustration. He had been talking with David Sproat, a Philadelphian loyal to Great Britain, who was serving as their Commissary-general of Naval Prisoners. Sproat's conduct, wrote Skinner, "I cannot account for." The problem was two-fold. "He denies having any hand in sending our poor fellows home in the *Yarmouth*, and though he acknowledged a balance due to Philadelphia, yet he absolutely refused to make the remittance."

Skinner did not hide how bitter he felt about the interview. "I could not help abusing him." Quickly, however, he softened the indictment. Sproat promised to send out certain captives, "but as he is a creature without power. I fear he will not be able to accomplish it." Possibly Skinner's anger was aimed less at Sproat than at the system in which both men worked and at their superiors who managed the system.

"I think it is high time something should be done." He was venting feelings, signalling for help, and prodding Congress to review the system, all three. At least Congress should abide by the terms of negotiation they had set: "Pray don't attempt letting a captain in the naval line or anyone under his rank name a parole." Again, "Don't on any account send a man until they send out some." Climax: "Believe me, there is not the least faith to be put in those people, and they really act with as much villainy as you can suppose."

Would they think he was only upset for the time being? "My God, was you to see the manner in which our officers and men are confined in their prison ships, you'd almost forget the rules of decency toward some of those people." Then he thanked Bradford to wish Mrs. Bradford a Merry Christmas.

Congress might have discounted the letter as special hygiene for an upset official, except for the accompanying papers. One (if authentic) was written by Sproat with exceptional candor, then intercepted on its way to a Captain Griffing: "You have too long been a witness of the distress and misery attending our imprisonment. You will therefore use your endeavors to get as many released as possible."

Another paper came from Boston, written by Congress' sometime member, Samuel Holten, as justice of the peace. His paper was a deposition, December 19, by one George Batterman, a recent captive taken while a passenger at sea, "respecting the cruel treatment of our people, prisoners with the enemy at New York." Holten's credibility was entire.

The fourth was a report by John Appleton, recently arrived at Boston, about Great Britain's confinement of Henry Laurens in the Tower of London. Laurens, former President of Congress, father of Col. John

Laurens, prominent South Carolina merchant, had been captured at sea while on a diplomatic trip to the Netherlands under the commission of Congress. The honor of Congress was manifestly involved.

Skinner's passion had fired Sullivan, Sharp, and Clark, the committee appointed by Congress. They reported in one day. Their report, written by John Sullivan, perhaps was designed in part for propaganda effect. It spoke of "insult, outrage, and cruelty." It complained that "our seamen taken upon the American coast have been sent to Great Britain and other parts beyond seas, to prevent their being exchanged or to force them to take arms against their country." The committee believed that "an exercise of the law of retaliation has become necessary."

Congress thereupon directed that the Commander-in-chief order his officers "to take particular care that the British prisoners receive the same allowance and treatment, in every respect, as our people who are prisoners receive from the enemy."

Huntington transmitted copies of the act, with the letters and papers, to Washington on January 6, to Greene and to the states on January 9.

"By these dispatches," he wrote to Washington, "you will see the cruel treatment exercised by the enemy toward the prisoners in their hands, and that in the opinion of Congress an exercise of the law of retaliation is become necessary." He called the British practices "unwarrantable and inhuman."

His message to the states was similar, and he added: "It is especially recommended to the executive of the states respectively to take effective measures for carrying into execution the acts of Congress of the 13th of January, 1780, respecting prisoners taken by the citizens, troops, or ships of particular states" — that is, to turn them over to continental authority.

On February 18, Washington ordered Skinner to "ascertain the ration allowed by the enemy to land prisoners of war and make the same allowance to those in our possession."

The vote for retaliation did not relieve the anxiety of Congress. On January 8, they called on the states from New Hampshire to North Carolina to procure for the use of officers in captivity their respective quotas of specie, or bills of exchange on New York. "It is presumed," wrote Huntington, "the necessities of those officers, the distresses they have already suffered, and the more disagreeable situation they must yet be reduced to for want of the means of subsistence, unless these supplies are attained, will be sufficient to induce a compliance with this resolution as speedily as possible."

———➣●€———

At breakfast of berries and milk, Huntington once asked a companion: "What, sir, would the princes of Europe say, could they see the first magistrate of this great country at his frugal repast?"

—Legend

———➣●€———

Neither Huntington nor his colleagues seem to have felt much excitement about Congress' considerable move toward a separate executive sphere of government, discussed during the late months of 1780 and voted in January, 1781. To them it was simply a necessary expedient.

The American people were beginning to realize that their effort for independence was not yet potent enough. Like bidders at an auction, they had named a price which they thought would gain what they desired. Now they saw that they would have to bid higher. Great Britain was not quitting, even after the formation of effective state governments, even after Saratoga and the French alliance, even after the logistical strain of supplying New York and Charleston from across the Atlantic. The American people believed they could go on suffering enemy coastal raids, monetary inflation, tension with their loyalist neighbors. But when d'Estaing quit Savannah, Arnold defected at West Point, and Gates failed at Camden, it was time for a higher bid.

One particle of the bid was recruitment of men, longer terms of commitment to military service, provision for officers' pensions. The attempt to increase revenues by means of impost levies was another. But the creation of executive departments and the appointment of Robert Morris as Superintendent of Finance were the most ingenious of all.

Huntington had been waiting for a resurgence of public spirit. "A free people must feel before they will unite in the necessary measures," he had commented in the letter to Jonathan Trumbull, Jr. A most insightful comment. He could endure the duties of leadership during the worst season of the Revolution because he could accept polarities, impatience, and patience, pain and hope, simultaneously. While to the senior Trumbull he revealed his bitter dissatisfaction at the people's withholding needed contributions although "there is a fullness in the country," to the junior Trumbull he revealed composure. He was bewildered by evidence that individual Americans "have laid aside all thoughts of danger, and are pursuing their private gains in opposition to the public." But meanwhile he continually expected a change. "The importance and necessity of a substantial compliance... are so obvious that nothing further seems necessary to be added to excite the most vigorous exertions" is the theme he expressed again and again. Eventually a general awareness by the people of the "necessity" he posited began to catch up with his early awareness of it.

In July, 1780, when he wrote to Cogswell of "a spirit rising in this part of the country to exert themselves in the common cause," others who stood with him at the pole of impatience were talking about resort to military dictatorship. So he was among the minority who voted against removing the clause "within the United States" from the grant of authority to the Commander-in-chief. For him, the issue had nothing to do with confidence in Washington. He had that. Writing to Washington the next day, he treated the matter as routine. The issue was others' desire to widen the powers of the Commander-in-chief still farther. By September, talk about "dictatorship" had intensified.

In the past Congress had provided emergency dictatorial powers. Huntington had been chairman of a committee which, in October, 1776, reported a plan to obtain horses and carriages required for public use. Quartermasters were to avoid impressment as much as possible and, to discharge impressed horses and carriages as soon as possible. "No violence whatever" was to be done to persons or their horses and carriages. Yet the quartermasters were authorized to impress. The plan was adopted.

In May of 1781, he would again support a bill, moved by Madison, permitting General Wayne to impress required provisions and forage.

Particular emergencies were one question. Broad grants, another.

John Mathews, recalled from headquarters, moved in Congress that Washington be "fully authorized and empowered to carry into execution in the most compleat and ample manner such measures as shall appear to him best calculated for raising and bringing into the field "an army" to continue in the service of these United States during the present war with Great Britain, to provide arms, ammunition, clothing, military and hospital stores and camp equipage of all kinds." Also, to appoint army officers, to bring officers to trial and to execute sentences awarded by courts-martial, and to call forth militia. He might draw on the treasury of the United States to defray expenses incurred in consequence of those powers.

James Lovell called that proposal "most scandalous," and "the product of camp education." Congress disregarded it.

At about the same time, Schuyler was at the New York legislature. He wrote to Alexander Hamilton, "Some here are for appointing a dictator and vice-dictators, as if it was a thing already determined on." He also wrote, "To the convention to be held at Hartford. I believe I shall be sent with instructions to propose that a dictator should be appointed."

Hamilton, according to a letter he wrote to James Duane, was then thinking how to enlarge the powers, not of the Commander-in-chief, but of Congress. He could not approve of dictatorship. Soon afterward he wrote to John Laurens that some persons saw him "as a friend to military pretensions, however exhorbitant;" in fact, however, "I am not overly complaisant to the spirit of clamour," so he was "losing character" at camp.

Camp was indeed clamoring. Nathaniel Greene wrote to Lewis Morris: "Many talk of a dictator." Not Greene. "I am in great doubt whether there would be as prompt obedience from the people at large under a dictator as under a Congress with full and ample powers."

James Duane even doubted whether Hamilton's idea of enlarging Congress' powers was practical. As for the idea of the New York legislature, he had still more doubt. Governor Clinton, and others had dissuaded the legislature from voting the instructions which Schuyler predicted. They did vote approval, whenever Congress saw that a state was deficient in the money or supplies it forwarded, that the Commander-in-chief be directed to march the army into that state and compel it to contribute. Duane and John Morin Scott agreed between them to hush that resolution. "The compulsion clause," Duane wrote to Clinton, "is not perhaps proper for publick inspection."

On November 11, one delegate from New Hampshire met in the convention at Hartford with three from Massachusetts, one from Rhode Island, two from Connecticut, two from New York. Their objective was to consult and advise on ways to supply the army. Those attending included a current member of Congress (George Partridge, Massachusetts), three former members (Thomas Cushing of Massachusetts, Eliphalet Dyer and William Williams of Connecticut), and two future members besides Dyer (John Taylor Gilman of New Hampshire, Egbert

Benson of New York). Two of them, Williams and John Sloss Hobart, were sons of prominent Connecticut clergymen.

The Hartford convention adopted ten recommendations for action by the states, and four aimed at the reform of Congress by its own action. Those recommendations reflected and summarized a thoughtful discussion, in and out of Congress, concerning wartime government. They took into account Mathews' idea, Hamilton's idea, and the idea of the New York legislature.

Hamilton's was documented in his letter to James Duane from Liberty Pole. A newly authorized and defined "President of War" should take charge; not the Commander-in-chief. General Schuyler, he thought, would be excellent in that position. (In December, Hamilton would marry Schuyler's daughter, Elizabeth.) Army officers should be assured of half-pay for life. And he visualized a uniting of "ways" to finance military supplies: "a foreign loan, heavy pecuniary taxes, a tax in kind, a bank rounded on public and private credit."

Just as Mathews assumed that Congress had power to vest a dictator, so Hamilton assumed that Congress could adopt his plan for meeting the nation's crisis. They could exercise "the discretionary powers I suppose to have originally vested in them for the safety of the states." R.R. Livingston had been urging that view. So had the committee at headquarters in its May 28 advice to Congress.

There was a second possibility, Hamilton thought: "Calling immediately a convention of all the states, with full authority to conclude finally upon a general confederation", including explicit powers granted to Congress. It is due to that suggestion that Hamilton is frequently credited with germinating the U.S. Constitution.

Both Mathews and Hamilton proposed change by orderly means and sanctioned by existing authority. Neither proposed bypassing the states in collecting revenue for government's needs. Mathews stipulated that the Commander-in-chief should be empowered to draw on the continental treasury. States were presumably to continue their duty of supplying the treasury. Hamilton was still clearer: Congress should have complete sovereignty, he thought, "except as to that part of internal police which relates to the rights of property, and life among individuals, and to raising money by internal taxes. It is necessary that everything belonging to this should be regulated by the state legislatures."

So his letter did not sound too dangerous. "You told me my remedies were good," he wrote his fellow-officer John Laurens, "but you were afraid would not go down at this time." Of course, not all of Hamilton's ideas did go down.

By the time of the Hartford convention, its members had pondered and talked about Hamilton's and others' proposals. They moderated all the proposals, inclining perhaps toward Hamilton's. For instance, they did not address Mathews' idea of putting the Commander-in-chief in power for all executive functions. Rather, they advised the establishment of efficient executive offices, separate from Congress.

They recommended taxes, duties, or imposts, as an ingredient of Congress' finances, connecting those revenues especially with the obligation to discharge interest on loan certificates.

Faintly like the New York state legislators, they recommended that states instruct their congressional delegates to empower the Commander-in-chief "to take such measures as he may deem proper and the publick service may render necessary, to induce the several states to a punctual compliance with the requisitions" for 1780 and 1781. This formulation omits some words voted by the New York assembly, "to march" and "by military force." Furthermore, it specifies permission in advance from the states.

Possibly the New York men at the convention, Benson and Hobart, did not press for keeping the exact proposal. In early November, Clinton had written to Hobart about going to Hartford; Schuyler, although chosen a delegate, would not be going, he said. Possibly Clinton and others had awakened significant second thoughts since the assembly's vote.

In further recommendations, the Hartford convention favored earlier communication by Congress about the requisitions and adoption by Congress of a mode of trial and punishment for misdeeds of its civil appointees.

On December 12, Congress heard a letter from the president of the Hartford convention, William Bradford of Rhode Island, with a copy of the proceedings. The committee to whom these were referred consisted of Mathews (chairman), Root, Montgomery, Witherspoon, and Madison. It became Mathews' pleasure to report a possible reformation of Congress in one detail. A new committee should be formed to sort out all "public dispatches" received by Congress, referring some to the proper departments and selecting only those which needed special attention for presentation to the whole membership of Congress. Also he reported a draft of a law which would "constitute a court of judicature for the trial and determination of all causes relative to offences committed against the United States in the civil departments."

Later the report was debated and re-committed. Apparently it never came to a vote.

The provision for trial of offending civil appointees later was merged into the plan for empowering such action by the new Superintendent of Finance.

Measures such as seeking authority from the states to levy an impost and establishing new executive departments, already of interest to Congress, apparently superseded the work of the committee.

Congress did buzz when the recommendation about military inducement arrived from the Hartford convention. John Witherspoon wrote to Governor William Livingston that he would never advocate use of the army to induce compliance "unless you or my constituents should specifically direct it, perhaps *even not then*." He did not think Washington would accept or act in consequence of such powers, and believed the proposal would have few advocates. Washington's recurrent misgivings about impressment, later his vehement rejection of Lewis Nicolai's army-based suggestion that he become king and, of John Armstrong's momentous Newburgh Address, show that Witherspoon judged him rightly.

While Huntington sat in the chair, Duane worked on the floor. They guided the moves to seek an impost and to establish executive departments.

The motion to appoint a planning committee on new arrangement of the civil executive departments was put, August 29, by Livingston, seconded by Joseph Jones. A prestigious start. Congress agreed. Both Livingston and Jones took appointment to the committee, as did James Lovell, whose long and sometimes half-hearted labor of letter-writing for the old Committee of Foreign Affairs would be touched by the planning. The committee met often enough to sketch a new arrangement.

As we have seen, Congress' executive boards at first were composed only of members of Congress; Sam Adams never gave up his preference for that mode. It reflected a deep distrust of bureaucrats, stemming from years of dealing with the British Board of Trade. By now, however, the treasury and admiralty boards were composed of two members of Congress, three nonmembers, and aided by civilian employees. The war board now was composed only of non-members; they opened their business to Congress constantly, however, asking approval for all major policies.

Members of Congress felt real fatigue from executive duties, added to legislative. Even so, of course, they could give only divided attention. Whenever they left Congress, attending off and on, their leaving broke the boards' continuity. In and out of Congress, thoughtful people were suggesting a permanent executive system.

In September, both Livingston and Jones left Congress for a time, but Duane arrived from a time off. Jones wrote to Madison, "I was also of a committee to arrange or reform the civil departments of Congress, and it was in contemplation to place at the head of the Foreign Affairs, the Admiralty, and Treasury, some respectable persons to conduct the business and be responsible. Has anything been done in these matters?"

Duane, it would have pleased Jones to know, was steering the arrangement toward finality. Sullivan soon reported to Washington: "The several departments are arranging." When Congress began to discuss Duane's own plan for the foreign affairs department, Lovell was ruffled. He would have been writing letters, he informed Franklin, but felt "prevented from doing by an arrangement being but partially accomplished, which Congress has thought fit to connect with these affairs."

Huntington was ready to accept the new plans. They should not be too ambitious; but within proper bounds, he thought them helpful. On January 6, Congress appointed four new members, including Duane, to the planning committee. On the 10th, Duane's own plan authorizing a secretary for foreign affairs was adopted. And on the 13th the total scheme, written up by Duane, was reported and read. Debate absorbed parts of several sessions from then on, until on February 7, Congress voted to create three new offices: executives for treasury, war, and marine.

Huntington examined the journal of Congress carefully and made some small corrections. He wanted the journal to show precisely what they had agreed to. Seeing finances as the one great piece of ever-unfinished business on their agenda, Congress was thinking more about the finance department than any other. Where a secretary had used the title "Financier" three times, Huntington struck it out and substituted "Superintendent of Finance." That executive, that is, would not singlehandedly raise and spend the money. He would manage a process by which all America provided it for the continental government, and by which government utilized it for all America.

Also Huntington noticed a problem about the new executive's power to deal with delinquencies. The secretary's entry stated that the executive "in his official character" was empowered "to prosecute...for all delinquiencies." Huntington foresaw difficulties in locating the proper court before which a delinquent would be charged and the code of laws which properly pertained to the offense. So Huntington made two insertions: after "in his official character" he added "or in such manner as the laws of the respective states shall direct;" and after "delinquiencies" he added "respecting the public revenues and expenditures." (Later, Joseph Jones explained these difficulties to Jefferson. "Can Congress, in other than military and maritime laws, subject any citizen to death or other punishment than the laws of the state he belongs to inflict for such offenses?") Huntington's insertions probably express a consensus by Congress which the secretary had not caught. They would enable the executive to prosecute effectively when someone was a delinquent while preventing any assertion of unintended official power. Later, Huntington pursued this issue to its settlement. Congress, debating the power of the Superintendent of Finance to control the personnel of the department, once struck out a provision for a "procurator or solicitor" in each state "to carry on prosecutions against persons delinquent." But eventually they passed a more precise grant of authority, "to appoint by letter of attorney, or otherwise, such person or persons as he may think proper to prosecute or defend for him in his official capacity or in behalf of the United States, in all places where the same may be necessary." Therefore on May 1, Huntington notified Congress' appointee, Robert Morris, of the action "authorizing the Superintendent of Finance to appoint attornies to prosecute or defend in his official capacity."

Congress' decision in January to authorize a Secretary of Foreign Affairs, and in February to authorize executives of finance, war, and marine, excited candidates for the appointments and their backers. Alexander Hamilton suggested Schuyler for war, McDougall for marine, and Robert Morris for finance. Sam Adams heard that Hamilton himself, or Gouvernor Morris, was proposed for finance and Livingston for foreign affairs, and worried about "a compleat New York administrations." Burke thought that William Bingham was "the most proper person I can think of" for foreign affairs. Sullivan considered himself a candidate for war, and felt that Sam Adams opposed him as an "apostate from the New England faith."

On February 20, Congress elected Robert Morris to be Superintendent of Finance. The vote was unanimous, although Sam Adams and his colleague Artemas Ward abstained. "It is hoped," Huntington wrote him officially, "that this important call of your country will be received by you, sir, as irresistable."

On February 27, they named Alexander McDougall to be Secretary of Marine. The next day, they postponed a vote on the secretary of war; it was October before they filled the office. Nor did they decide on a secretary of foreign affairs until August. By the time of those latter choices, Huntington had gone home.

The appointees' conditions for acceptance of their offices, received soon, immediately led to new discussions in Congress. McDougall's case was the simpler. He wished to retain his active army status, without pay but with rank, on call for military duty while administering a civil department. Congress rejected that stipulation. McDougall, who had told Governor Clinton that he could not think of quitting the field, then declined his appointment.

Morris wished to keep his commercial connections while administering a department; furthermore, he wished sure control over hiring and firing the departments personnel. He said this included removals for cause of every continental agent who spent public money, whatever the department, civil or military.

Huntington opposed allowing him to keep his commercial connections, since it would involve obvious conflicts of interest. On March 20, Congress voted against a motion, "Congress do not require Mr. Morris to dissolve any commercial connections" formed before taking office. Seven others joined Huntington in the negative. More members than eight voted affirmative, an insufficient vote for passage.

But Duane narrowed the motion by reference to the connections which Morris had described in an explanatory letter, whereupon two members switched to the affirmative (Huntington "no") and the motion carried. Sentiment in Morris' favor was strong. Not only was he a former member of Congress and the leader of Congress' financial measures at that time. He was also a patriotic standout among the great, successful merchants of the land. Not long before, he had led the association of Philadelphia merchants who subscribed a private fund to supply the army. The prominence of his energetic, decisive-personality in Philadelphia gave him visibility to members of Congress.

Huntington favored allowing Morris the power to appoint and remove his own assistants. On March 21, Congress voted affirmatively on that point. Four members including Sam Adams opposed it.

Power to remove and prosecute all others who spent public money or kept public accounts was more troublesome. A favorable report by Houston, with Burke and Wolcott, nevertheless put forward a few restrictions: "limited to the duration of the present war," "not extend to interfere with the rank or commission of any officer in the line of the army," "report to Congress the reasons for such removal," "not extend to those who are, or shall be, duly entrusted with money for secret services." But Congress was not satisfied that the restrictions were adequate. They wanted to retain more control. They voted against the resolution.

Then Houston, with Burke and Wolcott, in another report, proposed to reduce the power rather than to deny it. The Superintendent might be able to remove persons "not immediately appointed by" Congress but only "to suspend" persons Congress did appoint, "reporting forthwith their names and the reasons for suspension. Those and associated powers could be exercised "during the pleasure of Congress" and, not beyond the duration of the war. This modified resolution was adopted.

So on May 14, Morris accepted office. On the 17th, he presented his plan for establishing a national bank. Congress knew his thoughts by now, for meeting the financial problem.

Morris' principal measures were: establishing the bank, urging states to repeal their legal tender laws (laws which aided private debtors to pay off creditors cheaply) and projecting to fund the government's debt by confederal methods. He effectively attracted private credit as a reinforcement to public credit offering a substantial amount of his own credit for that purpose in what came to be called "Morris notes." Otherwise his policies proved identical with old policies which Congress had adopted and attempted to use. His managerial skill and vigor tended to succeed where previous administrators had failed to control expenditures. He wrote appeals to the states, as Congress had done. But even when he sent collectors eastward and southward, they gathered little increase in revenue from the states. His encouragement of payments in hard money continued the policy Congress began with their specie requisition of August, 1780. Because the general supply of specie was still limited, states still responded insufficiently. His return to the method of contracting with private vendors for the needs of the army brought back the abuses of that method deplored by Congress when they switched to requisitioning specific supplies. (The abuses by Comfort Sands provoked Washington to a crescendo of complaints in the summer of 1782.)

Morris had emphatically approved the design of Congress' act of March 18, 1780, to call in old paper money while limiting the issue of new. He firmly maintained that policy during his administration.

The arrival of French loan money just before Yorktown, followed by the shutdown of the war after Yorktown, were circumstantial boons to his dedicated struggle for financial order.

Congress sensed his essential agreement with their traditional methods and were therefore prepared to favor his bold proposal for the bank. He proposed that a subscription be opened for $400,000, payable in gold or silver. Shareholders were to elect twelve directors, without pay, who were to choose a president, appoint other necessary officers, dispose of the money and credit of the bank for the benefit of the proprietors, and from time to time issue dividends out of profits. Bank capital could be increased by opening new subscriptions occasionally. Chosen inspectors were to report daily to the Superintendent of Finance the cash account and the notes issued and received. The bank's notes were to be made receivable by law in the duties and taxes of each state and the payments of states to the U.S. treasury.

On May 26, Congress acted on a resolution to approve the plan for a bank as worked up by Morris. The bank was to be incorporated under the name "The President, Directors and Company of the Bank of North America." Incorporation was to occur as soon as the subscription was filled, the directors and president chosen, and an application from them received by Congress. Huntington, with 19 other members, voted "yes." Four voted "no."

Congress then proceeded to recommend to the states the enactment of supportive laws. During its brief corporate lifetime the bank would loan a large amount of money to the United States, discount government notes, and circulate its own notes as an acceptable medium of exchange. Morris was able to retire a considerable part of the outstanding old continental and state paper money, replacing it with bank notes.

When Governor of Connecticut, in 1789, Huntington wrote to "Respected Friend James Pemberton," of Philadelphia, enclosing by request an extract of Connecticut statutes concerning slavery. He noted, "You will observe that from the operation of those laws slavery must be entirely abolished, and the slave trade prevented, so far forth as it is in the power of one state to prevent the same."

For a time, Huntington owned a black slave. Then he freed him.

Also when Governor, Huntington addressed the convention at Hartford, January, 1788, debating the proposed U.S. Constitution. He commented concerning the diversity of people: "Even among the American states, there is such a difference in sentiments, habits, and customs, that a government which might be very suitable for one might not be agreeable to the other." Later in the same address, he said: "While I express my sentiments in favor of this Constitution, I candidly believe that those gentlemen who oppose it are actuated by principles of regard to the public welfare. If we will exercise mutual candor for each other, and sincerely endeavor to maintain our liberties, we may long continue to be a free and happy people."

———⟫●⟪———

While white Americans and the king's whites fought each other, the red native Americans puzzled. They had supposed that British victory over France in 1763, after repeated conflicts, might have introduced a time of stability. "What have we to do with your contentions?" asked Samson Occom, the Christian Mohegan preacher, of a white English friend.

At a council of the Iroquois' Six Nations at Albany, August, 1775, Congress' commissioners said: "This is a family quarrel between us and old England. You Indians are not concerned in it. We do not wish you to take up the hatchet against the king's troops. We desire you to remain at home and not join on either side." The chief of the lower Mohawks, Little Abraham, spoke for the Six Nations in pledging neutrality. Oliver Wolcott was present. He may well have reported it to his friend Huntington, afterward.

A few months later, however, in January, 1776, Philip Schuyler after receiving reports that Sir John Johnson was arming at his British headquarters in Johnstown, led 700 men from Albany to investigate. Little Abraham met him on the way. The Mohawks, said the chief, objected to the passage of an armed force into their territory. They wanted both Johnson and Schuyler to keep the peace, citing the Albany agreement. Schuyler offered them what reassurance he could and, nevertheless, went on to disarm Johnson. The Mohawks were apprehensive.

Little Abraham remained committed to peace. In early 1780, he joined an embassy from Schuyler to the British at Fort Niagara — two leading Oneidas and two leading lower Mohawks. A conference between the embassy and the people, white and red, at Fort Niagara, ended bitterly. Little Abraham voiced his desire for peace with both sides of the Revolutionary conflict, eloquently urging the Six Nations to lay down arms if they had become involved, and go home. The four messengers were put into an unheated stone vault. Little Abraham died in the confinement.

Samuel Huntington was interested in the attempt to assure native American neutrality. As a delegate to Congress in 1776, he had heard about it, and in July was appointed to the Indian affairs committee. When Schuyler informed Congress of a new treaty of neutrality, made at the German Flats, they were so impressed that they sent a copy to George Morgan. Indian agent for the "middle department," in hopes he could negotiate something like it.

"We have intelligence," Huntington wrote colleagues in Connecticut that August, "that the Indians in the southern department have commenced hostilities on the frontiers of Carolina and Georgia." He knew of a punitive military reaction: "An expedition is forming from those states to march into their settlements and extirpate them unless they submit to reasonable terms of peace." The words indicate his humane wish for peace, a wish he expressed with reference to British in other statements, now with reference to native Americans; but also his readiness to apply force for the terms which he considered "reasonable."

Congress had no time for reflection on the issue. They inherited the whites' attitude of uneasy vigilance toward native tribes, as white settlement spread from the coastline westward. The insecure peace had frequently been broken. Two cultures were at odds, especially two incompatible philosophies of land tenure.

"From the middle and northern departments," Huntington continued, accounts of Indian relations were more favorable. "A treaty in the middle department is now negotiating at Pittsburg, and from the account of the treaty which Col. Butler held with the Indians met at Niagara this summer,...it appears the chiefs and sachems are determined to observe a strict neutrality in the present war."

"In what manner" he had learned this, he wrote mysteriously, "may not be made public at present." (In fact, George Morgan had eased a spy from Pittsburgh into the council meeting.)

Huntington enjoyed passing on a story. "Col. Butler opened the treaty by inviting them to join the British forces. He told them the Americans were mad and foolish, that they were weak, boys and women. They had no powder or ammunition, then they made a little but it was no better than dirt, and that if they would join the British forces, they would soon drive the Americans into the sea. Next morning the Indians by a sachem replied, "You told us yesterday the Americans were mad etc., but we say, 'tis you are mad. They are wise, for they advise us to be still and quiet and let you and them fight it out, which we intend to do. If they have no powder, are weak, boys and women, why do you want us to help you?" Relaying the story used up more writing paper than he was in the habit of needing.

"By the late treaty at the German Flats with our commissioners, the Indians engaged to remain neuter and to call home their young warriors which had been entered, as they say, to go into Canada, and it seems was without the consent of their sachems." He closed: "We have reason to hope the Indians in general in the middle and northern departments well remain neuter, unless some more unfavorable events take place in our armies and cause them to change their minds, which God prevent."

The change of minds would soon occur. After the loss of Long Island and the British occupation of Philadelphia, the reputation of American arms dimmed somewhat. More important, sorrow over the memory of Sir William Johnson, British Indian commissioner from 1756 until he died in 1774, affected many who had known him. He understood Iroquois society and spoke its own speech, honored its tradition and aspiration, married Iroquois women. His young Mohawk protege, Joseph Brant, arrived from a trip to Great Britain at about the time when Huntington's responsibility for Indian affairs began. Visiting the Iroquois communities one after another, Brant spoke on behalf of the British cause. He persuaded many, especially among Mohawks, Senecas, Onondagas, and Cayugas. Germans Flats was forgotten. By the summer of 1777, Brant was leading a considerable number in support of Col. St. Leger's siege of Fort Stanwix.

When Huntington returned to Congress in 1778, the hope for red natives' neutrality was largely past. The ambush at Oriskany had wrecked it: two red and white sets of fighters had inflicted severe mutual casualties. After an Oneida sachem had effectively warned the Americans about St. Leger's strategy, thus assisting the defense of Fort Stanwix and disabling St. Leger's planned junction with Burgoyne at

Saratoga, one of Sir William's wives, Mary Brant, warned the British of Nicholas Herkimer's attempt to relieve Fort Stanwix, occasioning the Oriskany ambush. Emotions warmed.

Congress in 1778 authorized Schuyler's and LaFayette's recruitment of Oneida and Tuscarora warriors. They were alarmed that Schuyler's arch-opponent, Col. John Butler, led his own white Tories, with Senecas under Cornplanter, Cayugas, and other Indian units, into the Wyoming River Valley where they massacred many settlers. They also heard that Joseph Brant was preparing harmful action. The Board of War, told Congress that large-scale war with hostile natives could be expected.

Huntington left Philadelphia in July and did not return until late in May, 1779. During that interval, Brant and others inflicted a massacre at Cherry Valley; Washington and Schuyler projected an expedition against Fort Niagara. Congress' May 6 Fast Day Resolve drafted by Gouvernor Morris mentioned "the fatherless children, who weep over the barbarities of a savage enemy."

On his return, Huntington found that the plan for an expedition against Niagara had been scaled down somewhat. Major-general John Sullivan would command a large operation into Iroquois country. Correspondence about the plan dragged on between Washington and Congress, although Washington was in frequent correspondence with Schuyler. Sullivan's ideas differed from Washington's in some particulars.

From May 7 to June 18, Sullivan was at Easton, Pa., directing preparations. From August 10 to 26, he was at Tioga, N.Y., where a force under Brigadier-general James Clinton joined him. Washington impatiently tried to propel Sullivan's movement. On the 29th, Sullivan's force made contact with Tories and Indians at Newtown, followed by an elaborate attack, and prevailed. They swept forward, destroying Iroquois villages and crops, their adversaries retiring before them. Near Gennesee, Butler and several Iroquois chiefs, with their men, planned to attempt a stand, but instead surrounded a scouting party when it surprised them from the rear; they killed several, captured, tortured and dismembered both the white lieutenant in command and an Oneida scout. Next day, Sullivan's main columns passed without resistance. Deciding to terminate the sweep before they did provoke a major stand, Sullivan was back in the Wyoming Valley by September 30.

"I have the pleasure," Huntington wrote to Sullivan two weeks later, to send an act of Congress "expressing their thanks and the other brave officers and soldiers under your command for effectually executing the important expedition against such of the Indian nations as, encouraged by the councils and conducted by the officers of his Britannic Majesty, had perfidiously waged an unprovoked and cruel war against these United States."

The language follows that of Congress' resolution. Nonetheless. Huntington chose to repeat words like "perfidiously," "unprovoked," and "cruel." From his viewpoint the repetition seemed just. As for perfidy, he doubtless had in mind the neutrality pledged at Albany in 1775 and the German Flats in 1776. Congress had received no forthright notice that the pledge was revoked. On the other hand, pro-British Iroquois could interpret as provocation various punitive expeditions, such as one in October, 1778, under Thomas Hartley. The supreme provocation, of course, from the native American viewpoint, was the continual westward movement of settlers from the states, entailing occupation of land which Indians claimed. Although the United States did not want war with Mohawks, Senecas, and others, the westward movement was neither well-negotiated nor well-regulated. But if British government in Indian territories had survived the war, the white movement surely would not have been shut off.

The United States competed with Great Britain, meanwhile, in commissioning leading Iroquois warriors as army officers. Agents from both sides sought to exploit Indian grievances in wooing their friendship. And both sides kept spinning the sad wheel of frontier vengeance.

Both Washington and Congress took for granted that Sullivan's strike at the Iroquois villages might quiet the frontier. In actual consequence, however, the unfriendly Iroquois were forced by the strike to huddle miserably and resentfully in a British refugee camp at Fort Niagara. When they had an opportunity, deprived and angry, they sprang back in a series of vengeful raids. Those raids started at Skenesboro the next March and included burning Oneida and Tuscarora settlements in July. So the next winter, it was the Iroquois allies of the United States who had to huddle — at Schenectady.

In November, 1780, Congress voted $6,464 to provide clothing for 406 friendly Oneida, Tuscarora, and Aaughnawaga, "obliged by the enemy to abandon their habitations and take refuge in the state of New York." Again in April, 1781, Congress agreed to expenses for similar relief. If the remarkable Iroquois enterprise in establishing farming villages and fields had not been scorched away, would the future of red wardship under white bureaucracy have veered in another direction?

The Cayugas had been divided over which white nation to favor, once they breached neutrality. Their great leader Fish Carrier sided with the British, but there was a party who favored the Americans and kept in touch with Schuyler. He received a message from the Cayuga leader Tegatlaronwane, transmitted by Oneida messengers. It proposed peace in exchange for the release of prisoners. Schuyler gave the message more credit than Sullivan had done, during his invasion. An astute Iroquois-watcher, Schuyler also intervened on behalf of the Fort Hunter Mohawks, who had remained neutral, after Sullivan sent a force to capture them.

On the strength of the Cayuga signal, Schuyler proposed a general accommodation with all Iroquois. Congress did not respond promptly, but when he came to Congress in November, 1779, Schuyler lobbied for the accommodation. Not aware that hostile Iroquois were then at Fort Niagara, fraternizing with the British agent Guy Johnson and preparing for more frontier terror. Congress gravely discussed whether "to grant peace." On November 27, a committee which unpropitiously included both James Forbes and Gouvernor Morris from states then disputing about land policy, offered a report. It began: "Notwithstanding the many injuries committed by the savages, Congress are disposed to peace."

Conditions for peace were to be: "It shall be supplicated on the part of the enemy," "they shall surrender all the Americans in their hands," "they shall expel all British agents and emissaries," and "they shall Covenant not to take up the hatchet again under penalty of being driven from their country." They were also to give hostages for their adherence to those pledges. So far, the proposal seems to have been drafted by Forbes.

An additional paragraph, however, discloses that reconciliation with the Iroquois was not the only issue on Congress' mind. It dealt with "offers of territory." In Gouvernor Morris' handwriting, it wished for land concessions from the Iroquois, which might "serve as the most pointed marks of their contrition," at the same time wishing Congress to decline any such offers of territory, "to convince them of the superior generosity of America, compared with their experience of others." But Forbes wanted to add that Congress would accept territory if ceded not to a state but to the United States, "reserving to any particular state their right of prior claim." The New York delegates, to forestall loss of New York land, parried immediately. Livingston moved, Schuyler seconded a substitute "which cession shall be for the benefit of such state as may have a prior right." What had happened to America's "superior generosity"?

Finally the motion to accept cession for the benefit of the United States was sidetracked. Huntington voted with twelve others to defeat it; the debate had become absorbed in the larger dispute over land policy. "We had reason to apprehend," Schuyler later told the New York legislature, "that several who were opposed to the motion rounded their opposition on the necessity of a reconciliation with the Indians, against which they imagined the spirit of the motion would militate."

So on November 29, Huntington was able to inform Schuyler of Congress' votes "Notwithstanding the many injuries... Congress are disposed to peace." It was to deliver word of that vote that Little Abraham travelled to Fort Niagara, and died.

At Fort Pitt, Col. Daniel Brodhead, the American commander, tried to discourage encroachment by new settlers on land traditionally claimed by Indians of the Ohio Valley. "Congress have resolved to support you," Huntington assured him, (April, 1780). Their support entailed political intervention against the lawsuit of two settlers against the colonel. Huntington appealed to Pennsylvania and Virginia for "proper measures adopted to prevent Col. Broadhead being unjustly vexed on account of any orders or act" while on duty.

And, on a plane above where Joseph Reed and he stood in their states' land contest, he transmitted to Pennsylvania's Council President Reed an act "for removing, every subject of jealousy and discontent" in the defense of the Wyoming River Valley. The Commander-in-chief, if he concurred, was asked to replace troops of Pennsylvania and Connecticut with new continental troops. Likewise he transmitted the act to Governor Trumbull, commenting that the post was necessary and important "not only to protect the inhabitants in the vicinity, but as a barrier to the frontier in general."

Limited as was Huntington's opportunity to think philosophically about the relations of whites to native Americans, he wrote this sentence to Thomas Jefferson (October, 1780):, "The expedient you have adopted to invite some of the chief Indian warriors to visit Congress and General Washington appear to me good policy." Amicable encounter and augmented understanding between the two groups suited his practical search for a settlement of the issues.

The Maryland assembly, having pushed along an accord on the question of western lands, were free to debate whether to ratify the Articles of Confederation. In early February, 1781, they ratified. Their delegates returned to Congress with the news, whereupon Congress planned a festive observance of the "completion" of the union. They set March 1 as the date.

Maryland acted, said their assembly, "conscious that this state hath, from the commencement of the war, strenuously exerted herself in the common cause." They desired "to conciliate the affection of the sister states" and "to destroy forever any apprehension of our friends, or hope in our enemies, of this state being again united to Great Britain." They became still more explicit: "It hath been said that the common enemy is encouraged by this state not acceding to the Confederation to hope that the union of sister states may be dissolved."

On March 1, John Hanson and Daniel Carroll, for Maryland, signed the embossed copy of the Articles of Confederation which Huntington and others, for eight states, had signed in July, 1778. (By the end of 1778, three more states had ratified. In 1779, Delaware.)

The Confederation of thirteen states being completed, at 12 noon the bells of Philadelphia rang and a salute of 13 cannon shots sounded from the hill and from John Paul Jones' frigate, specially decorated, in the harbor.

At 2 p.m., President Huntington received the members of Congress, the French minister, the Council President of Pennsylvania and members of his council and assembly, and federal and state military officers, at his house. He provided a "cold collation" and accepted congratulations as the ceremonial chief of the United States.

That night there was an elegant fireworks display in the city.

On March 2, Congress convened as usual, except that now their name was "The United States in Congress Assembled." They resumed the business which the old Congress had referred to them by vote on February 28. Huntington remained in the chair, nobody raising a question whether to accept members' credentials freshly or to elect a President freshly. Everybody seems to have assumed that he would preside until the first Monday in November, the day set by Article V, the first paragraph, for the start of a new congressional year. Only four months had passed since the start of the current year.

On the same day, Huntington sent a brief letter to the heads of state governments: "By the act of Congress herewith enclosed your Excellency will be informed that the Articles of Confederation and Perpetual

Union between the thirteen states are formally and finally ratified by all the states. We are happy to congratulate our constituents on this important event, desired by our friends but dreaded by our enemies."

Writing four days later to General Greene, again enclosing a copy of the act, he suggested: "It will be proper to announce this important and happy event to the army when circumstances will admit."

Although Congress assumed continuity of their identity and organization, they also felt obligated to comply with certain of the Articles more strictly than before. Both New Hampshire and Rhode Island, for instance, were technically under-represented. Each had only one delegate present, whereas Article V stipulated no less than two. Might those states vote now, as formerly? No. Their single delegates might speak but not vote. Sullivan of New Hampshire objected that his state had not received due notice about this requirement. As for Rhode Island, Congress could solve the problem by seating General Cornell, whom they had appointed to the Board of War while he was still accredited to serve in Congress. But they decided that he was more acutely needed at the Board of War.

Thus aware of newly-pressing questions of procedure, they created a committee to frame revised house rules. There had been no revision throughout Huntington's term in the chair and the occasional addition of only three or four rules. This slowdown of introspection and procedural anxiety was in large part a credit to Huntington's aptitude, fairness, and good temper.

On March 3, they considered the question whether a member of Congress who had already served three years might now retain his seat, in light of another stipulation within Article V, limiting delegates to three out of a period of six years, but they decided to start counting at the time of Confederation.

On March 5, Huntington posed still another question. How many states had to be represented in order for Congress to do business? The familiar practical problem of thin attendance made it pertinent, as well as a mixed prescription in Article IX, paragraph 6: nine states must assent for Congress to exercise certain powers such as war, treaties, alliances, coinages; a majority must assent on any other point. And Articles X and XI also mentioned nine states. The house rules adopted in 1776 and 1778 had stated, "As soon as nine states are represented in the house, the Congress may proceed to business." Members debated their reply to the president's inquiry. Witherspoon, Duane, Madison and others were of the opinion that nine states still were required.

However, Burke argued persuasively for seven, on the grounds that seven meets a longstanding concern that not less than a majority should determine a question and, that a tactical combination of five states voting against eight might negate the majority if nine were the mere requirement. The next day, they wearily decided to require the presence of nine for a quorum, but the assent of seven for an affirmative vote on a question. The newly appointed committee to revise rules accordingly proposed, later, "As soon as seven states are met," members shall take their seats; but Congress substituted, "As soon as the President assumes the chair," allowing some discretion.

On March 14, the new committee brought a report on rules. Congress finished revising May 4. Now the house would operate under 32 rules. In 1774, there were four, but by May, 1778, the most recent list, there were 18 and a dozen had been added occasionally afterward, mainly during the turbulence of 1779.

One change was in the sequential arrangement of the new list. For instance, the previous list put rules on the order of daily business as numbers 16, 19, and 20. Now it was a compressed rule number two. "No member shall speak more than twice in any one debate" was number six in 1776 and 1778, now number 13.

"No member shall read any printed paper in the house during the sitting thereof" was in the draft, but did not endure through the final revision. The old rule, "No member shall leave Congress without permission of Congress or of his constituents," now was dropped.

John Mathews' reform measure of last December now became a rule of considerable importance for saving Congress' work time. It introduced a "committee of the week." Every Monday, Congress would appoint a committee of three to suggest dispositions of all "public dispatches" received by Congress. Congress struck out one provision in the draft of this rule, concerning rotation of appointees to the committee of the week; Mathews seems to have been considered a candidate for future President of Congress, but may have lost momentum when Congress struck out the rotation provision, as well as striking out another new proposal he seems to have sponsored: "The habit of a member of Congress in future shall be a plain purple gown with open sleeves, plaited at the bend of the arm. And that no member of Congress be allowed to sit in Congress without such habit." Sam Adams probably gasped when that proposal came up.

One of the most notable of old rules, contained in the lists of 1774 and 1778, now was incorporated into Article V, paragraph 4: "In determining questions in the United States in Congress Assembled, each state shall have one vote." This was the outcome of a major disagreement when the Articles were forged in 1776. It expresses the principle of the equality of states which was carried over into the Constitution, by assigning a set of powers to the upper house, the Senate, represented by two from each state. In 1776 the more populous states wanted voting in proportion to the sizes of states' population.

Article IV of the Confederation, on the other hand, significantly if fleetingly, recognized people as such, in contrast to entities such as states or a union of states. "The better to secure and perpetuate mutual friendship and intercourse among the people of the different states in this union, the free inhabitants of each of these states, paupers, vagabonds and fugitives excepted, shall be entitled to all the privileges and immunities of free citizens in the several states." Those who were counted as "free inhabitants" owned rights, fixed by this article, which would later be extended, for instance by Article I.9 of the Constitution and by the Bill of Rights of the Constitution. Many of the new state constitutions did include explicit wording about such rights as *habeas corpus* and fair trial, as well as free speech and free press, in the spirit of the Declaration of Independence. Therefore, in those states the "free inhabitants" of all other states now shared the same explicit rights.

Furthermore, Article II of the Confederation kept for the states "every power, jurisdiction, and right" not expressly delegated to the United States in Congress Assembled, a way of limiting confederal government in the same spirit as they had sought to limit government by the British crown.

The Articles of Confederation, like the Declaration of Independence, contained some religious language. Seeking independence from Great Britain, the people did not want to lose it to a new American government which was too powerful. Yet they saw the importance of unity; foreign governments would not wish to make thirteen treaties but would prefer to make one treaty; unity was important for establishing continental credit for loans and currency. How else was unity important? Some thought it was important to God. The final Article therefore began: "And whereas it hath pleased the great Governor of the world to incline the hearts of the legislatures we respectively represent in Congress, to approve and authorize us to ratify the said articles..."

****

That language was probably borrowed from Psalms, where expressions like "Incline thou my heart" were familiar; or "the Lord looks forth on all the inhabitants of the earth, who fashions the hearts of them all." If they believed that the Governor of the world was inclining hearts to unite for common defense, for the security of their liberties, and for the mutual and general welfare (see Article III), probably they recalled the words of a prophet, "In that day, says the Lord of hosts, every one of you will invite his neighbor under his vine and under his fig tree." The quest for sufficient unity led some Americans, including Samuel Huntington, along the path of prayer and religious vision.

Huntington's tenacious hopefulness during the gloomy events of mid-1780, including Charleston's fall and Congress' intractable problems about supply, took strength from one trend, the widening opposition of Europe to Great Britain. No longer was France alone in patronage of America's cause. Spain did not recognize United States independence, but joined France at sea in the hostility. Denmark and Sweden, soon other nations, joined Russia in a league to defend neutral shipping against British naval attempts to stop trade with America. Huntington felt pleased.

"Dispatches not only from all parts of the United States daily arrive," he wrote Cogswell "but frequently from various powers and parts of Europe. We have lately received intelligence that the United Netherlands with Denmark, Sweden, and the empress of Russia at their head, have determined to maintain a neutrality and protect their trade. This is an important stroke and all that America would wish for on the subject."

Not long after, he wrote Governor Trumbull that Great Britain "seems left without a single ally or any assistance, except what she has obtained from the petty states of Germany."

It was too early, at that time, to see that the European patrons whose actions he welcomed were little concerned about American war aims. They had aims of their own. He knew, of course that, like Spain, the neutral signatories had not recognized the independence of the United States. He knew that William Lee, diplomatic representative to the courts at Vienna and Berlin, had been received coldly. John Jay was feeling increasingly frustrated by the avoidance tactics of the court at Madrid.

The obvious focus of Spain's unhappiness with Great Britain was not America but Gibraltar and Minorca. Although Spain was dissatisfied with the 1763 cession of Florida, now they expected to undo it with France's help but without obligation to Florida's neighbors of English background. In South and Central America Spain held colonies, up to the border of the United States. The idea of colonies' independence was not attractive to them, as Francisco Miranda and Simon Bolivar would soon learn. In fact, Spain aspired to control of western territory in North America and to control of Mississippi River shipping; Huntington knew that.

Still, the armed neutrality, if not totally a good sign, seemed a hopeful development. So at first he discounted "reports" which were worrying the southern states, where British power was prevailing. The northern states, according to those reports, might let the Carolinas and Georgia remain British conquests, in exchange for their own independence.

"Our enemies in New York," he wrote Cogswell, "figure to publish" the armed neutrality "as favorable to Great Britain, to prevent ill impressions among them or for some other purpose not more honorable with regard to the truth." The hints of disunion of the states, he assumed, were similar crafty propaganda.

But on June 23, 1780, Congress had countered those hints by a resolution "designed to prevent any false and insidious reports that have been made in the southern states," he wrote to Governors Rutledge and Howly, "and to assure the good people of South Carolina and Georgia that these United States will support and defend them as well as any other part of the United States against the common enemy."

What else Huntington did not know yet was that non-British diplomats, both neutral and friendly, were themselves beginning to discuss possible dismemberment of the United States. He would know soon. John Adams meanwhile sent news of proposals by Josiah Tucker, dean of Gloucester in England, "to the English, Americans, French, and Spaniards, now at war." The dean proposed that Great Britain keep Newfoundland, Labrador, Canada, Nova Scotia, and territory to the Penobscot River; that they cede to the Americans territory from the Penobscot to the Connecticut River, also from the Delaware to the north boundary of South Carolina; that New York, Long Island, New Jersey, and a little adjacent territory be retained by Great Britain, but West Florida ("chiefly barren sand") and Gibraltar ("totally useless") be ceded to Spain; and that England exchange its parts of the East

Indies for France's parts of the West Indies. To consider those proposals, Adams thought, "would be wasting time."

Adams sent other news about peace proposals by English critics of the war. His letter of June 12 perhaps caused Congress more disquiet than others did. Thomas Pownall, former Governor of Massachusetts, before that Lieutenant-governor of New Jersey, had proposed a truce between Great Britain and the United States. But in naming the states, he omitted Georgia. Was this significant? Was he thinking that Georgia would remain under British sovereignty?

Had Huntington known at the time that Empress Catherine of Russia, her minister Count Panin, and perhaps other interested neutrals were thinking about possible benefits which could be shared in Europe if England were drawn to peace on condition of keeping some territory in America, probably he would not have felt great surprise. Regret, doubtless, but not great surprise. Calvinism and jurisprudence had taught him a realistic view of human nature. He had participated without illusions in the formulation of peace terms in 1779.

Vergennes found Catherine's idea quite thinkable. His letter to Luzerne, September 24, indicates that he also was giving weight to the opinions of Silas Deane. "So veracious and patriotic" a man as Deane, he said, was suggesting to him that America might settle for something less than independence. And Vergennes needed help, whether from Deane or from Luzerne, trying to grasp the attitude of most Americans toward their war. Adams and Franklin, at Paris, were not interpreting the situation to him in exactly the same way. What should be believe? When Francis Dana talked with Deane three months later, he learned that Deane imagined America to be conquered already, the armed neutrality sure to be crushed. Vergennes felt friendly with Deane, enough so to lend him money, and for the time being was influenced by the former agent's bitterness. John Laurens arrived in France none too soon.

Two of John Adams' letters from Paris became the occasion of an agreement in Congress, October 18. To guide him in his eventual negotiations with Great Britain for peace and commerce, they agreed that a truce could be accepted — if on Great Britain's part it were "a virtual relinquishment of the object of the war," and "provided the removal of the British land and naval armaments from the United States be a condition of it." Further, no stipulation to re-admit persons who left the United States; no stipulation to restore property seized from Tories or British unless balanced by compensation to Americans for war-damaged property; no stipulation to give British subjects "any of the rights and privileges of citizens of the United States," nor to give them equality with French subjects, "unless such a concession should be deemed by the said minister preferable to continuing the war on that account."

By November 18, Congress knew about the readiness of Europe to think seriously about dismemberment of the United States as a possible step to peace. A delegate for Georgia, Richard Walton, supported by his colleague Richard Howly, moved resolutions which combined two matters. First, the chance of alliance with Spain. Second, the urgency of retaking lost American territory. The armed neutrality had become linked in the news with a projected meeting of neutral powers to plan a mode of peace. "It is not improbable," according to Walton's preamble, "overtures of peace may be made, and that the principle *uti possidetis* may be the foundation" (the principle that a belligerent keeps the territory it occupies at the close of a war). Walton did not feel neutral about that: "a principle utterly inadmissible by these states."

Assuming that the claim of certain states to free navigation of the Mississippi River was the "only bar to an alliance with Spain," one of the resolutions would instruct John Jay, at Madrid, to give up Congress' 1779 instruction about the navigation. It proposed ceding the navigation wholly to Spain, along with territory east of the river to Mobile and north to Cape Anthony, provided Spain enters an alliance, grants an annual subsidy for 25 years or an annual loan during the war, and agrees not to make a peace without concurrence of the United States.

Another resolution favored Congress' sending a special envoy to France, to represent the United States "in concert with Mr. Franklin." On his way, perhaps he could deliver the new instruction to Jay.

The first of the resolutions influenced Congress' commissioning John Laurens, who had sailed off to France before Congress, February 15, voted that Jay should not try unalterably for free navigation below the 31st degree n. latitude, as an inducement for Spanish aid.

For the moment, Spanish relations were less troublesome than the reluctance of the Virginia legislature to support relaxing the old instruction. Virginia was one of the states directly interested in river navigation, having claimed territory to the east bank. However, Theodorick Bland quickly recommended Virginia's assent. Soon, with less enthusiasm, Madison and Jones helped obtain it.

Indeed the threat of partition was fast becoming a new breeder of national purpose. Great Britain, wrote Oliver Wolcott at the beginning of the new year, "may hope, if she shall be successful, to settle the terms of peace upon an *uti possidetus*." Like Walton's, his judgment was firm: "But this will not do. The terms upon which the war is to be carried on, or peace established, stand as they did."

In the spring, Congress received more and more explicit messages about what had been rumored and surmised. John Laurens, among others, sent a message. Quoting from Vergennes, he informed Congress through Huntington: "The courts of Petersburg and Vienna have offered their mediation. The king has answered that it will be personally agreeable to him, but that he could not accept it as yet because he has allies whose concurrence is necessary. Dr. Franklin is requested to acquaint Congress of this overture and the answer, and to engage them to send their instructions to their plenopotentiaries. It is supposed that Congress will eagerly accept the mediation."

On May 26, Luzerne wrote of it to Congress through, Huntington. He stressed the importance of Congress' giving their plenopotentiaries "instructions proper to announce their disposition to peace and their moderation," as well as to convince the powers of Europe that "independence of the thirteen United States" is really their war motive. He asked for a meeting with a congressional committee on matters related to the mediation.

A committee met with Luzerne and on the 28th, reported. Luzerne had told them that Vergennes liked Congress' support of the armed neutrality while questioning their decision to send Dana as diplomatic representative to the Russian court. (Those were references to acts of Congress in early October and mid-December.) Dana's mission, Vergennes feared, could compromise Catherine's neutrality. He also questioned the conduct of John Adams, especially Adams' wish to deal directly with the British. Vergennes urged consultation with France at every step.

Adams and Vergennes did not get along well. They differed in temperament and style as well as in advocacy of separate national interests. Each was wary of the other. "In case this minister, by aiming at impossible things, forming exorbitant demands which disinterested mediators might think ill-rounded, or perhaps by misconstruing his instructions," the report went on, "should put the French negotiators under the necessity of proceeding in the course of the negotiation without a constant connection with him, this would give rise to an unbecoming contradiction between France and the thirteen United States."

The pressure from Vergennes would have a brief effect, but in 1783 his bad dream of a "contradiction" would come true.

The committee reported, further, that Spain was staying true to her engagements with France, despite the efforts of a British emissary to Madrid, Richard Cumberland; that Russia and Austria were offering to mediate, and Great Britain was accepting the offer; and France, while not responding until Spain and the United States consented, wanted eventually to accept also. "Several states being invaded by the enemy." Vergennes suggested with tactful restraint, "the French Council thought it inconvenient to begin a negotiation under these unfavorable circumstances." He hoped the planned French military diversion would prevent Great Britain from worsening things.

Finally, Congress should "rely on the justice and wisdom" of the mediating monarchs. France would defend the cause of the United States zealously. Congress should take care not to divide the allies and, to carry on the war with vigor.

"A great object," Luzerne warned, "was to secure the United States from the proposition of *uti possidetis*." (In February, Luzerne had written Vergennes, advising that union of the states was an advantage to France, partition would be an advantage to Great Britain.) His hint that dismemberment might be in the thought of some mediators was Luzerne's grave ending to the conference with Congress' committee.

After receiving their committee's report, Congress debated until mid-June on a new set of peace ultimata. On June 1, Congress sent a confidential letter to the states. Two days later, Huntington wrote to Nathaniel Greene, to inform him of the Russo-Austrian mediation offer, "which was embraced with apparent eagerness on the part of Great Britain, and will probably be accepted on the part of France and Spain, and we are called upon by our ally to prepare for negotiation as soon as possible."

Then he went to the main point: "This important intelligence we have communicated to the several governors, with caution that it be not disclosed at present, and a most earnest recommendation that the states make the most vigorous exertions at this critical juncture to drive the enemy from all their interior posts and, if possible, to expel them from these states."

On June 6, Congress formally accepted the co-mediation offer. They declared, however, that no treaty would be acceptable which does not specify the independence of the thirteen states. On a motion by Witherspoon the same day, they also voted that their negotiating minister should prudently use his own judgment about a treaty defini-tion of territorial boundaries, relaxing the previous instruction. Hun-tington voted "no," as did Sherman and others, including Madison. By states, the vote was 5-4.

Foreseeing Adams' difficult position, the next day they returned to the question of boundaries. All members agreed that the minister should at the outset try to win the boundaries according to previous instructions. But if the previous instructions proved unacceptable to the others negotiating, seven out of eight states favored delaying spe-cific north and west boundary lines until a future agreement. If delay-ing also was not acceptable, five states (Huntington, "aye") voted against three that the minister should simply seek whatever advantages he could get.

Meanwhile they had been debating whether to instruct their min-ister to consult France at all points of the negotiation. Luzerne began to press for a still stronger instruction to "govern yourself by" French advice. The vote on this question came June 11. Two states, "no" (in-cluding the entire Connecticut delegation: Huntington. Sherman, Ellsworth) but six states, "aye." Trusting Adams' sagacity, New England (except Sullivan, who typically sided with the French minister) wanted to preserve Adams' freedom of judgment. But Congress already, on June 9, had agreed by a narrower vote to Commission other negotiators, joined with Adams, as their peace-bargainers. All the New England states voted "no," but the majority seem to have lacked confidence in Adams' delicatesse, whatever they may have felt about his acumen.

On June 13, they added Jay to the enlarged peace commission. The next day, Franklin, Jefferson, and Henry Laurens, although the latter was still a British prisoner. "Congress have thought proper to add four other plenopotentiaries to the Honourable John Adams, Esquire, to assist in the expected negotiations," Huntington wrote Jefferson, "of whom you are elected one." (Jefferson did not serve; the four others did).

When he wrote to Franklin, besides notifying him of the appoint-ment, Huntington enclosed two versions of the document stating ac-ceptance of the co-mediation; on one, the emperor was named first, on the other, the empress, "to be made use of as circumstances shall render it expedient."

Throughout their peace terms debate, Congress consistently guarded against allowing Great Britain to possess any part of the thirteen states. Although Huntington voted against the majority on three questions, he voted in favor of several terms they adopted.

The diplomatic dispatch from Marbois at Philadelphia, to Vergennes, July 14, contains some interesting comments about the recent doings of Congress.

He says, for one thing, that the President of Congress had spoken with him, expressing concern over popular opinion in America if adherents to the king prevail in the peace terms revision and if the peace does not turn out to be so favorable as some expect. It might lower popularity of the alliance. Marbois seems to have been in communication with several members of Congress. Huntington, for his part, had dissuaded Luzerne from writing his own firm letter to the states and urging compliance with Congress' requisitions, during the doldrums of March, 1780. It would set a bad precedent, he told Luzerne.

Marbois now commented, further, identifying New York, Maryland, and the three southern states as nearest the French wishes on the issues of peace terms: Massachusetts, as followers of Samuel Adams, least satisfactory; Virginia, not too satisfactory; Connecticut, independent of the eastern states tie, yet loyal; New Jersey, in the person of "Doctor Witherspoon," breaking from the eastern tie.

Disorders in Vermont "will oblige General Sullivan, probably, to go there, but he has promised to come back here and, of course, his presence is extremely necessary." Later, Marbois noted that a change in the delegation of New Hampshire could "re-establish the old tie" with eastern states policy.

Across the land there are dry creek-beds which seasonally take in runoff water. The water spills in from high ground, and at first jerks forward, fast downslope but slow if the bed flattens or a rocky, dusty hump arrests water movement.

The flow of the American War for Independence was similar. In 1780, the movement was slow but Samuel Huntington, knowing dry creek-beds on the old home farm and knowing human moods, distractions, and motivations, never really mistook the slowness for an actual defeat. Even if he said. "Do thus, or the army must disband" and the cause must be ruined, he also waited for its flow to exceed the impediments.

In 1781, he noticed a forward jerking of the creek.

When he was continued in office "longer than expected," after a presidential term of one year, Huntington had to request money from the Connecticut state treasury. He assured the treasurer, "I should not make this request if I could with decency or comfort subsist without the money."

Congress provided him with the house of the Philadelphian Joseph Pemberton, as a residence, and every quarter authorized support for his household. In November, 1780, he wrote to Jeremiah Wadsworth, saying he had sent the post rider with a carriage to bring Martha, his wife, to Philadelphia. She was escorted out of Norwich one December day, so the local newspaper reported, "by a number of gentlemen and ladies of the first character."

After joining her husband, she "did the honors at the table" when they entertained guests. A French guest, the Marquis de Chastellux, described her as "a stout, rather good-looking woman approaching middle age." She "helped everybody, without saying a word."

Thomas Rodney wrote in his diary that, one night, he "dined at the house of Mr. Huntington, President." Leading Members of Congress and a number of army officers were present. They talked over "a variety of sentiments on the war etc." and after dinner enjoyed several rounds of toasts.

The Huntingtons' entertainment had not lasted long, however, when colleague Oliver Wolcott predicted that "Mr. Huntington and Mr. Root will probably continue here till the latter end of April, at which time they will return" to Connecticut. He was half correct. Root returned, as did Wolcott, in mid-April. For seven weeks, Huntington was the only delegate from Connecticut and therefore, although his individual vote was recorded it was not counted for decisions. Presidential duties did not lighten thereby. He not only presided at Congress' sessions, but docketed the business, carried on the official correspondence, signed documents, received official visitors, and formally represented the government at ceremonies. His correspondence included summarizing news of the day, because he was at the source of a considerable amount of it. At times he permitted personal feelings to show modestly in his letters, if ordinarily he went to the point tersely. For instance, when informing his onetime fellow in Congress and New England compatriot, William Whipple of New Hampshire, that he was appointed to the Board of Admiralty, he expressed "hope for the pleasure of your company soon at Philadelphia."

Livingston wrote Schuyler at the end of March that the chair soon would be vacant due to Huntington's retirement. Duane, Jones of Virginia, and Mathews, were being mentioned as possible successors.

On April 30, Huntington wrote to Governor Trumbull: "I hope, before this, some delegates from Connecticut are on the way to Congress, as I am once more left alone from the state and shall not be able to attend any considerable time longer myself."

According to the journal of Congress, it was May 8 when he made that announcement that he must return to Connecticut. So May 10 was set as the day for an election. But on election day, according to Witherspoon, no candidate received more than two votes. "I believe," he wrote to R.H. Lee, "if your colleague Mr. Jones would have agreed to serve, he would have been chosen."

Congress asked Huntington to remain in office, again, and postponed election day. Witherspoon thought probably he would remain until fall. In case of new balloting, Jones or Jenifer would be elevated.

Back home, Wolcott wrote. "I am glad that you consented to tarry longer than I expected, as I know that your services are much wanted in Congress."

On June 6, 9, and 10, Congress attempted inconclusively to elect a new President. Jones was not accepting. Significantly, they were interested in another jurist. Huntington's model was attractive.

A "man to the south" would accept the office. McKean wrote to Sam Adams. (Was it Mathews?) "I question whether he will be elected."

And on July 10, McKean himself, a jurist, a moderate, was elected. Secretary Thompson informed the state governors about Huntington's decisions "the state of his health would not permit him to continue longer in the exercise of the duties of President."

"My health is so impaired by long confinement and application as compels me to retire from Congress," Huntington wrote Washington. He informed the general of McKean's election.

Viewed in light of the plentiful official correspondence between them, the relationship of Huntington and Washington, principal civilian and military officers, is well suggested by their letters at this time. There was genuine mutual regard, without fraternity.

Huntington: "It also gives me much satisfaction on retiring to see our public affairs wear a more promising aspect than heretofore." Probably he was thinking of Confederation, of the Philadelphia merchants' fund and the French loan, of the increased French naval commitment, of Greene's field ability. But also he was praising Washington's own contribution.

"The enemy at present in every part of the United States seem to be reduced to a situation merely on the defensive, and should the states improve the opportunity with proper and vigorous exertions, we have reason to hope from the smiles of Providence yet more favorable events."

Along with the military situation, Huntington thought of his own main burden for a year and three-fourths: "The distresses we have suffered from the deranged state of our finances begin to be relieved, and the arrangements taken by the appointment of a Superintendent of Finance etc. and the measures he is adopting give me great encouragement on that most important subject." The two men had written back and forth often on the subject.

"I am now to take leave of your Excellency with respect to my official correspondence, but be assured, sir, my warmest wishes still continue to attend you, that our military operations may be prospered and crowned with the most desirable event, a speedy and honorable peace..." As his passive verbs indicate, Huntington assumed that the event would be providential. Possibly he was conscious of a contrast in assumptions between himself and the Commander, who was more the uneasy activist.

He went on: "...and that you may experience many days of tranquility in the enjoyment of the happy fruits of your important and arduous service in the cause of your country." Neither man at the time could predict the shape of future days and years, nor their own public roles.

Having risked a small expression of sentiment, Huntington warmed to the words "your country." He wrote. "Whatever my future situation in life may be. I shall always love my country. In her happiness and prosperity will consist my own personally."

Finally, he suggested that, "should my state of health permit me the pleasure," he might have an opportunity to visit with the Commander.

Toward the end of July, Washington, who had already joined forces with Rochambeau for their felicitous campaign, replied to Huntington. "I am constrained to take this method of returning my thanks and expressing my sincere wishes for the re-establishment of your health."

He expressed happiness if political affairs were better off but, typically, a less optimistic view than Huntington's on military readiness.

"The station which you have lately filled with so much honor has given you an opportunity of making yourself intimately acquainted with our real situation." So he recommended that Huntington impress those at home with the needs of the army for recruits and supplies.

At about the same time of Washington's letter, Yale's President Ezra Stiles, in New Haven, noted, "President Huntington from Congress passed through town this day. Advised that the prime minister of Russia in a private letter to one in Holland assures that he will use his influence that Russia takes part, and not lay down arms till the Dutch be indemnified..., American independency be acknowledged, and the armed neutrality be supported."

After Huntington reached home, he heard from his friend, Princeton's President Witherspoon: "With great satisfaction I observe by the public papers the joyful and honorable reception you met with on your arrival, so expressive of that affection and approbation which to you will be the most grateful tribute of praise your country can bestow, and next to your consciousness of your having labored how to establish the liberties of America, will be the greatest happiness you can enjoy."

Huntington's own concerns at the moment were less grand, even if Witherspoon's words contented him. On August 27, he wrote to President McKean that a letter-bearer "will herewith deliver your Excellency the two coach horses which are kept for the use of the President of Congress. After they had brought me home, their shoes were immediately taken off, and I ordered them kept in the best manner. They are now in very good order."

"Your care in forwarding Mr. Jay's letter to me merits my thanks. The accident of opening the letter needs no apology."

⇒⋙●⋘⇐

On January 2, 1781, Huntington had written Washington, posing a question about the year's campaign strategy. "Your opinion is desired on the expediency of ordering the forces of his most Christian Majesty now at Newport in Rhode Island to take post in Virginia."

Samuel Huntington

Epilogue

Between late April and late May, Cornwallis and his army marched from North Carolina into Virginia.

> *"No means in the power of Congress will be left unessayed to give you all necessary aid. I am informed some arms are now on the way for Virginia, and the Board of War are still using their endeavors, not without prospect for success, to procure more arms to supply such troops from Maryland and this state as may be raised and march to join the Marquis de LaFayette."*
> **—Huntington to Governor Jefferson,**
> June 3, 1781

> *"The Count de Barras prepares himself for a zany bid into the top secret expedition to the Chesapeake, and is resolved to do it.*
> *"Around the middle or the end of the month, if he is able to arm the fantastic boat which till now is out at sea... and if Lord Cornwallis has not by this time pulled back his forces, and if we can stop the English fleet from entering the Chesapeake, the situation of the English will be very critical."*
> **—Marbois to Vergennes,**
> July 8, 1781

May 6, the Count de Barras Saint Laurent had arrived with the Count de Rochambeau, into Boston from France aboard the *Concorde*. Respectively the army commander and the navy commander, the two men apparently discussed strategy during their trip and agreed upon a focus in the Chesapeake. They both were to have met with Washington at Wethersfield, May 22, but Barras was drawn into a sea battle instead. Washington and Rochambeau discussed Washington's idea of attacking New York and Rochambeau's of attacking the Chesapeake area, but Rochambeau did not reveal that a French naval force under the Count de Grasse, assigned to the West Indies waters, might come to the North American theater. Washington thought they agreed on the New York plan, but Rochambeau and Barras covertly were planning on the Chesapeake.

"The Minister of France having communicated to me his intention to take a journey to camp, and that during his absence you would perform the duty his most Christian Majesty's charge de affairs, it is unnecessary for me to repeat the sentiments of Congress expressed on a former occasion, that they will readily honour you with their confidence in all respects, as you may be assured that their esteem and regard as well as my own for you is not abated but increased by further and more intimate acquaintance."

—Huntington to Marbois,
July 5, 1781

Marbois wrote to Vergennes, July 11, that Huntington was sincerely attached to the alliance and was a forthright and unpretentious man, "one of the finest citizens of America, whose conduct we have always found praiseworthy."

On June 29, Bland of Virginia had moved in Congress that warships, as soon as equipped, be ordered "to join the fleet of our ally, now under command of Mons. de Barras, and put themselves under his order."

"Between the 12th and 18th [of August] plan of operation was totally changed. The attack upon New York from its first contemplation had been deemed eventual and contingent, dependent on the exertions of the states and the place of the arrival of the French fleet. At this period the General, having intelligence from the fleet that their first appearance would be in the Chesapeak-bay, from this circumstance and the slow and ineffectual preparations of the states, took his resolution to abandon his first object, and to meet and cooperate with the fleet in the Chesapeak with a view to reduce the British army in Virginia under the command of Lieut-general the Earl Cornwallis."

—Col. Jonathan Trumbull, Jr.,
of Washington's staff, Minutes of Occurrences

At Yorktown, the capitulation was signed on October 19,
Cornwallis
Thos Symonds
G. Washington
le Cte de Rochambeau
Barres — "Le Cte de Barras, en mon nora & celui de Comte
de Grasse"

"We have had a report that the enemy were preparing at N. York to make us a visit at Norwich, which gave us some trouble to be in readiness for their reception. The capture of Cornwallis may alter their plans. We have not yet received the particulars of this glorious event."

—Huntington, at Norwich, to a
Connecticut delegate in Congress,
November 8, 1781

RESTING TO RUN

Two ran on a wooded slope.
The child could run no longer;
"Give me better legs," he cried.
Instead, the man knelt in moss,
Lowered his head to a spring.
The child drank, too, claimed his breath,
Soon both were running again.

RESTORATIONS

They still buy old, abandoned farms and try to restore them. Some want to farm there, others to sleep there after driving to different workplaces. Not all old places can be restored, however. Too broken down.

Has the line from Calvin through the Geneva Bible to John Milton, Oliver Cromwell, Locke, English Whigs, republicans of the American Revolution, broken down irreparably? Are the disciplines prized by Huntington and Laurens, Witherspoon and Adams, now dilapidated past restoring? How much patience with face-to-face communication is left? With well-shared deliberation and agreed action? How much realistic hope in finite measures while only grace is infinite? See-saw of liberties and responsibilities?

AN AFTERQUIZ

Have you noticed that young people leave the farm and seek life in town?

"It's pointless to plow a field if you can easily go to the flour mill. It's pointless to shave a log smooth and square if you can easily go to the saw mill."

And is it pointless to listen to speeches if you can easily scan statistical printouts? To concern yourself about enslavements to tyranny if you can easily rush a film to the enslaved which explains the technical and managerial systems they need?

"What's that you're saying?"

I can't say more. In the thirteen newly-bonded states, it's still anachronism.

ANOTHER

Don't cry. Suck a popsicle. Turn on your earphones and listen to a rhythm tape. Select sun glasses.

"What's that you're saying?"

I can't say more. Anachronisms.

AND ANOTHER

The purpose of a human being is to glorify God.

"Ho! Did God win our Independence? Did you see God out on the village green, marching with musket and drum?" I didn't.

"Well, you saw me! Give me the glory."

"I am fully of opinion that the great council of the union must have a controlling power with respect to national concerns. There is at present an extreme want of power in the national government, and it is my opinion that this Constitution does not give too much…

"While I have attended in Congress, I have observed that the members were quite as strenuous advocates for the rights of their respective states, as for those of the union. I doubt not but that this will continue to be the case, and hence I infer that the general government will not have the disposition to encroach upon the states. But still the people themselves must be the chief support of liberty."

—Huntington to the convention
debating the proposed U.S. Constitution,
Hartford, January 4, 1788

Preamble: "Considering the great and manifold favours which Almighty God hath, manifested to this land, and to this state in particular, from the first settlement thereof through succeeding generations to the present times and the numberless mercies and blessings conferred upon this state in the course of the current year, which demand the sincere praise and thankful acknowledgments of a professing people…"

Praise: "For the continuation of the blessings of peace, and the quiet enjoyment of our happy Constitution, religious and civil privileges, the general state of health enjoyed; the competent supplies of the fruits of the earth in general and the plentiful productions thereof in many parts of the state; the continuation of the inestimable privilege of the gospel and the means of grace…"

Prayers: "That he may be graciously pleased to bless the federal council of our nation with wisdom and fidelity, and succeed their deliberations to promote the happiness and prosperity of the United States; that it may please him to smile upon and bless the people of this state; to inspire them with a becoming zeal to maintain, support, and preserve their constitutional rights and government; that it may please him to bless us in our husbandry and the labour of our hands, give success to our trade and navigation, prosper the means of grace, and education, and make us a people of his praise..."

— Governor Huntington's thanksgiving
proclamation for Connecticut,
October 27, 1786

CONCLUSION

An original purpose of this study of Huntington's presidency was to inquire into the relation of his religious faith to his public service. But in these pages so far, perhaps you have counted up only a few glances at the question. I trace more attitudes and acts than wordy thoughts. Huntington was sparing in words but quite eloquent in a style of action. So this book has been organized less topically than chronologically, like a sequential narrative.

Huntington, one can say surely, represented Calvinism in the "classical" phase of European and American culture. A man of faith in the tradition of the "Savoy Declaration" of 1658 and of Watts' psalms paraphrases, his personal religion reminds one of the Olney hymns of Cowper and Newton. But, of course, he was himself not a verse-writer nor a creed-maker. He was a republican citizen, a jurist and statesman. By his trail of deeds we must find him, if anywhere at this date.

The crucial contribution of his faith to his deeds, I think, was composure while enduring the "embarrassments" of historical experience. "Embarrassments" in the code of his time meant failures, disappointments, frustrations, as well as feelings of awkwardness and ineptitude. Open-eyed and alert, he realistically accepted the embarrassments: recall his letters of July 22, 1780, to Governor Jonathan Trumbull and to James Cogswell, and his February, 1781 circular letter to the states. But politically his tradition was that of the liberal Calvinists such as Locke and certain promoters of the English Bill of Rights, 1689. By faith he was able to persist in the drive for American independence without downscaling its very aims, dear to the liberal Calvinist tradition: without delegating Congress' powers to a dictator, nor yielding much of the consensual public vision to initiatives of self-interested private groups; not replacing slower and riskier civilian controls over the struggle by emergency enhancements of the military, nor diminishing the international breadth of the allies' plan by fretful recoil into a solitary nationalism.

While several other leaders were interpreting the numerous difficulties of the struggle desperately, hardly hoping unless Congress would permit their own favorite downscalings, Huntington steadfastly kept on believing that independence, peace, and development of free society were God's own aim in God's own time. Although he also believed in human responsibility and soberly took for granted his own urgent commission to "improve the opportunities" presented to him and his generation by providence, still human responsibility was for him a counterpoint with divine sovereignty. No philosopher or theologian has yet expressed such a counterpoint in clear, rational words. But a few sturdy believers of Huntington's sort have exemplified it in action. This book has sketched chronologically what the action was in his case.

BIBLIOGRAPHY

What follows is not a recommended reading list so much as an ac-
knowledgment of sources for this book. It is reduced from a longer list,
at cost of omissions which are nearly as important as many of the titles
included.

I. Primary sources.

Huntington's manuscript letters.
> Manuscripts and Archives, Yale University Library
> Connecticut Historical Society Library
> Historical Society of Pennsylvania
> Manuscript Division, Library of Congress
> New York Historical Society

Manuscript letters to Huntington, or from and to associates of
> Huntington, same libraries

Microfilm. Huntington's President's Letterbook.
> Microcopy N. M247, Roll 24
> National Archives of the United States

Typescript. Huntington, Henry L. Letters of Samuel Huntington
> as President of Congress.
> Connecticut State Library

Photocopy. Marbois, Francois, Marquis de
> Diplomatic Dispatches
> Correspondance Politique Etats Unis. No. 17
> Archives des Ministere des Affaires Etrangeres, France

In print:

Burnett, Edmund Cody
> Letters of Members of the Continental Congress, vv. I-VI
> Washington: Carnegie Institution, 1931

Ford, Worthington C. (vv. 4-15), and
Hunt, Gaillard (vv. 16-20)
> Journals of the Continental Congress
> Washington: U.S. Government Printing Office, 1906-1912

Fitzpatrick, John C., ed.
    The Writings of George Washington 1745-1799, vv. 5-22
    Washington: U.S. Government Printing office/
    Indianapolis: Bobbs Merrill Co, 1933

Hoadly, Charles J., et al, eds.
    Public Records of the State of Connecticut 1776-1784
        particularly:
    appendix, The Hartford Convention, 1779
    appendix. The Hartford Convention, 1780
    appendix, Ratifying Convention. January, 1788
        (cf. Elliot, Jonathan, Debates of the Several State
        Conventions, Philadelphia, 1836)
        with speech by Huntington

Trumbull Papers
    Massachusetts Historical Society

Trumbull, Jonathan. Jr.
    Minutes of Occurences Respecting the Siege of York in Virginia
    Massachusetts Historical Society, April, 1876

Sparks, Jared
    The Diplomatic Correspondence of the American Revolution
    Boston: Nathan Hale and Gray and Boney, 1829-30

Paullin, Charles Oscar, ed.
    Out-Letters of the Continental Marine Committee and Board of
        Admiralty
    New York: Naval History Society, 1914

Hunt, Gaillard, ed.
    The Writings of James Madison, v. 1
    New York: G..P. Putnam's Sons, 1900
        (cf. Hutchinson. William T., et al, eds., The Papers
        of James Madison, 1977)

Cushing, Harry Alonzo, ed.
    The Writings of Samuel Adams, v. 4
    New York: G.P. Putnam's Sons, 1908

Ferguson, E. James; Catanzariti, John, eds.
  The Papers of Robert Morris 1778-1784, v. 1
  Pittsburgh: University of Pittsburgh Press, 1973

Clark, J. Reuben, ed.
  Emergency Legislation Passed Prior to 1917
  Washington, U.S. Government Printing Office, 1918

Ford, Worthington C., ed.
  Letters of Joseph Jones of Virginia 1777-1787
  Washington: Department of State, 1889

Proceedings of a Court Martial for Trial of Major-general
  Schuyler, October 1, 1778
  New York: N.Y. Historical Society Collections, 1880

Klett, Guy S.
  Minutes of the Synod of New York and Pennsylvania
  Philadelphia: Presbyterian Publishing House, 1976

Fitch Papers
  Connecticut Historical Society, 1920

Bailyn, Bernard, ed.
  Pamphlets of the American Revolution 1750-1776, v. 1
    particularly:
  Fitch, Thomas, et al, "Reasons Why the British Colonies in
    America Should Not Be Charged with Internal Taxes"
  Cambridge: Harvard University Press, 1965

Walton, E.P., ed.
  Records of the Governor and Council, State of Vermont, v. 2
    particularly:
  Appendix G, "Action of Congress in Reference to Vermont,
    February 7 to October 6, 1780"
  Montpelier: J. and J.M. Poland, 1874

II. Studies of Samuel Huntington

Gerlach, Larry R.
  Connecticut Congressman: Samuel Huntington 1731-1796
  Hartford: The American Revolution Bicentennial Commission of
    Connecticut, 1976

particularly:
Chapter, "President of the United States" pp. 52-74
Chapter's reference-notes, pp. 119-124
"Note on Sources," pp. 133-135

VanDusen, Albert E.
Samuel Huntington: A Leader of Revolutionary Connecticut
Connecticut Historical Society Bulletin (19.2), 1954

Strong, Joseph
Sermon Delivered at the Funeral of His Excellency Samuel
Huntington, Governor of Connecticut
Hartford: Hudson and Goodwin, 1796

Also brief sketches in Dictionary of American Biography, various encyclope-
dias, surveys of the signing of the Declaration of Independence, and the like

III. On the Huntington Family

Shipton, Clifford K., ed.
Early American Imprints, 1630-1800 (Readex Microprints)
Worcester: American Antiquarian Society

Dexter, Franklin B.
Biographical Sketches of the Graduates of Yale College
New York, New Haven: 1885-1912

Root, Grace Cogswell
Father and Daughter: A Collection of Cogswell Family Letters and
Diaries 1772-1830
West Hartford: American School for the Deaf

Bayles, Richard M., ed.
History of Windham County
New York: W.W. Preston and Co., 1889

Dankert, Clyde
Dartmouth Essays (inc. "Joseph Huntington")
Hanover: Dartmouth College

Chandler, Winthrop
   Portraits, 1770, Ebenezer Devotion, Martha Devotion
   Brookline: Brookline, Mass., Historical Society

Waugh, Albert E.
   Samuel Huntington and His Family
   Stonington: The Peuquot Press, 1968

Knox, William
   The Claim of the Colonies to an Exemption from Internal Taxes
      Imposed by Authority of Parliament Examined: In a Letter from
      a Gentleman in London, to his Friend in America
   London: for W. Jonston, 1765

Devotion, Ebenezer
   The Examiner Examined, A Letter from a Gentleman in Connecticut,
      to his Friend in London
   New London: Timothy Green, 1766

Huntington, Joseph
   Calvinism Improved, the Gospel Illisrated as a System of Real Grace
      Issuing in the Salvation of All Men
   New London: Samuel Green, 1796

IV.   Related Subjects.

A.   American Religion, Connecticut Churches

Ahlstrom, Sydney E.
   A Religious History of the American People, v. 1
   New Haven: Yale University Press, 1972

_____ Annuit Coeptis: America As the Elect Nation, the Rise and Decline
      of a Patriotic Tradition
   Leiden: E. J. Brill, 1979

Bainton, Roland H.
   Yale and the Ministry
   New York: Harper and Brothers, 1957

Dexter, Franklin B., ed.
> The Literary Diary of Ezra Stiles
> New York: Scribner's Sons, 1901

Stokes, Anson Phelps
> Church and State in the United States, v. 1
>> particularly,
> Chapter, "The Official Acts and Utterances of the Founders Regarding Religion and Religious Freedom Prior to the Constitution"
> New York: Harper and Brothers, 1950

Morgan, Edmund S., ed.
> Prologue to Revolution, Sources and Documents on the Stamp Act Crisis 1761-1766
> Chapel Hill: University of North Carolina Press, 1959

____ The Gentle Putitan: A Life of Ezra Stiles
> Chapel Hill: University of North Carolina Press, 1962

____ Puritan Political Ideals
> Indianapolis: Bobbs Merrill, 1965

____ The Putitan Ethic and the American Revolution
> William and Mary Quarterly (24:1), 1967

Bacon, Leonard: Dutton, S.W.S, eds.
> Contributions to the Ecclesiastical History of Connecticut, v. 1
> New Haven: William L. Kingsley, 1861
> (Hartford: Connecticut Conference, U.C.C., 1973)

Fowler, William Chauncy, ed.
> Centennial Papers, Congregational Churches
> Hartford: Case, Lockwood, and Barinard Co., 1877
> (Hartford: Connecticut Conference, U.C.C., 1976)

Foster, Herbert Darling
> The Political Theories of Calvinists Before the Puritan Exodus to America
> American Historical Review, 1916

____ International Calvinism through Locke and the Revolution of 1688
> American Historical Review, April, 1927

Kingdon, Robert M.; Linder, Robert D., eds.
  Calvin and Calvinism, Sources of Democracy?
  Lexington: S.D.C. Heath and Co., 1970

Smith, Page
  Religious Origins of the American Revolution
  Missoula: American Scholars Press, 1976

Tucker, Louis Leonard
  Puritan Protagonist, President Clap of Yale College
  Chapel Hill: University of North Carolina Press, 1962

_____ Connecticut's Seminary of Sedition: Yale College
  Hartford: The American Revolution Bicentennial Commission of
    Connecticut, 1974

Clap, Thomas
  The Annals or History of Yale College in New Haven in the Colony of
    Connecticut 1700-1766
  New Haven: John Hotchkiss and B. Mecom, 1766

Lovejoy, David S.
  Samuel Hopkins: Religion, Slavery, and the Revolution
  Philadelphia: United Church Press, 1976

Eggleston, Percy Coe
  A Man of Bethlehem: Joseph Bellamy and His Divinity School
  Bethlehem: Bethlehem, Conn. Tercentenary, 1936

Meyer, Freeman W.
  Connecticut Congregationalism in the Revolutionary Days
  Hartford: The American Revolution Bicentennial Commission of
    Connecticut, 1977

Baldwin, Alice M.
  The New England and the American Revolution
  Durham: Duke University Press, 1928

_____ The Clergy of Connecticut in Revolutionary Days
  New Haven: Yale University Press for Tercentenary Commission of
    Connecticut, 1936

Hatch, Nathan O.
    The Sacred Cause of Liberty: Republican Thought and the Millenium
        in Revolutionary New England
    New Haven: Yale University Press, 1977

Greene, W. Louise
    The Development of Religious Liberty in Connecticut
    Boston, New York: Houghton Mifflin and Co., 1905

Shipton, Clifford K.
    "James Dana" in Sibley's Harvard Graduates, v. 13
    Boston: Massachusetts Historical Society, 1965

Manuals of Connecticut Churches, collection
    Yale Divinity School Library

Pope, Robert G.
    The Half-way Covenant
    Princeton: Princeton University Press, 1969

Gaustad, Edwin Scott
    A Religious History of America
    New York: Harper and Row, 1966

_____ Historical Atlas of Religion in America
    New York: Harper and Row, 1962, 1976

Baird, Robert
    Religion in America
    New York: Harper and Brothers, 1844
    (Arno, 1969)

Humphrey, Edward Frank
    Nationalism and Religion in America 1744-1789
    Boston: Chipman Law Publishing Co., 1924, 1966

Haroutanian, Joseph
    Piety versus Moralism: the Passing of the New England Theology
    Hamden: Anchor Books, 1964

Foster, Frank Hugh
>A Genetic History of the New England Theology
>Chicago: Chicago University Press, 1907

Albanese, Catherine L.
>Sons of the Fathers: the Civil Religion of the American Revolution
>Philadelphia: Temple University Press, 1976

Richey, Russell E.; Jones. Donald G., eds.
>American Civil Religion
>New York: Harper and Row, 1974

Cross, Arthur Lyon
>The Anglican Episcopate and the American Colonies
>New York: Longmans, Green & Co., 1902

Stout, Harry S.
>Religion, Communications, and the Ideological Origins of the American
>>Revolution
>William and Mary Quarterly, 1977

Newlin, Claude M.
>Philosophy and Religion in Colonial America
>New York: Philosophical Library, 1962

Heimert, Alan
>Religion and the American Mind from the Great Awakening to the
>>Revolution
>Cambridge: Harvard University Press, 1966

Cherry, Conrad
>God's New Israel: Religious Interpretations of American Destiny
>Englewood Cliffs: Prentice Hall, Inc., 1971

B. American Society, Connecticut Society

Main, Jackson Turner
>Social Structure of Revolutionary America
>Princeton: Princeton University Press, 1965

_____ Connecticut Society in the Revolutionary Era
Hartford: the American Revolution Bicentennial Commission of
Connecticut, 1977

_____ The Upper House in Revolutionary America 1763-1788
Madison: University of Wisconsin Press, 1967

East, Robert A.
Business Enterprise in the American Revolution Era
New York: Columbia University Press, 1938

Morris, Richard B.
A People's Revolution
American Historical Review (82.1), 1977

Lockridge, Kenneth A.
Social Change and the Meaning of the American Revolution
Journal of Social History (6.4), 1973

Jameson, J. Franklin
The American Revolution Considered as a Social Movement
Princeton: Princeton University Press, 1926

Grinds, Donald A. Jr.
The Iroquois and the Foundling of the American Nation
San Francisco: Indian Historian Press, 1977

Graymont, Barbara
The Iroquois in the American Revolution
Syracuse: Syracuse University Press, 1972

Logan, Gwendolyn Evans
The Slave in Connecticut During the American Revolution
Connecticut Historical Society Bulletin (30.3), 1965

Hastings, George Everett
Life and Works of Francis Hopkinson
Chicago: University of Chicago Press, 1926

Tyler, Moses Coit
The Literary History of the American Revolution
New York: G.P. Putnam's Sons, 1897

C. The American Revolution

Bailyn, Bernard
    Ideological Origins of the American Revolution
    Cambridge: Harvard University Press, 1967

Morris, Richard B., ed.
    The Era of the American Revolution (essays)
    New York: Columbia University Press, 1939

Flexner, James Thomas
    George Washington in the American Revolution 1775-1783
    Boston: Little Brown and Co., 1967

Hutchinson, William T., et al. eds.
    The Papers of James Madison, v. 2 (with notes, comments)
    Chicago: Chicago University Press, 1977

Jensen, Merrill
    The Articles of Confederation: An Interpretation of the Social-Constitu-
        tional History of the American Revolution 1774-1781
    Madison: University of Wisconsin Press, 1940

_____ "The New Nation: A History of the United States During the Confed-
        eration 1781-1789
    New York: Random House (Vintage), 1965

_____ essay in Journal of American History (57), 1970

Peckham, Howard H., ed.
    The Toll of Independence
    Chicago: University of Chicago Press, 1974

Banning, Lance
    The Jeffersonian Persuasion: Evolution of a Party Ideology
    Ithica: Cornell University Press, 1978

Mitchell, Broadus
    Price of Independence: A Realistic View
    Oxford: Oxford University Press, 1974

Buel, Richard. Jr.
>   Time, Friend or Foe of the Revolution?
>>   essay in Higginbotham. Don. ed., Reconsiderations on the Revolutionary War
>   Westport: Military History (14), 1978

Bowman, Larry G.
>   Captive Americans: Prisoners During the American Revolution
>   Athens: Ohio University Press, 1976

Lindsey, William R.
>   Treatment of American Prisoners During the Revolution
>   Emporia: Kansas State Teachers College, 1973

Ketchurn, Richard M., ed.; Lancaster, Bruce, and Plumb, J.H., narrative
>   The American Heritage Book of the Revolution
>   New York: McGraw Hill, 1958

Boatner, Mark M., 3d
>   Encyclopedia of the American Revolution
>   New York: David McKay, Inc., 1966

Wheeler, Richard
>   Voices of 1776
>   Greenwich: Fawcett Publications Inc., 1972

DuPuy, Trevor N., Hammerman. Gay M., eds.
>   People and Events of the American Revolution
>   Dunn Loring: DuPuy Associates, 1974

D. The Continental Congress

Burnett, Edmund Cody
>   The Continental Congress: A Definitive History of the Continental Congress from Its Inception in 1774 to March, 1789
>   New York: W. W. Norton and Co., Inc., 1941

____ Washington and the Committees at Headquarters
>   American Historical Society, Annual Report, 1932

_____ The More Perfect Union: the Continental Congress Seeks a Formula
The Catholic Historical Review (24.1), 1938

Henderson, H. James
Party Politics in the Continental Congress
New York: McGraw Hill, 1974

_____ Constitutionalists and Republicans in the Continental Congress 1778-1786
Pennsylvania History (36), 1969

_____ Congressional Factionalism and the Attempt to Recall Benjamin Franklin
William and Mary Quarterly (27.2), 1970

Gerlach, Larry R.
A Delegation of Steady Habits: The Connecticut Representatives to the Continental Congress 1774-1789
Connecticut Historical Society Bulletin (32), 1967

Rakove, Jack N.
The Beginnings of National Politics
New York: Knopf, 1979

Brown, Richard G.
The Founding Fathers of 1776 and 1787: A Collective View
William and Mary Quarterly (27.2), 1970

Dutcher, David C.
The Presidents of Congress 1774-1788
Philadelphia: Independence National Park Bulletin (33), 1974

Marshall, W. Joan
Arrangement of Tables in Assembly Room, Independence Hall
Philadelphia: Independence National Park Bulletin (61), 1975

Dreher, G.K., ed.
Now Alarming, Now Promising Fast Day and Thanksgiving Day Resolves of Congess 1775-1783
Hartford: Connecticut Conference, U.C.C., 1976
(Mystic: Longshanks Book, 1976)

E. Government

Ferguson, E. James
   The Power of the Purse: A history of American Public Finance 1776-
      1783
   Chapel Hill: University of North Carolina Press, 1961

Studenski, Paul
   Financial History of the United States
   New York: McGray Hill, 1952

Carson, Hampton Lawrence
   The Supreme Court of the United States: Its History
      particularly:
   chapter on appeals: case of the sloop *Nancy*
   Philadelphia: J.Y. Huber Co., 1891

Ubbelohde, Carl
   The Vice-admiralty Courts and the American Revolution
   Chapel Hill: University of North Carolina Press, 1960

Jameson, J. Franklin, ed.
   Essays in Constitutional Development
      particularly:
   "The Predecessor of the Supreme Court" by Jameson
   "Development of Executive Departments" by Jay Caesar Guggenheimer
   Boston: Houghton Mifflin, 1889

Cometti, Elizabeth
   Civil Servants of the Revolutionary Period
   Pennsylvania Magazine of History and Biography, 1951

Johnson, Victor LeRoy
   The Administration of the American Commissariat During the Revolu-
      tionary War
   Philadelphia: University of Pennsylvania thesis, 1941

Risch, Erna
   Quartermaster Support of the Army: A History of the Corps
   Washington: Quartermaster Historian's Office. Office of the Quartermas-
      ter, 1962

Wells, Thomas L.
   The Resignation of Nathanael Greene
   Greenville: East Carolina College thesis, 1960

Kohn, Richard H.
   The Inside Story of the Newburgh Conspiracy: America and the Coup
      d'Etat
   William and Mary Quarterly (27), 1970

Brewster, William
   The Fourteenth Commonwealth: Vermont and the States That Failed
   Philadelphia: George S. McManus Co., 1960

F.   Connecticut Participation

VanDusen, Albert E.
   Connecticut
      particularly:
   Chapter, "Connecticut Fights for Independence" and chapter's
      reference notes pp. 435-439
   New York: Random House, 1961

Gerlach, Larry R.
   Firmness and Prudence: Connecticut, the Continental Congress, and the
      National Domain 1776-1786
   Connecticut Historical Society Bulletin (53.2), 1966

_____ Connecticut and Commutation 1778-1784
   Connecticut Historical Society Bulletin (33), 1968

Roth, David M.; Meyer, Freeman
   From Revolution to Constitution: Connecticut 1763-1818
   Chester: the Pequot Press, 1975

Destler, Chester M.
   Connecticut: the Provisions State
   Hartford: the American Revolution Bicentennial Commission of
      Connecticut, 1973

Mix, Irene H. compiler
   Connecticut's Activities in the Wars of This Country: a Summary

particularly:
chapter, "Revolutionary War 1775-1783"
Washington: U.S. Government Printing Office, 1932

Dreher, G.K.
Chow for the Continental Army: Commissary Leadership of Joseph
    Trumbull and Jeremiah Wadsworth
Manuscript material for a talk to adult groups

G.   Individual Leaders

Flexner, James Thomas
George Washington in the American Revolution 1775-1783
Boston: Little Brown and Co., 1967-68

The Traitor and the Spy
Boston: Little Brown and Co., 1975

_____ The Young Hamilton
Boston: Little Brown and Co., 1978

Mitchell, Broadus
Alexander Hamilton: A Concise Biography
Oxford: Oxford University Press, 1976

Morris, Richard B.
Seven Who Shaped Our Destiny
New York: Harper and Row, 1973

Roth, David M.
Connecticut's War Governor: Jonathan Trumbull
Hartford: the American Revolution Bicentennial Commission of
    Connecticut, 1974

Collier, Christopher
Roger Sherman's Connecticut: Yankee Politics and the American
    Revolution
Middletown: Wesleyan University Press, 1971

VerSteeg, Clarence L.
Robert Morris, Revolutionary Financier
Philadelphia: University of Pennsylvania Press, 1954

Young, Eleanor
    Forgotten Patriot: Robert Morris
    New York: Macmillan, 1950

Lossing, Benson J.
    The Life and Times of Philip Schuyler, v. 2
    New York: Sheldon and Co., 1873

Gerlach, Don R.
    Philip Schuyler and the American Revolution in New York 1733-1776
    Lincoln: University of Nebraska Press, 1964

Dangerfield, George
    Chancellor Robert R. Livingston of New York
    New York: Harcourt Brace and Co., 1960

Alexander, Edward P.
    A Revolutionary Conservative: James Duane of New York
    New York: Columbia University Press, 1938

Champagne, Roger J.
    Alexander McDougall and the American Revolution
    Schenectady: Union College Press for New York State
        American Revolution Bicentennial Commission, 1975

Coleman, John W,.
    Thomas McKean: Forgotten Leader of the Revolution
    Rockaway: American Faculty Press, 1975

Rowe, G. S.
    Thomas McKean and the Coming of the Revolution
    Pennsylvania Magazine of History and Biography (96.1), 1972

Clarfield, Gerard H.
    Timothy Pickering and the American Republic
    Pittsburgh: University of Pittsburgh Press, 1980

Pell, John
    Ethan Allen
    London: Constable and Co., Ltd, 1929, 1972

Holbrook, Stewart H.
   Ethan Allen
   New York: The Macmillan Co., 1940

Stohlman, Martha Lou Lemmon
   John Witherspoon, Parson, Politician, Patriot
   Philadelphia: Westminster Press, 1976

Royster, Charles
   The Nature of Treason: Revolutionary Virtue and American Reactions
      to Benedict Arnold
   William and Mary Quarterly (36.2), 1979

H. International Scope

Morris, Richard B.
   The Peacemakers
   New York: Harper and Row, 1965

Christie, L. R.
   Crisis of Empire: Great Britain and the American Colonies 1754-1783
   New York: W.W. Norton and Co., 1966

Langford, Paul
   Modern British Foreign Policy, the 18th Century 1688-1815
   London: Adam and Charles Black, 1976

Wright, Esmond
   Benjamin Franklin and American Independence
   Mystic: Lawrence Verry, Inc., 1966

Meng, John J., ed.
   Despatches and Instructions of Conrad Alexandre Gerard 1778-1780
   Baltimore: Johns Hopkins Press, 1939

Stinchcombe, William C.
   The American Revolution and the French Alliance
   Syracuse: Syracuse University Press, 1969

Persons, James Breck
   France in the Revolutionary War
   Boston: Houghton Mifflin Co., 1911

Van Doren, Carl
    Benjamin Franklin
    New York: The Viking Press, 1938

Savelle, Max
    "The American Balance of Power and European Diplomacy 1713-78"
    essay in Morris, The Era of the American Revolution, op. cit.

Thanks to these sources of illustrations:

Front Cover—Samuel Huntington, detail of John Trumbull's "Declaration of Independence" at the U.S. Capitol, Washington, D.C., from Architect of the Capitol

p. i[1]—StateHouse Row 1778, water color by Rembrandt Peale

p. ii—engraving of Samuel Huntington by John Chester Buttre. From the Connecticut Historical Society, Hartford, Connecticut.

p. vi[2]—engraving by Burnet Reading

p. viii[1]—John Witherspoon, Charles Wilson Peale, artist

p. ix[1]—John Adams, Charles Wilson Peale, artist

p. x[1]—Richard Henry Lee, Charles Wilson Peale, artist

p. xi[1]—Thomas McKean, Charles Wilson Peale, artist

p. xvii[1]—George Washington, Robert Edge Pine, artist

p. xviii[2]—engraving by B.B. Ellis

p. 11—Marquis de Lafayette at Yorktown, Jean Baptiste lePaon, artist. From Lafayette College, Easton, Pennsylvania.

p. 18[2]—engraving by Benoit Louis Prevost

p. 136[1]—Ben Franklin, Duplesis, artist

p. 180[1]—Samuel Huntington, Charles Wilson Peale, artist

p. 216—Governor Samuel Huntington, George F. Wright, artist, 1862. Courtesy Museum of Connecticut History.

1. Supplied by Independence Historic Park, National Park Service, Philadelphia, Pennsylvania.
2. After Pierre Eugene du Simitiere supplied by the National Portrait Gallery, Smithsonian Institution, Washington, D.C.

A Biographical Sketch:
George Kelsey Dreher, 1919–1994

Born June 10, 1919, in Milwaukee, Wisconsin, George Kelsey Dreher was the only son of a bank president. His father, George Cameron Dreher, was a jovial man and known for his funny dinner stories. Having started working as a bank teller he had become one of Milwaukee's important bankers. The work ethic was deep in the family tradition. He would tell young George a story of his uncle who would eat a large bowl of oatmeal every morning then go to the shore and singlehandedly pick his fishing boat up over his head and carry it to the water. Their early years were spent in Wauwautosa, an affluent community on the shore of Lake Michigan. His mother, Marguerite Kelsey Dreher, was also of good humor and talented at the piano. She hired household help and maintained an active social calendar which included lots of crocheting and bridge. He had one sister, Dorothy, who was younger.

Young George possessed an active imagination which initiated many stories and at one time he sent out arbitrary letters authored by a "talking canary" which actually generated responses to the embarrassment of his parents. A woman in the community humored him with several rounds of return letters to this canary. The neighborhood had several families with young children and life was pretty normal with numerous pranks and shenanigans. As he grew older he had private tutors in voice, piano, dance, and French.

His family was well off, yet moved to Eau Claire, a smaller town, as a result of the depression and high level powerplays within the Milwaukee banking establishment. Attending high school there, he was in the band and on the swimming team. The family spent their summers on Star Lake and he developed an appreciation for the great outdoors, fished for Muskie, and canoed. Some winters were spent in Florida to help young George's health. He was active in the Congregational church and civic life, aspiring to be a journalist or possibly a publisher.

He went to Dartmouth College where his uncle served as Dean of English. He was in the glee club and was a serious student. There he experienced a radical affirmation of faith and became a very devout Christian, even giving away his tuxedo and other worldly possessions. He was president of the Christian Student Union and a conscientious objector. He graduated in 1941 with a major in English Honors, a keen interest in Shakespeare, and a feeling that possibly the ministry would be right for him.

He subsequently earned degrees from Oberlin Graduate School of Theology and Yale Divinity School in an exciting theological climate. At Yale he began writing papers on the history of New England religion and became a Congregational historian. A friend introduced him to his future wife, Kathryn Rice, a rural Georgian, stunt pilot, and ex-Bulldog cheerleader who had graduated cum laude from the University of Georgia. She was then studying at Union Theological Seminary under Reinhold Niebuhr. George was ordained on June 3, 1946, in Bethany, Connecticut, where he had been student minister.

After some years of courting, and a somewhat fish out of water visit to her family's farm, they were married on July 1, 1947, at James Chapel, Union Theological Seminary. Kay served one year on the professional staff of the New York State Student Christian movement and it was decided that she wouldn't seek ordination. He found a new parish and they moved to Mountain Home, Idaho, in the summer of 1946. Their first child, a daughter, was born in August, 1948.

This small community afforded a pastoral setting. He wrote a devotional called "Abel Was Innocent" during that time. That piece was greatly influenced by the local shepherds in the surrounding mountainsides. It fascinated him to experience their method of sharing irrigation water via ditches under the auspices of the ditchmaster. There was a nearby air base that contributed a sizable part of the congregation. He relished the rugged western terrain of the Snake River Valley and wanted to remain in the region but he was young and needed to move.

He was called by a church with a nearly defunct congregation of eleven members. So in 1950 they moved to Bountiful, Utah. He helped to start a new church and they had three more children. Bountiful was a hilly suburb of Salt Lake City and the house was filled with growing babies. They built a new sanctuary and became strong under his leadership. The greater Salt Lake area was fervently religious, and the mountains were beautiful, but anticipating more intellectual excitement in the Berkeley area, he moved his family including a newborn daughter to Kensington, California, in August, 1955.

San Francisco was visible from their front yard, and atop a giant redwood there one could view the bay bridges, Alcatraz, and beyond to the smoky hills of 'Frisco. He enjoyed taking his family camping in the Russian Gulch and Yosemite National Park and would whisk his wife away for a day here and there along the Big Sur coastline. The Arlington Community Church was rather large, the church well established, yet he didn't get very close to the intellectual activity at Berkeley. The exciting possibility of starting a new church captivated him and he soon moved to Wichita, Kansas, to begin from scratch. In the summer of 1957 the family headed east with a fishtank of guppies on the floorboard between his pregnant wife's feet in their '49 Plymouth with the luggage rack overflowing.

There they had two more children which made six. He was a religion and philosophy lecturer at Wichita U., as well as minister of a fledgling congregation at Concord Church. Services were first held in the parsonage basement using a foot pump organ, and then at the elementary school until a church building could be built. With six children to feed much time was spent building church membership by calling on new families as they moved into newly built homes in the middleclass housing development. And he prepared lectures which left little time for his family which was then getting large. Grading students' papers was an agonizing process which he gladly passed on to student professors if possible, but making the rounds in the community and bringing new people into his parish was pleasurable.

Using an A.B. Dick mimeograph machine he published a weekly newsletter which he delivered to the main post office on the other side of town. These weekly trips across town allowed him to stop at the bakery thrift stores to supply his family for another week. Used and hand me down clothes were brought home for his children.

He began to write again and various pieces were published in United Church periodicals. He stopped lecturing and wrote a play called "Romain Will Knock" based on a protagonist dedicated to the humane campaign against hunger. He gave the manuscript as a Christmas present to his awestruck wife who was wondering if his writing would ever help feed the family. At the time, a prosperous neighbor who was retired wheat farmer, was flying around the world to help other countries raise better crops. The vast wheat fields on our great plains were overflowing the grain elevators with rotting wheat berries as the huge B-52's being manufactured locally were flying overhead. The play was intended to be performed on Broadway but it wasn't. Was the drama too intellectual? Or is interest in humanitarian campaigns faddish?

By 1964, despite preaching for fairhousing and nuclear disarmament, he had built a healthy church congregation amidst a new housing development on the edge of wheat fields at the outskirts of a military industrial based city. He wanted to move back to New England to be closer to bigger libraries to pursue his research. He would miss the church family camps he led during the summers at Estes Park that allowed him to fish for trout, grow a beard, and to write. But one evening an unknown caller left a message for him with the children and asked that he call the pastoral search committee at the Mystic Congregational Church. The Rockies, West, and Mid-West would soon become memories as he made only rare return visits. Trading off their '53 Chevy he loaded his family into a new Volvo station wagon and pulled out of Wichita headed east. Once there, his itchy feet were finally nailed to the floor and he spent the rest of his life on the picturesque Connecticut coast.

But on one return trip he took four of his children and wife to the top of a 12,000' peak in Northeastern New Mexico on a visit to his son living near Taos. Later, he went to Albuquerque to participate in another son's marriage. And he visited a daughter working in Silicon Valley and a son working in the Texas oilfields. There were more visits too, but he was dynamically returning east having gone a full circle.

While living in Mystic, Connecticut, a sailors haven, he did the bulk of his writing and undertook a study of George Peele's 16th century drama researched at Yale University libraries from 1964–1974. This resulted in his publication of "The Chronicle of King Edward The First (surnamed Longshanks) with the Life of Lluellen (Rebel in Wales)" a retroform which provided a few unriddles in the text, modern spelling and punctuation, and an introduction. He also published samples from Peele's "The love of King David and Fair Bethsabe" and reference portions form the Bible in the translation by Miles Coverdale, selected and modernized, with comment.

Following out an interest in the impact of the Bible on later literature, he presented papers to small groups on Fulke Greville, Giraudoux' "Judith" and Peele's "David and Bethsabe." It was the latter which led to the study of "Edward I."

His environment in Mystic was more inspiring for his writing though he was still jammed for time. In the late 60's he again was excited by his play "Romain Will Knock" and converted it to prose, picking away in his two fingered style at the typewriter. He was intent, but still the manuscript was not published until 1995, though he had even offered it gratis to be used to raise money to fight hunger. The prose underwent many revisions and is more lively than the play, even using some lingo he learned from a son's friend who had lived in an eastern ghetto. It is still mainly intellectual, challenging the reader to consider choices and consequences. The setting is an American city in the 1960's encompassing all walks of life, depicting many contrasts with only a few shades of gray.

Like a Camus novel, the content is philosophical. Like a Brecht play, the style is didactic with some alienation. But unlike Ibsen, he was willing to convert his playscript to prose, which left elegant flowing dialog. He passionately wanted to diminish hunger and felt this could contribute.

At this time his household was bustling with activity from six children who kept him busy going to school sporting events, concerts, plays and musicals, and closely watching their studies. And he introduced them to events like the Newport Folk Festivals and Broadway plays, urging them to become involved in lots of activities.

Then in the 70's he completed a journalistic study of human power drives titled "And Still We Lost" which is not yet published. His mother, who had been a house mother at Beloit College and was living out her retirement years in Mystic as he wrote this piece, died in 1978. He took her ashes to Milwaukee to lay next to her husband who had died in the early 1950's and her only daughter who had died in her twenties from Addison's disease.

For the bi-centennial he published a book "1775–1783, Now Alarming, Now Promising, Fast Day-Thanksgiving Day Resolves of Congress." This book provides authentic texts for re-enacting a Revolutionary fast day or thanksgiving day. And it provides case material for discussing "Does American have a tradition of civil religion? If so, can Christians live with it?" and "Do Christians' attitudes when America won independence help us understand independent nationalism in the Third World today?"

His church was still his main thrust, filling the days with its surrounding concerns. Many hours were spent on into the evenings and on Saturdays into the early morning hours preparing sermons. Sometimes his sermons were heavily theologically bent, once prompting one parishioner to ask, "Is he angry?" He was generally serious in the pulpit but would tell humorous stories to lighten the atmosphere on occasion. When guest preaching on family visits to Georgia he was always urged to use scripture more heavily when he spoke.

True to his intent, he was spending any spare moment in various libraries researching Peele and the American Revolutionary period. His little Ford Vega and then Fiesta cars were virtually worn to the ground making these 100 mile round trips. While his wife was working as an educator, his few hours away from parish work were spent writing. Only occasionally could his family drag him away for a few hours of relaxation on the beach.

In 1980 his parish gave him a partial sabbatical in conjunction with a Fellowship from Yale University to write an essay on the letters of Samuel Huntington, President of Congress 1779–1781. Finally, he was given some relief from his career-long struggle between ministering and writing. This resulted in possibly his most ambitious manuscript, the essay titled "Longer Than Expected." (Samuel Huntington to John Lawrence, treasurer of Connecticut, December 1, 1780: "As I find myself under a necessity to remaining in Congress much longer than I expected, for it was my wish and full expectation to have returned home in October last, I am under necessity or requesting one hundred pounds in hard money may be sent to me...") The theme is the marvelous ability of the American political system (whatever its concurrent faults) to practice FREEDOM, derived from a prior development of the Christian tradition.

It shows the presidency of Huntington in the light of New England religion. The current debate over the separation of church and state is integral to these letters. And though the original intent was merely to write an essay on a local signer of the Declaration of Independence, it became a "study to determine if Huntington's religious New England background was a significant factor in his attitudes and capabilities." "Issues...were the beginnings of the federal judicial branch, the creation of the first executive departments, currency reform with the devaluation of the Continental paper money, negotiation of a peace treaty with Great Britain and final ratification of the Articles of Confederation and the formal start of the Union." As Huntington's home was Norwich, a neighboring town at the head of the Thames River, local research was available at Connecticut College and the Mystic Seaport but many original papers were found in Hartford and New Haven as well.

During this time he trimmed his involvement from the many committees he had been participating in on the regional, state and local level. He had always tried to be involved and encouraged others to be, but his concentrated effort was required for this essay which he completed, but was never able to publish.

All his children being grown, he retired in 1984, already sensing the beginnings of a neurological deterioration which eventually resulted in his death on October 18, 1994, at the age of 75. The last congregations he served were made up of people involved in national defense though he himself was a pacifist. He ministered in Wichita which is a major base for the Strategic Air Command and a major manufacturer of military aircraft. And he ministered in Mystic which is adjacent to Groton which is a major submarine base, home of the Naval Underwater Warfare Center, and a major manufacturer of nuclear armed and powered submarines. He was a deep thinker in the realm of Christian ethics and was able to serve these parishes wholeheartedly.

When he retired, his wife remained a remedial reading therapist in the local school system and he tried to think and write at home, but he was deteriorating. While in retirement he was able to complete "Kings of Judah," ten plays for amateurs which is not yet published. The theme is the human benefit to which David and the successor kings of Judah either validated or failed to validate their kingship, not sheerly in terms of Divine Right of Kings—so preparing us partially for the messiaship of Jesus Christ. It has very sparse trappings and minces no words, seeming to capture blocks of thoughts in single phrases.

He suffered a series of small strokes. The first he was aware of hospitalized him while he was attending a seminar and doing research when visiting one of his daughters in England. He was examined by specialists in Boston but the exact nature of his illness was never determined. Unknowingly, one would assume it was Alzheimer's disease.

He belonged to a group of theater goers who were regulars at the Yale Repertoire and the Eugene O'Neill Theater but by then he was unable to promote his work. Even a local theater group in Stonington was beyond his reach by the time he completed "Kings of Judah" as his condition left him indecisive and docile.

In 1991, though he was unaware, his manuscript "Ourselves & One Other", a devotional book, was published as a medley of images tied together by a view of faithful response to Jesus theme. This included devotions, poetry, music, comments on scripture using metaphors and paraphrases, and prayers that he had written through the years in every parish. It was edited with photographs and illustrations. When he first received a printed copy of it he was able to express surprise and pleasure but was unable to comment on it due to his illness which left him unable to articulate what he was thinking.

"Now The Dog Is Quiet," the prose version of "Romain Will Knock," was published in 1995, eight months after his death, after sitting idle for over twenty five years. The main characters are businessmen but the theme is the humane campaign against hunger. It has many sides dealing with both social and business values but is secular and never actually mentions religion. A hopeful and strong ending which includes the entrance of a new character is climactic. It appears to offer a technique for Americans and the world to get along together.

There are many personal similarities to his life in the characters and events in the story. Perhaps Elson Miles is similar to his father, and Romain is similar to the other bankers he was working with. Perhaps John Wiro is similar to himself and Daphne Miles similar to his sister. His children remember some incidents with the family dog that are similar to ones in this story. It was entirely fitting that he gave such a personal story to his wife, for she too champions human rights, perhaps even more so, or at least they inspired each other. She also embraces other humane issues such as nuclear disarmament and regularly raises money to fight hunger through "CROP Walks" which matches dollars for miles.

He eventually offered it to be used to raise money to fight hunger through Church World Service-CROP. The inside back cover asks for donations to help fight hunger to be sent there.

In the words of some of his congregation, "He was a man who practiced what he believed." "A true Christian." "A selfless servant of God." "A man who truly lived his faith." Also, he was a great group leader. He could lead a church camp dining room in song and story telling as well as anyone. And he would listen to people's problems one on one, and usually was able to help.

He spent the last years of his life in a nursing home but never missed going to church, being wheeled over in a wheelchair by a friend, except for the last Sunday before his death. Becoming unable to swallow, he had stopped even trying to eat and drink and was overcome from lack of food and water.

He was never published by a major publisher, and this was great disappointment to him. He tried to gain a publisher until he was too ill to send his manuscripts off, and received rejection after rejection. This disappointment probably added fuel to his illness. His wife would say, "But George, what did you expect? Your subjects are so obscure." The books he self published on Peele, on Longshanks Book, are still selling after twenty years and received acclaim by several select scholars for his introduction, editing, and comments.

One of the 1995 summer blockbuster movies was based loosely on the story of King Edward I (Longshanks) through the very different eyes of William Wallace, a Scott and foe. In the fascinating 43-page introduction to "Edward I" he states, "Peele gave them [Welsh and Scottish nationalists] a voice, but implied that unification was the better policy." But then, "Peele's portrait of him is coherent and vivid enough that we feel curious about the actual Edward. We ask whether the portrait resembles the man. To relieve our curiosity, however, we first have to decide how much resemblance to expect..."

Iron Horse Free Press is posthumously publishing his remaining works. He IS being published and his life's works ARE becoming available with modest promotion should they find their way to readers. His remaining two unpublished known manuscripts are scheduled as projects.

It would be bittersweet for his recognition to come after his death, but not unusual for artists. His humility made him entirely the wrong person to promote his own work. He was more a serious writer and would have produced much more had he not become ill and had he received some encouragement from publishers. Not that he had ever written anything specifically with commerciality in mind. But, thinking ahead, he had looked for retirement spots in both Idaho and Vermont. He would have gone to the mountains, grown a beard (or red mutton chops), to write.

SNARLED ROPE

A slender rope, much tangled,
My fingers tugging at snarls
Rope fiber proves
Tougher than skin.
The friction rasps its offense.

A slender line of habits,
Glandular twined aptitudes,
Fixated style.
I am a rope
And harshly check untangling.

—George Kelsey Dreher

George K. Dreher

1945

1786·S·HUNTINGTON·1796

Index

Iron Horse Free Press/Longshanks Book offers these titles:

"Now The Dog Is Quiet" A novel with a 1960's setting, by George Kelsey Dreher, written in opposition to hunger. First written as a play and later converted to prose, the protagonist is dedicated to the humane campaign against hunger. John Wiro, proprietor of the Two-Bit Plate, not only helps feed the hungry but is able to help leaders of the community who are struggling for the courage to make changes: choices and consequences. ISBN 0-9601000-4-0

"The Chronicle of King Edward the First" surnamed Longshanks with "The Life of Lluellen" Rebel in Wales, by George Peele. Tudorian drama by a contemporary of Shakespeare. A retroform which provides a few unriddles in the text, modern spelling and punctuation, edited and with a fascinating introduction by George Kelsey Dreher. ISBN 0-9601000-1-6

"The Love of King David and Fair Bethsabe", by George Peele. Samples with reference portions from the Bible in the translation by Miles Coverdale, selected and modernized with comment by George Kelsey Dreher. ISBN 0-9601000-2-4

"Ourselves and One Other", by George Kelsey Dreher. A meditative medley of images tied together by a view of faithful response to Jesus theme. Taken from the pieces he had written through the years including prayers, devotions, poetry, hymns, and thoughts on selected scriptures. ISBN 0-9601000-3-2

"1775–1783, Now Alarming, Now Promising: Fast Day/Thanksgiving Day Resolves of Congress. Introduction by George Kelsey Dreher

and soon to be available:

"And Still We Lost", by George Kelsey Dreher. Written in the 1970's, a journalistic study of human power drives.

"Kings of Judah", by George Kelsey Dreher. 10 plays for amateurs. The theme is the human benefit to which David and the successor kings of Judah either validated or failed to validate their kingship, not sheerly in terms of Divine Right of Kings—so preparing us partially for the messiaship of Jesus Christ.

To order write:

Iron Horse Free Press
P.O. Box 10746
Midland, TX 79702

or call 800-484-6645 code 0661
or fax 915-686-0397
or e-mail: geodre@aol.com